The
CHILDREN'S
Factfinder

The CHILDREN'S Factfinder

zigzag

CONTENTS

MINIBEASTS 8

Growers • Developers • Hunters and trappers
Rotters, tunnellers and burrowers • Suckers • Flyers
Crawlers and runners • Hoppers, jumpers and skaters
Slitherers and wrigglers • Camouflagers • Tricksters
Flashers and warners • Singers and glowers • Carers

MONSTER ANIMALS 36

Monsters on land • Monsters of the sea • Monsters in the air
Hairy monsters • Scary monsters • Disgusting monsters
Fierce monsters • Fat monsters • Weird monsters
Deadly monsters • Masses of monsters • Rare monsters
Imaginary monsters • Extinct monsters

FANTASTIC SEA CREATURES 64

Coral creatures • Seashore creatures • Deep-sea creatures
Cool creatures • Microscopic creatures • Giant creatures
Coastline creatures • Clever creatures • Deadly creatures
Flying creatures • Scaly creatures • Strange creatures
Prehistoric creatures • Mysterious creatures

COUNTRIES 92

**Europe • North America • South America
Africa • Western & Southern Asia
Northern & Eastern Asia & Australasia**

WONDERS OF THE WORLD 120

**The Wonders of the Ancient World • Building wonders • Rocky wonders
Towering wonders • Superhuman wonders • Watery wonders
Tunnelling wonders • Entertaining wonders • Underground wonders
Religious wonders • Artistic wonders • Deep, Hot and Cold wonders
Engineering wonders • Phenomenal wonders**

NATURAL DISASTERS 148

**Earthquakes • Volcanoes • Thunder and lightning
Hurricanes and tornadoes • Floods • Avalanches and landslides
Drought • Forest fires • Ice ages • Sea dangers
Plagues • Plant and animal pests
World pollution • Dangers from space**

WARRIORS 176

What is a warrior? • Alexander the Great • Attila the Hun • Romans
Enemies of Rome • Irish warriors • Vikings • Genghis Khan
Crusaders • Aztecs and Incas • Sitting Bull • Warriors of the Orient
Freedom fighters • Warriors from mythology

INVENTIONS 204

Sources of power • Moving ahead • Sea and sailing • Flying machines
Looking closer • Weaving a fabric • Telling the time
Writing and printing • Record and playback • Keeping in touch
Photography and television • Electronics
Revolution in the home • Weird and wonderful

SUPERNATURAL 232

All kinds of ghosts • Ghosts around the world • Poltergeists
Funny ghosts • Haunted houses • Scaring away ghosts
Mysteries in the sky • Mysterious disappearances • Witchcraft
Fortune telling • Second sight • Amazing powers
Strange and bizarre • More spooky cases

OPTICAL ILLUSIONS 260

The eye and the brain • Lines and shapes • Dimensions • Comparisons
Colour tricks • Moving pictures • Stereo vision
Holograms and stereograms • Stage and screen • Magic tricks
Mirrors and distortion • Useful illusions • Natural illusions • Virtual reality

BALLET AND DANCE 288

The history of ballet • Popular ballets • Unforgettable dancers
Ballet around the world • Start to dance • Ballet steps
Stepping out • Modern dance • Costumes and make-up
Music and movement • On with the show
Dance for fun • National dance • Ballet school life

INDEX 317

Young **scorpions** are carried on their mother's back.

Many young minibeasts look like small versions of their parents. They simply grow into adults. Others look completely different. They develop into adults through stages.

Some young minibeasts that look like small adults, such as snails, grow very gradually. Others, such as insects, have a hard outer skeleton. They have to moult in order to grow.

They moult by making a new, soft skeleton beneath the hard one. The new skeleton is pumped up with air, and this splits the old skeleton. The young minibeast grows inside the new, hard skeleton.

Cockroaches lay their eggs in a hard purse-shaped case. When the young hatch, they look like small adults.

Cockroaches can produce 30,000 young in a single year!

Young **snails** look like miniature adults when they hatch from round, silvery-coloured eggs. As they grow, more coils are added to their shells.

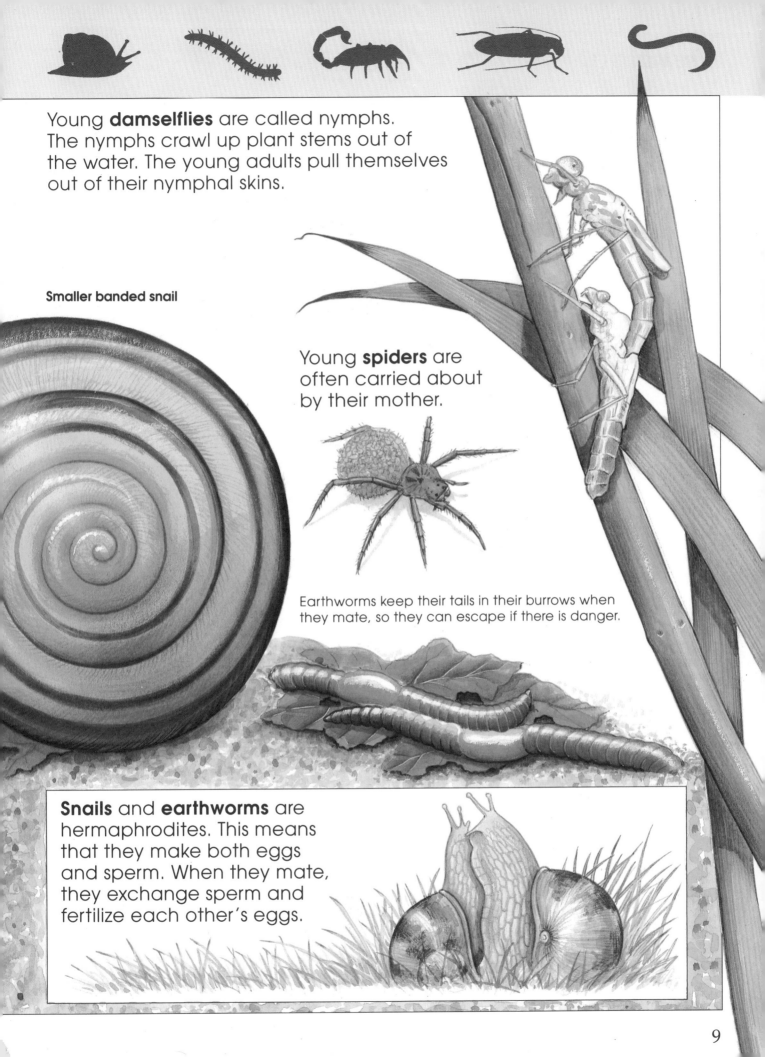

Young **damselflies** are called nymphs. The nymphs crawl up plant stems out of the water. The young adults pull themselves out of their nymphal skins.

Smaller banded snail

Young **spiders** are often carried about by their mother.

Earthworms keep their tails in their burrows when they mate, so they can escape if there is danger.

Snails and **earthworms** are hermaphrodites. This means that they make both eggs and sperm. When they mate, they exchange sperm and fertilize each other's eggs.

When they are born, many young minibeasts look completely different from their parents. They go through several stages to develop into adults.

The young that hatch from the eggs are called larvae. A larva feeds and grows. It eventually develops into a chrysalis, which is also called a pupa. Inside the chrysalis, the larva changes into an adult. After a time, the adult emerges from the chrysalis.

The development of a larva into an adult through these stages is called metamorphosis.

Ladybird beetles and their larvae feed on aphids.

Caddis fly larvae live underwater. They make homes to live in by sticking together pieces of plant, sand, shells and other material. They carry their homes around with them.

The larvae of **butterflies** and **moths** develop into adults through metamorphosis.

This egg has been laid by a **pasha** butterfly.

This **pasha** caterpillar will turn into a chrysalis.

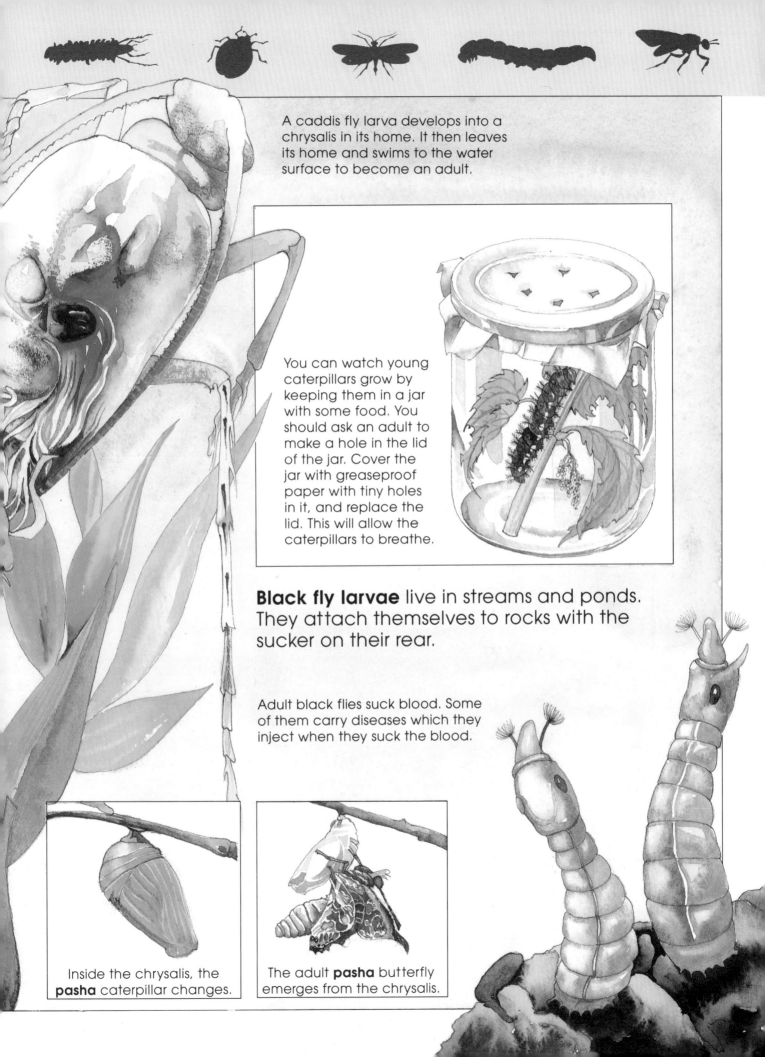

A caddis fly larva develops into a chrysalis in its home. It then leaves its home and swims to the water surface to become an adult.

You can watch young caterpillars grow by keeping them in a jar with some food. You should ask an adult to make a hole in the lid of the jar. Cover the jar with greaseproof paper with tiny holes in it, and replace the lid. This will allow the caterpillars to breathe.

Black fly larvae live in streams and ponds. They attach themselves to rocks with the sucker on their rear.

Adult black flies suck blood. Some of them carry diseases which they inject when they suck the blood.

Inside the chrysalis, the **pasha** caterpillar changes.

The adult **pasha** butterfly emerges from the chrysalis.

Hunters and trappers

Minibeasts have to find food to eat in order to grow. Some of them eat the leaves, shoots, flowers, fruits and roots of plants. Many minibeasts even eat other minibeasts!

Minibeasts find their food in different ways. Some of them eat rotten plants or animals, while others suck juices from plants, or even blood from animals!

Some minibeasts tunnel and burrow through the soil, while others hunt for a meal on the surface of the ground. Some minibeasts even make traps in which they catch their prey.

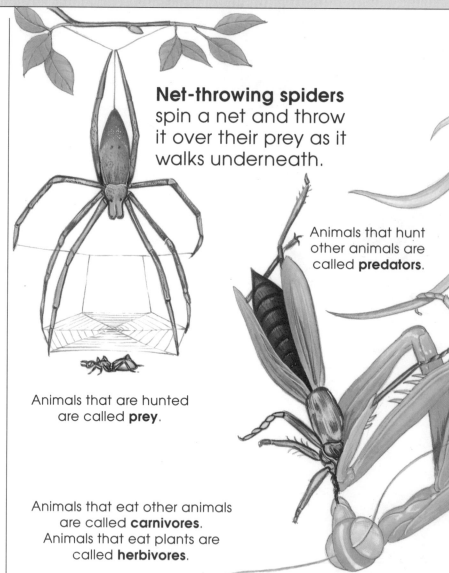

Net-throwing spiders spin a net and throw it over their prey as it walks underneath.

Animals that hunt other animals are called **predators**.

Animals that are hunted are called **prey**.

Animals that eat other animals are called **carnivores**. Animals that eat plants are called **herbivores**.

Long-jawed spiders are well camouflaged on grass as they wait for their prey to walk past.

Trap-door spiders hide in a silk-lined burrow with a trap door at the entrance. They throw open the trap door to grasp their prey.

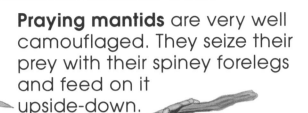

Praying mantids are very well camouflaged. They seize their prey with their spiney forelegs and feed on it upside-down.

Antlion larvae lie half-hidden at the bottom of a funnel-shaped pit. They flick sand at minibeasts that slip over the edge of the pit, so that the minibeasts fall down to the bottom.

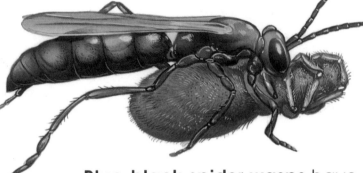

Blue-black spider wasps have a loud buzz which terrifies their prey.

Euglandina rosea attacking a *papustyla* snail.

Tiger beetles are fierce hunters. They use their strong jaws to kill and cut up their prey, which includes young lizards.

Snails sometimes attack and eat other snails. If the snail has withdrawn inside its shell, the attacker will drill a hole through the shell to eat the snail.

Rotters, tunnellers and burrowers

Nothing lives for ever. Plants and animals die and rot away. Many minibeasts feed on rotting material, helping to break it down into smaller particles.

Some of these pass into the soil, and are eaten by burrowing minibeasts. The particles contain nutrients which help minibeasts to grow.

Mole crickets dig burrows with their large spade-like feet. They eat the roots of plants and other minibeasts.

Scarab beetles make balls of dung, and bury them in a tunnel where they lay their eggs. The larvae discover a larder full of lovely food.

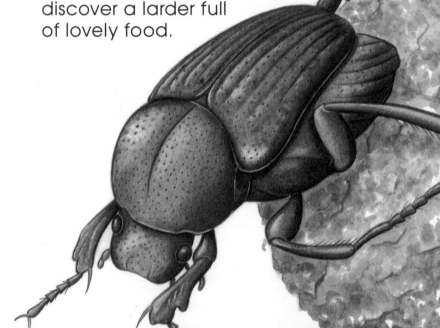

Mites help to break down the remains of dead plants in the soil. Some of them feed on fungi, while others hunt other mites.

Dermistid beetles help to tidy up the remains of dead animals.

Many different kinds of minibeasts can be found in compost heaps. To find them, place a handful of compost in a kitchen sieve and warm it gently with a lamp for two to three days. Remember to keep the tissue paper damp.

Stag beetle larvae live inside logs. They tunnel through the decaying wood for several years before they emerge as adult stag beetles.

Termites tunnel into wood or soil and build nests. These hang from trees, or are huge mounds rising from the ground.

Microscopic minibeasts live inside termites. They break down the plant food that termites eat.

Millipedes tunnel through the soil. They eat particles of rotten material which are rich in nutrients. They also eat fallen leaves, breaking them down into smaller pieces.

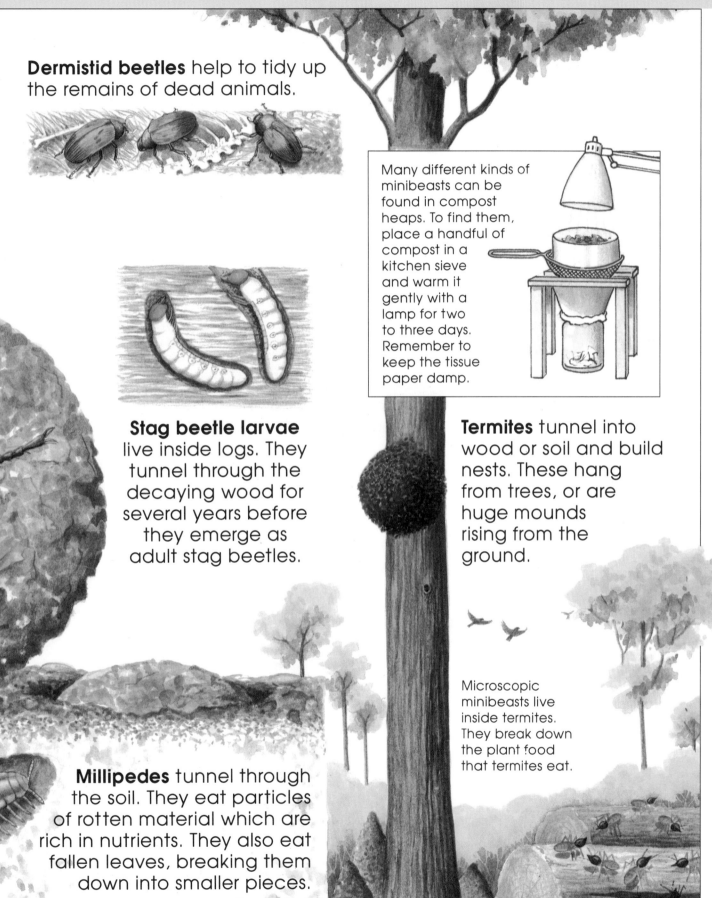

Suckers

Some minibeasts live on liquid food. They have extremely sharp mouthparts which they use to pierce the skin of an animal or the tissue of a plant.

They usually suck blood or plant juices through a sucking tube.

Fleas use the hooks and spines on their bodies to hold tightly on to the fur or skin of their hosts. Fleas can carry diseases which they inject into their hosts when they bite.

In the Middle Ages, the disease called the Black Death was spread by the rat flea. This disease killed millions of people.

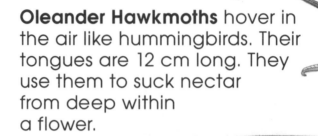

Oleander Hawkmoths hover in the air like hummingbirds. Their tongues are 12 cm long. They use them to suck nectar from deep within a flower.

Ticks are parasites. They sink their hooked mouthparts into the flesh of their host. As they suck the blood, their round, elastic bodies swell greatly.

Aphids feed on plant juices. Their delicate mouthparts pierce the sap vessels inside a plant, and the pressure forces sweet-tasting sap into the aphid's body.

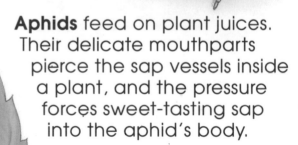

Some of the sap is passed out of the aphid as a drop of sweet fluid. This is sometimes eaten by ants.

Mosquitoes feed on blood and plant juices. Female mosquitoes have a meal of blood before they lay their eggs. Male mosquitoes suck plant juices instead of blood.

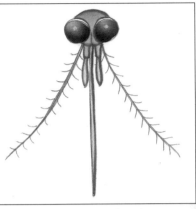

The long, needle-sharp mouthparts of a mosquito contain a sucking tube.

Female mosquitoes bite humans. A person can lose over half a litre of blood in an hour.

Jungle leeches suck blood. When they have had a blood meal, their body swells.

Thrips are tiny 'thunder-bugs'. They have mouthparts on one side of their mouth only, which they use to suck plant juices.

Thrips are pests, feeding on corn and other crops.

Animals that live and feed on other animals are called **parasites**. The animals that provide a home and food are called **hosts**.

Robber flies catch and stab their prey with their sharp mouthparts. Their victim is then sucked dry.

Cochineal bugs suck plant juices. They are used to make food colouring as they are dark red.

17

Minibeasts have to get about in order to find food, a mate and a new place to live. They also need to be able to escape from predators.

Minibeasts use many ways of getting about. Some of them crawl and others run. Some of them jump and others wriggle. Some of them can even fly.

Most minibeasts that fly have two pairs of wings which beat together.

Spiders are minibeasts that can fly but do not have wings!

A young **wolf spider** has released a long, silken thread. The wind will pluck the thread into the air, whisking the young spider away with it.

Beetles have two pairs of wings. The first pair is very tough and protects the delicate flying wings which are folded underneath when not in use.

Dragonflies chase other flying minibeasts by rapidly beating their outstretched wings.

Emperor dragonfly

Damselflies fly by fluttering their wings. They catch other flying minibeasts by grasping them with their legs.

Butterflies fly during the daytime. Most of them slowly flap their large, colourful wings.

The wings of the **painted lady** warn other minibeasts to keep away.

The wings of the **swallowtail** make a noise as they clap together.

Flies are the best acrobats of the minibeast world. They can even land upside down on a ceiling.

Flies have only one pair of real wings. The rear wings are tiny bat-shaped objects which beat very fast.

Hover flies can hover, dart backwards and forwards, and even fly straight upwards.

Midges have one of the fastest wing beats. Some beat their wings over 1000 times a second.

Fairy flies have delicate, feathery wings. They are one of the smallest flying minibeasts.

May bugs fly at dusk. They can fly over five kilometres in search of a mate.

Crawlers and runners

Many minibeasts get about by crawling or running. Some of them have lots of short legs which they use to crawl about.

Other minibeasts have fewer legs, but they are usually quite long. Long legs allow the minibeast to run about quickly.

Pseudoscorpions can run backwards as well as forwards! They are active hunters that crawl amongst decaying leaves in search of a meal.

Pseudoscorpions have long sensitive hairs on their rear to help them feel where they are going.

Caterpillars usually have plenty of food around them. As they do not need to move far to find a meal, they have short legs.

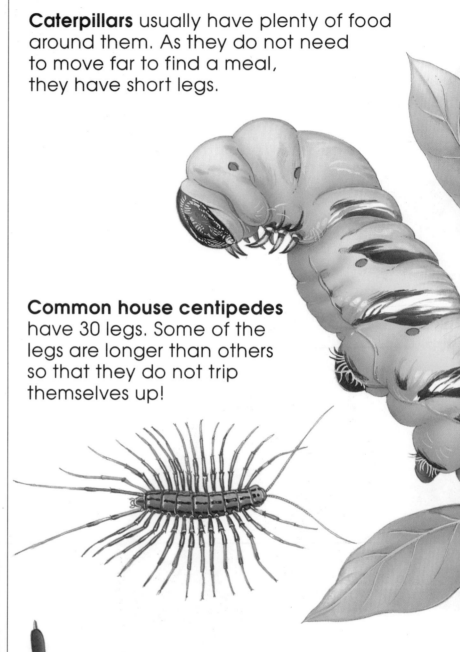

Common house centipedes have 30 legs. Some of the legs are longer than others so that they do not trip themselves up!

Harvest spiders have very long legs and a small body. To prevent them from toppling over, they bend their legs and keep their body close to the ground.

The legs of harvest spiders are not used for speed. The spiders crawl through the vegetation where they live.

Caterpillars have special suckers, called prolegs, on their bodies which keep them firmly fixed on to twigs and leaves, even in a strong wind.

Millipedes have over 100 pairs of legs which they use to crawl along the ground.

Jewel beetles scurry about in search of food. They have beautiful coloured wing cases. In South America, they are used as living jewellery which is why they are called jewel beetles.

Privet hawkmoth caterpillar

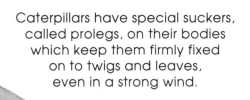

Huntsman spiders hide underneath the bark of a tree while they wait for their prey. They then race to catch it using their long legs.

Golden huntsman spider

Woodlouse-eating spiders have enormous jaws which are specially designed to catch woodlice.

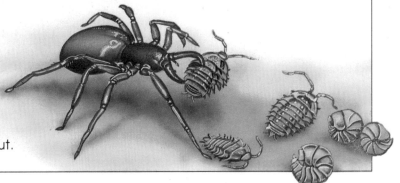

All spiders have eight legs, which they use to run about.

Hoppers, jumpers and skaters

Some minibeasts move about by hopping and jumping. Being able to jump suddenly is a good way to catch a meal, or to escape from a predator.

Other minibeasts skate across the surface of water in search of food or a mate.

Raft spiders stand half on the water and half on a water plant. They race across the water surface to catch their prey, which includes small fish.

Grasshoppers and **crickets** have huge back legs. They use the strong muscles in these legs to catapult themselves high into the air.

Fleas have large back legs which allow them to jump very high - well over half a metre.

Fleas jump on to animals, such as cats, where they make their home.

Treehoppers hop from tree to tree in search of food.

Pond skaters have waterproof hairs on their feet which help them to float on the water surface.

Grasshoppers attract a mate by rubbing their back legs against their front wings to make a singing sound.

Springtails can spring suddenly into the air using their special 'tail'.

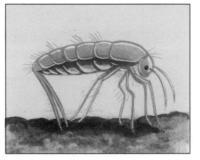

The 'tail' is tucked under the springtail's body.

The 'tail' straightens suddenly, making the springtail spring into the air.

Jumping plant lice have very strong back legs which means they can jump from plant to plant.

Click beetles have a peg on their bodies. When they lie on their backs and bend, the peg pops free with a loud click, and they jump into the air.

Apple suckers are jumping plant lice which live on apple trees.

Jumping spiders have excellent sight. When they see a fly, they will leap into the air to catch it.

Whirligig beetles skate quickly across the surface of a pond in a zigzag pattern.

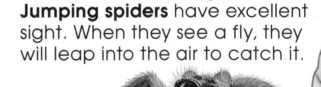

Slitherers and wrigglers

Legs can get in the way, so some minibeasts do not have any legs at all. They have soft bodies, and they move about by slithering along the ground or wriggling through the soil.

Earthworms make burrows which let air into the soil. They drag leaves into the burrows for food.

Leeches move along by using their suckers. They have two suckers on their bodies, one at the front and one at the rear. The one at the front has teeth as it is also their mouth.

The rear sucker sticks to the ground and the body stretches forward.

The front sucker sticks to the ground and the body is pulled forward.

African giant snail

Earthworms burrow through the soil by eating it. They grip the soil with very small bristles along their bodies.

You can make a wormery by putting some earthworms and compost into a plastic bucket with small holes in the bottom. As the earthworms eat the compost, you will need to add some more to the bucket.

Slugs and snails are special minibeasts that slither along on a trail of slime using one foot. If you place a slug or snail on a piece of clear plastic and look at it from underneath, you will see ripples moving along the foot as the minibeast moves forward.

Hover fly larvae look like little leeches. They wriggle along in search of aphids which they eat.

Fly larvae hatch from eggs laid on dung. They have small legs, or no legs at all. To move about, they wriggle through their squidgy food.

Soil centipedes have up to 100 pairs of tiny legs which help them to grip the soil.

Nematodes are minute roundworms which live inside many animals and plants, and in soil. They move about by wriggling their tiny bodies.

Some minibeasts hide from predators or prey, while others display bright colours, make noises, or glow at night to attract attention.

Many minibeasts use colours and shapes to disguise themselves. Some blend into their background, which is called camouflage. Others pretend to be fierce minibeasts.

Some minibeasts use bright colours to frighten or warn their predators. Others use sound and light to 'talk' to each other and attract a mate.

Assassin bug larvae look like the surrounding soil.

Peppered moths blend into the bark of the tree trunk on which they are resting.

Some Peppered moths are darker. They hide on tree trunks which have been blackened by pollution.

African bush-crickets are perfectly camouflaged among the leaves.

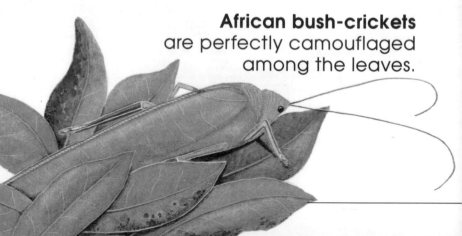

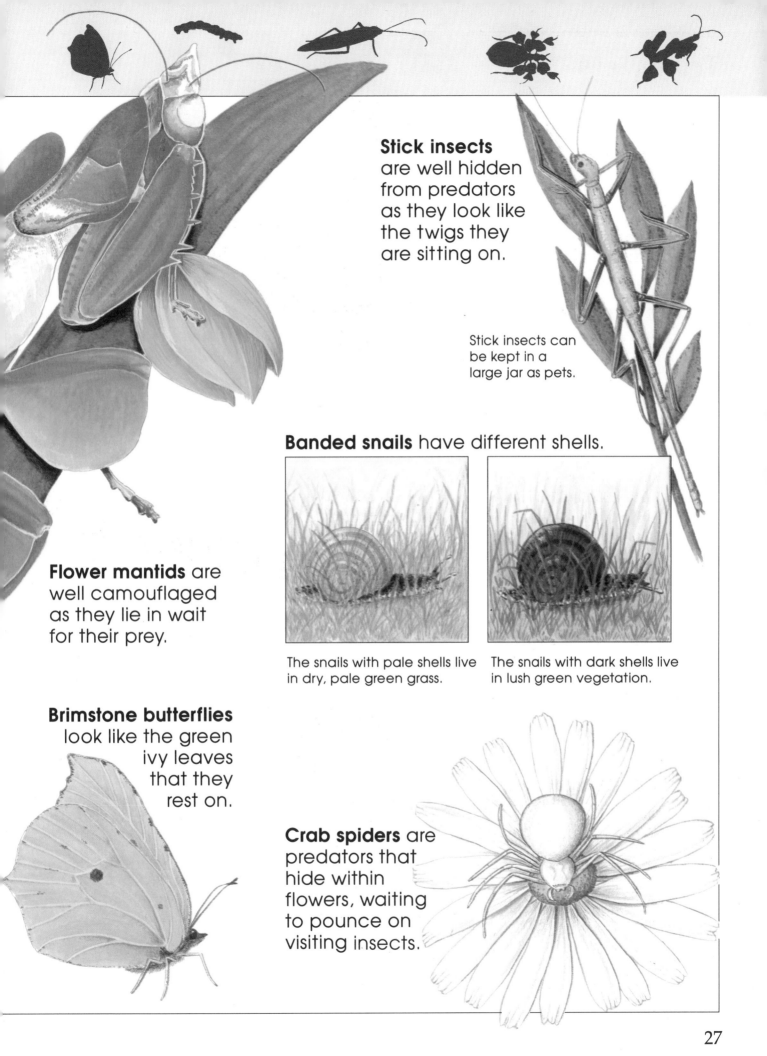

Stick insects are well hidden from predators as they look like the twigs they are sitting on.

Stick insects can be kept in a large jar as pets.

Banded snails have different shells.

The snails with pale shells live in dry, pale green grass.

The snails with dark shells live in lush green vegetation.

Flower mantids are well camouflaged as they lie in wait for their prey.

Brimstone butterflies look like the green ivy leaves that they rest on.

Crab spiders are predators that hide within flowers, waiting to pounce on visiting insects.

27

Tricksters

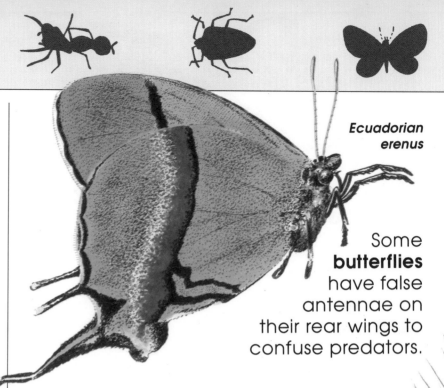

Ecuadorian erenus

Many minibeasts try to trick predators by using different disguises. Some of them have the same colours as minibeasts that are fierce or poisonous, so that predators will leave them alone.

Other minibeasts let predators approach them, but then they give them a nasty surprise. A few minibeasts even use false heads to confuse their predators!

Some **butterflies** have false antennae on their rear wings to confuse predators.

Tussock moth caterpillars have fine irritating hairs on their body which give predators a nasty shock!

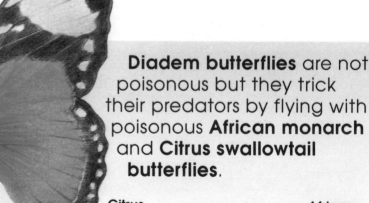

Diadem butterflies are not poisonous but they trick their predators by flying with poisonous **African monarch** and **Citrus swallowtail butterflies**.

Citrus swallowtail

African monarch

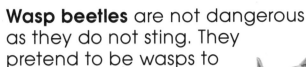

Wasp beetles are not dangerous as they do not sting. They pretend to be wasps to trick their predators.

Copying the colour of another creature is called **mimicry**. This helps to protect harmless minibeasts from predators.

Some **jumping spiders** mimic mutillid wasps to protect themselves.

The jumping spider's rear looks like the head of a mutillid wasp.

Shieldbugs ooze a stinking liquid when they are in danger. This is why they are also called stinkbugs.

Golden-silk spiders have bright colours. At a distance, these break up the shape of the spider, making it difficult to see.

Diadem

29

Many minibeasts use bright colours to protect themselves. Some of them frighten their predators by suddenly flashing bright colours at them.

Some minibeasts show their bright colours all the time. Predators learn that these are warning colours, telling them that the minibeast is dangerous.

There are only a few warning colours: black, white, yellow, red and brown. Minibeasts learn quickly that these colours warn of danger.

Peacock butterflies have large colourful eye spots on their wings.

Puss moth caterpillars shoot out long red tassles from tubes on their rear when they are frightened.

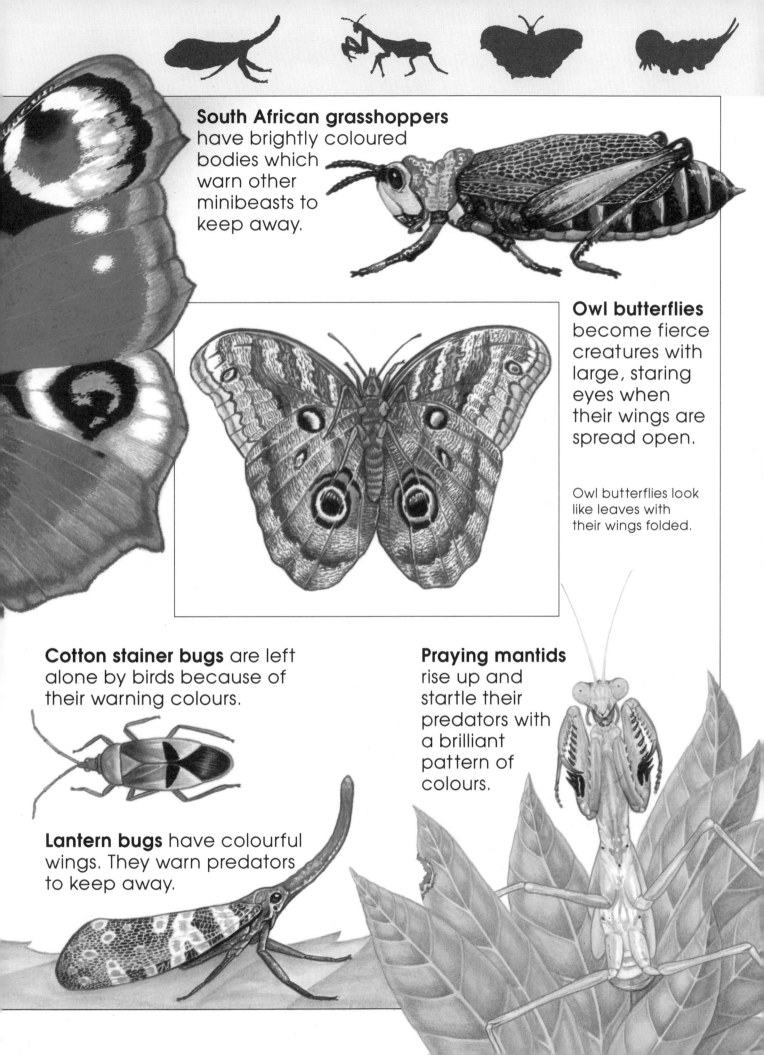

South African grasshoppers have brightly coloured bodies which warn other minibeasts to keep away.

Owl butterflies become fierce creatures with large, staring eyes when their wings are spread open.

Owl butterflies look like leaves with their wings folded.

Cotton stainer bugs are left alone by birds because of their warning colours.

Praying mantids rise up and startle their predators with a brilliant pattern of colours.

Lantern bugs have colourful wings. They warn predators to keep away.

Singers and glowers

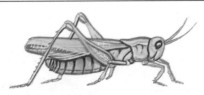

Many minibeasts use sound to attract a mate, or to warn off predators. Some of them make sounds during the day. If you walk through a field or a forest, you may hear all kinds of chirps and buzzes.

Many minibeasts make sounds at night, while others use light to attract a mate. The males or females glow in the dark, and their mates are attracted to them.

Katydids sing their repetitive song `katydid, katydidn't´at night. They sing by rubbing their left front wing against a ridge on the right wing.

Katydids and other crickets have ears on their legs.

Tree crickets make thousands of piercing chirps without stopping. Some tree crickets can be heard 1.6 km away!

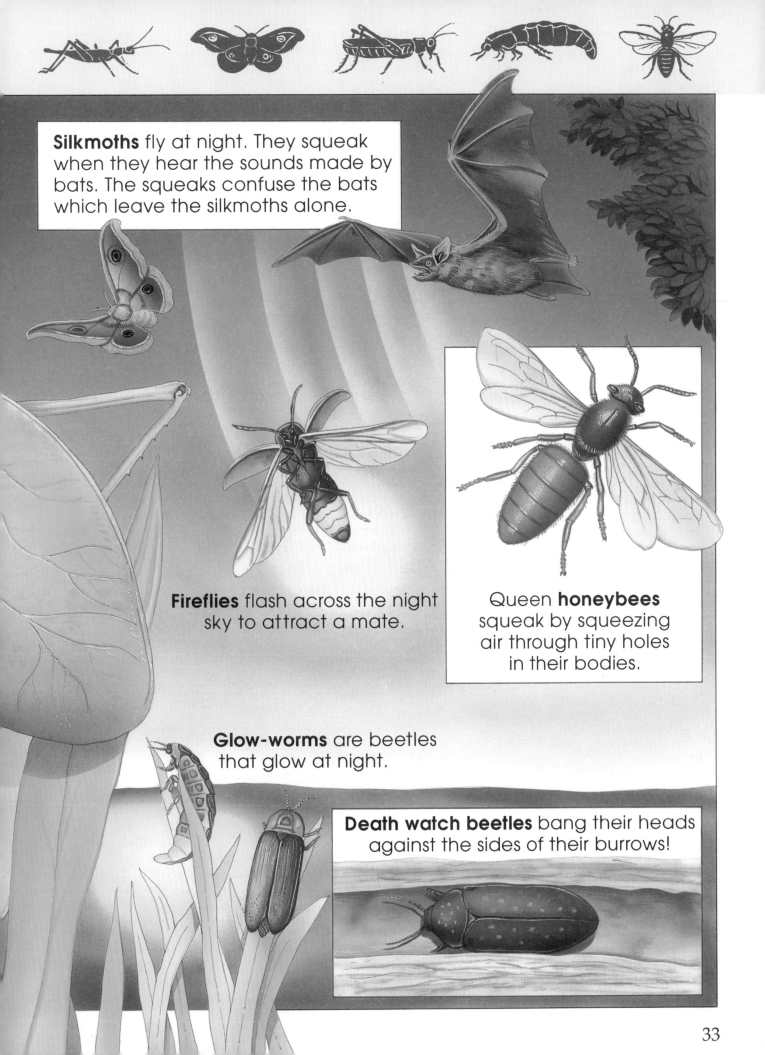

Silkmoths fly at night. They squeak when they hear the sounds made by bats. The squeaks confuse the bats which leave the silkmoths alone.

Fireflies flash across the night sky to attract a mate.

Queen **honeybees** squeak by squeezing air through tiny holes in their bodies.

Glow-worms are beetles that glow at night.

Death watch beetles bang their heads against the sides of their burrows!

Carers

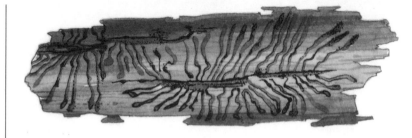

Most minibeasts leave their young to look after themselves. Many of the young starve to death, or are eaten by predators. To overcome this, many eggs are laid.

Some minibeasts care for their eggs and young, so fewer eggs need to be laid. Minibeasts such as female ants or bees work together to provide shelter and food for their young, giving them a better chance of survival.

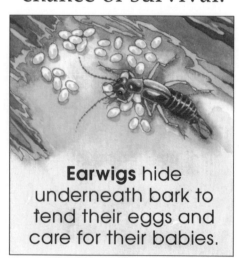

Earwigs hide underneath bark to tend their eggs and care for their babies.

Look at the bark of fallen trees and see if you can find the tunnels of bark beetles.

Elm bark beetles tunnel under the bark of a tree where they lay their eggs.

Termites live as a family in a huge nest. The king and queen live in the royal chamber. The queen's body swells to a huge size as she lays her eggs inside it. She can lay 30,000 eggs a day.

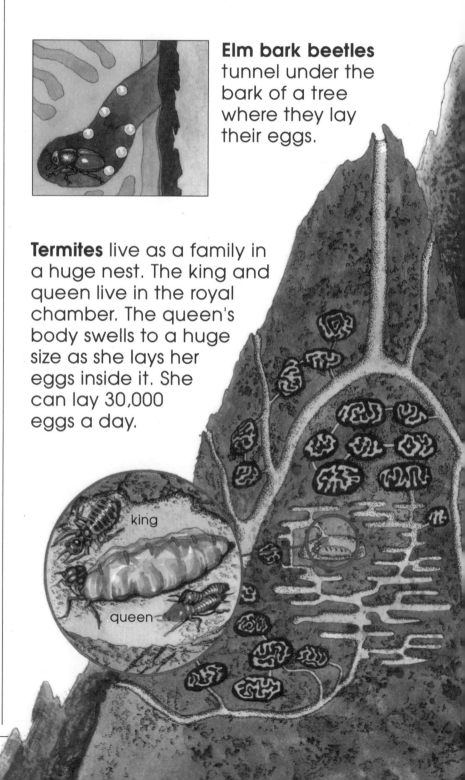

king

queen

Tailor ants make nests out of leaves. The workers sew the leaves together with silk made by the saliva glands of the larvae!

Pseudoscorpions carry their eggs on their bodies and feed them 'milk'. They look after their eggs and young inside a tiny nest made of silk.

Queen **bumblebees** build a wax honeypot in the nest where they lay their eggs, so they have plenty of food. They care for the young on their own.

Sandwasps catch and sting a caterpillar. This sends it to sleep. They put it in a burrow in the sand, and lay an egg on it.

When the egg hatches, the larva feeds on the sleeping caterpillar.

Oak gall wasps lay their eggs on the rib of an oak leaf. The rib swells and forms a gall which is a safe home for the larvae that grow inside it.

Galls come in all shapes and sizes. The aleppo gall is used to make special permanent ink which is used by banks.

35

Monsters on land

Happily there are few really monstrous large animals. Smaller monsters are much more common.

Pythons swallow their prey whole.

Giant **pythons** coil their powerful bodies around their helpless prey until they suffocate it.

Many large animals might look frightening, but usually they do not attack unless they are threatened.

The **elephant** is the largest land mammal. A full grown male (bull) African elephant can be over three metres tall and weigh eight tonnes.

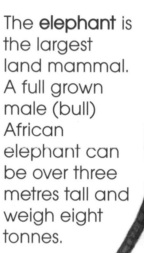

The enormous **Komodo dragon** prowls through the forest on lonely Indonesian islands.

This fierce lizard, nearly three metres long, will even attack people.

A **tiger** has huge, sharp teeth which grip and kill its prey.

The **giraffe** is the tallest mammal on Earth. However, it is not fierce and eats only leaves.

Grizzly bears tower a frightening three metres when they stand upright on their hind legs. They have big, sharp claws for tearing at food.

Gorillas are the largest primates. When threatened, a male gorilla will beat his chest with his hands, roar and rush towards the enemy.

The **Goliath beetle** is a heavyweight champion of the insect world. It can carry a load 850 times its own weight. That is similar to a human carrying 60 tonnes.

Some of the strangest monsters can be found swimming and living in the sea.

Large ones like the whales and sharks swim in the open ocean. Others, like giant sponges, hide deep down on the seabed.

Lurking at the bottom of the sea near Japan are **giant spider crabs**. With their claws outstretched they can measure nearly three metres.

The suckers on a 15-metre **giant squid** measure 10 cm across. But sucker scars on whales have been seen as long as 45 cm!

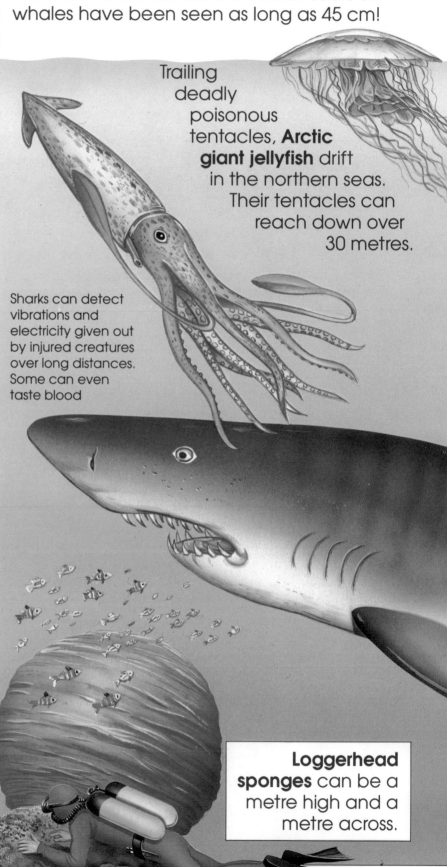

Trailing deadly poisonous tentacles, **Arctic giant jellyfish** drift in the northern seas. Their tentacles can reach down over 30 metres.

Sharks can detect vibrations and electricity given out by injured creatures over long distances. Some can even taste blood

Loggerhead sponges can be a metre high and a metre across.

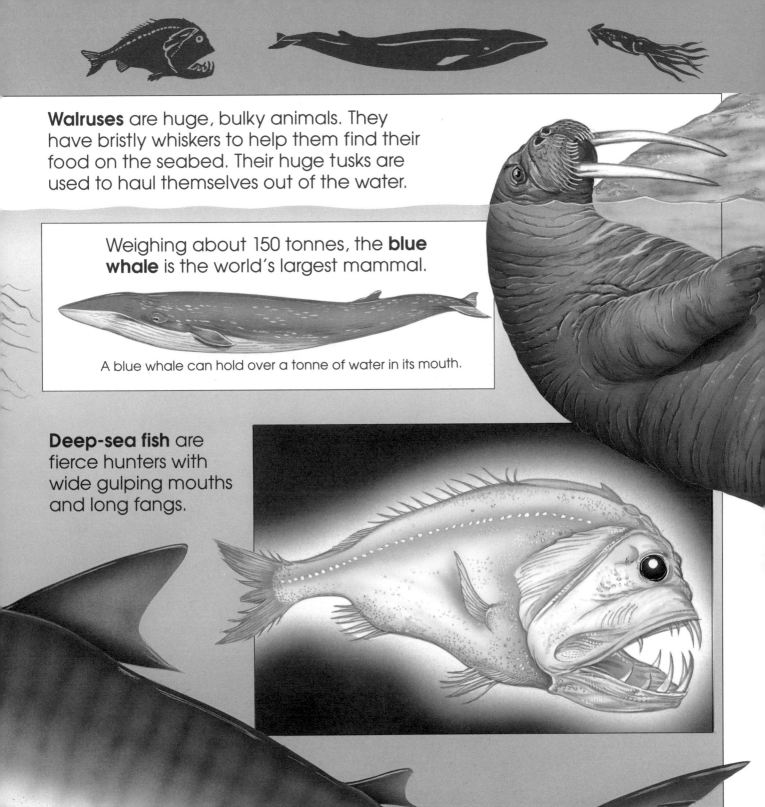

Walruses are huge, bulky animals. They have bristly whiskers to help them find their food on the seabed. Their huge tusks are used to haul themselves out of the water.

Weighing about 150 tonnes, the **blue whale** is the world's largest mammal.

A blue whale can hold over a tonne of water in its mouth.

Deep-sea fish are fierce hunters with wide gulping mouths and long fangs.

The **tiger shark** with its sharp teeth is a fierce predator in the sea.

Monsters in the air

Birds, bats and insects all have wings and can fly. Some are fierce hunters in the air and can grow very large.

Others use their long, needle-sharp claws, called talons, to catch and kill.

Monstrous **robber flies** hunt other insects in the air, piercing them with sharp mouthparts, and sucking out the contents of their bodies.

Bats are the only mammals that can truly fly. The largest bat is the **flying fox** which can have a wingspan of over two metres.

The **Andean condor** is the world's largest bird of prey and can weigh over 11 kgs.

Albatrosses circle the Earth, only coming to land when they want to breed.

The wings of an **albatross** can span more than three metres. They enable it to fly hundreds of kilometres at a time.

The wingspan of the largest moth in the world, the **atlas moth**, is 26 cm.

Pelicans dive to catch fish. Nearly half a metre long, their huge bills scoop up several fish at a time which they then swallow.

This evil-looking **wasp** has paralysed another insect with its terrible sting.

Hairy monsters

Monster animals covered with hair can look very strange. They are hairy for many reasons.

Some live in very cold places and need to keep warm. Others use hair for camouflage.

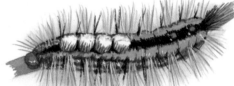

Poisonous hairs protect against attack. Hairs are even used to help some animals breathe underwater.

The hairs on this **Japanese Dictyoploca moth caterpillar** irritate and hurt any predator trying to eat it.

The body of a **porcupine** is covered with special hairs. When frightened the animal rattles these needle-sharp quills.

Some porcupines can even shoot quills out at their enemy.

The 'old man of the forest', or **orang-outang**, has very long, golden red hair.

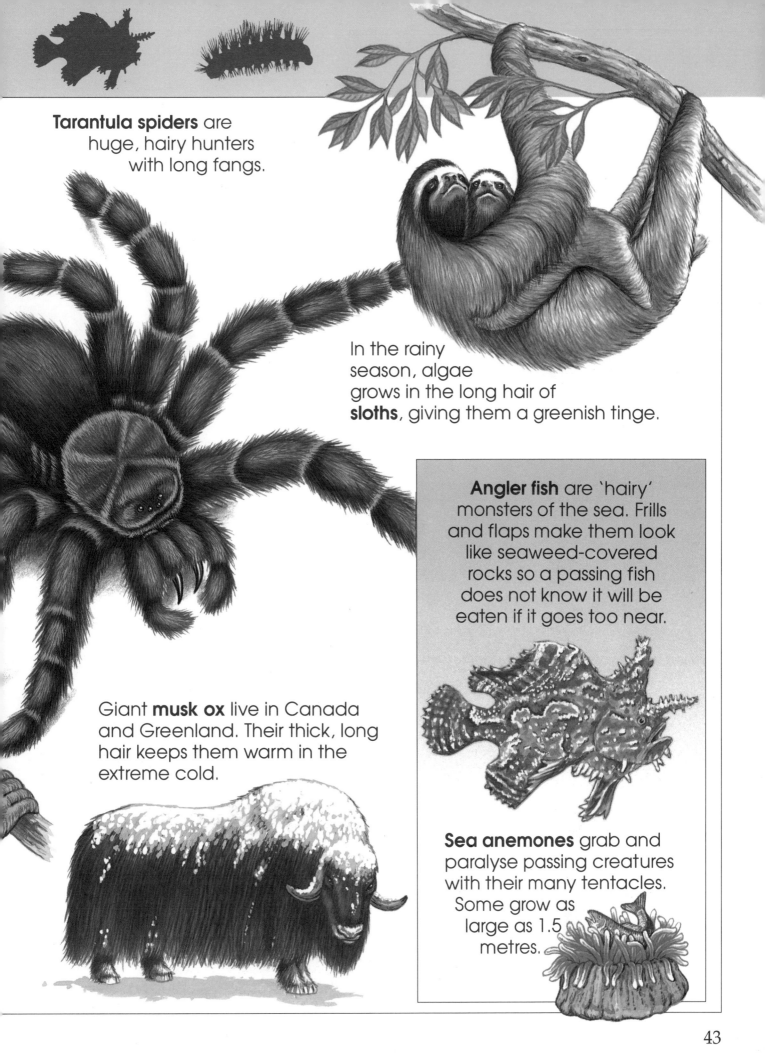

Tarantula spiders are huge, hairy hunters with long fangs.

In the rainy season, algae grows in the long hair of **sloths**, giving them a greenish tinge.

Angler fish are 'hairy' monsters of the sea. Frills and flaps make them look like seaweed-covered rocks so a passing fish does not know it will be eaten if it goes too near.

Giant **musk ox** live in Canada and Greenland. Their thick, long hair keeps them warm in the extreme cold.

Sea anemones grab and paralyse passing creatures with their many tentacles. Some grow as large as 1.5 metres.

To protect themselves from being attacked or eaten, many animals are monstrous looking.

Some look frightening all the time, while others can make themselves scary when they have to.

Roaring and puffing up their bodies are just some of the methods used.

Death's head hawkmoths can enter beehives and steal honey without being stung.

The strange skull-like markings on the **death's head hawkmoth** give it a deathly appearance.

This is not a fierce prehistoric monster, but a **frilled lizard**. This harmless lizard puts on an impressive display when it is frightened.

Male **stag beetles** have huge, fearsome jaws. They cannot bite with them, but instead joust with other males over females.

Stag beetles use their huge jaws to try and flick their opponent over.

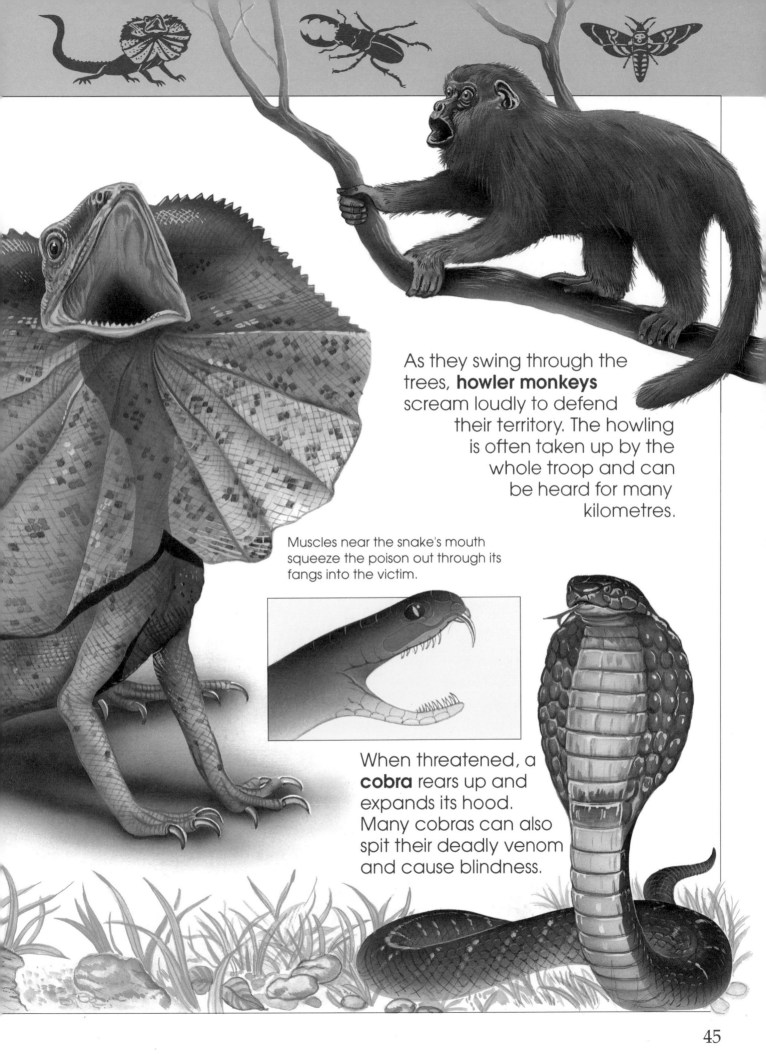

As they swing through the trees, **howler monkeys** scream loudly to defend their territory. The howling is often taken up by the whole troop and can be heard for many kilometres.

Muscles near the snake's mouth squeeze the poison out through its fangs into the victim.

When threatened, a **cobra** rears up and expands its hood. Many cobras can also spit their deadly venom and cause blindness.

Some monster animals use horrid smells to frighten their predators.

Others live in smelly places or have disgusting habits.

Eating dung and rotting corpses is not particularly nice, but without these animals to clear up, the world would be even smellier!

Big **dung beetles** carefully roll dung into balls which they hide in tunnels underground for their grubs to eat.

When a **vampire bat** finds a sleeping animal, it bites into the skin with its razor-sharp front teeth and laps up the blood with its tongue.

Vultures have bald heads and necks. This stops them getting too mucky with blood as they poke their heads inside a corpse to feed.

Lampreys cling to other fish with their strange circular mouths surrounded by hooks. They gnaw the flesh and even wriggle into their host's body.

Leeches attach themselves to animals and suck blood causing their bodies to swell. Some can grow as long as 20 cm.

Flies are attracted to dead bodies where they feed and lay their eggs. Once hatched, the maggots help to break down the rotten flesh.

Phew! The pungent odour of a **skunk** is disgusting. Skunks spray their scent to mark their territory and put off attackers.

Many animals are hunters, preying on other creatures. To catch and kill they have to be cunning, powerful and quick. Most have special teeth, jaws and stings to help catch, hold, kill and devour their victims.

Some of these fierce monsters are quite small. Others grow enormous and will even attack and eat people.

Giant **Colombian horned toads** are aggressive and will attack animals much bigger than themselves - they even bite horses!

Over a thousand people a year are killed by the world's largest and fiercest crocodile, the **Indo-Pacific crocodile**.

A **scorpion** grabs its prey with sharp claws and then bends its tail with its deadly sting over its head and into the victim, killing it with the poison.

Using their razor-sharp pointed teeth, **killer whales** can snatch a seal from a beach by rushing on to the shore on a wave. People stranded on ice-floes have also been tipped off and eaten.

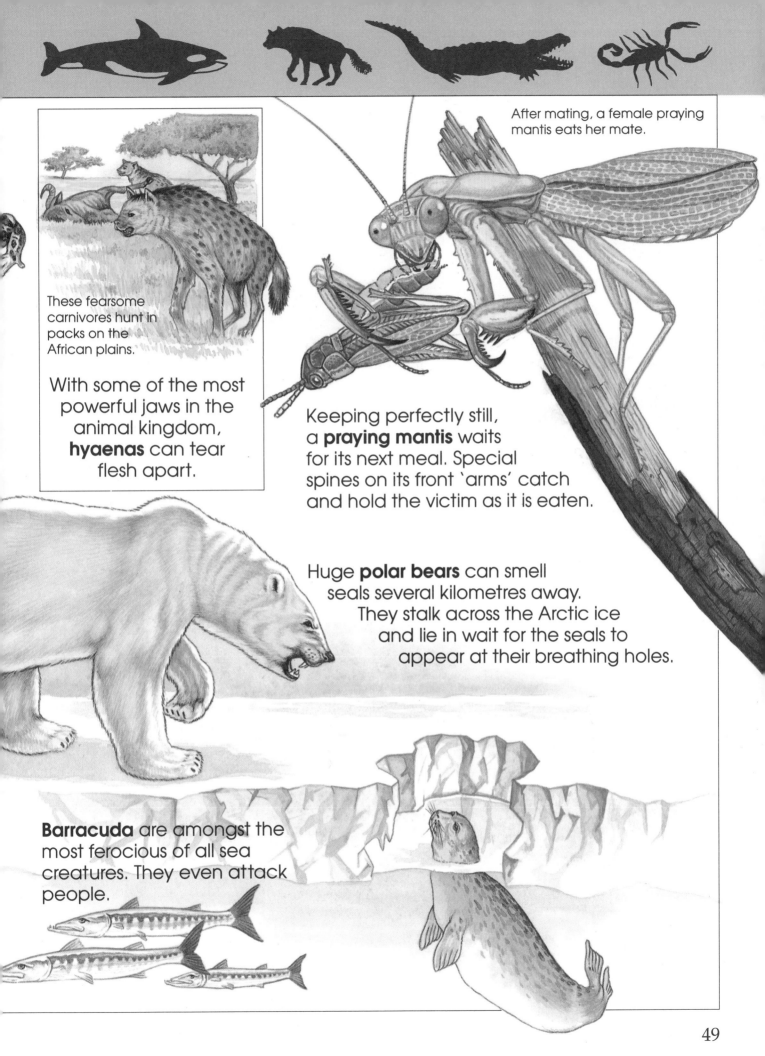

After mating, a female praying mantis eats her mate.

These fearsome carnivores hunt in packs on the African plains.

With some of the most powerful jaws in the animal kingdom, **hyaenas** can tear flesh apart.

Keeping perfectly still, a **praying mantis** waits for its next meal. Special spines on its front 'arms' catch and hold the victim as it is eaten.

Huge **polar bears** can smell seals several kilometres away. They stalk across the Arctic ice and lie in wait for the seals to appear at their breathing holes.

Barracuda are amongst the most ferocious of all sea creatures. They even attack people.

Fat monsters

Some animals are monstrously fat. Many of them spend most of their time in the water where the weight of their bodies is supported.

Fat bodies can hold a lot of food for times when there is little food around. They can also be used to scare off attackers.

The fat **Vietnamese pot-bellied pig** is kept as a pet in some parts of the world.

Herds of **elephant seals** wallow on the beach. An adult male can weigh almost four tonnes. When males fight each other they often crush the babies on the beach.

Hippopotamus means 'river horse'. Although they look fat and clumsy on land, when they are in water they can swim fast.

Hippos use their large teeth for digging up water plants and fighting.

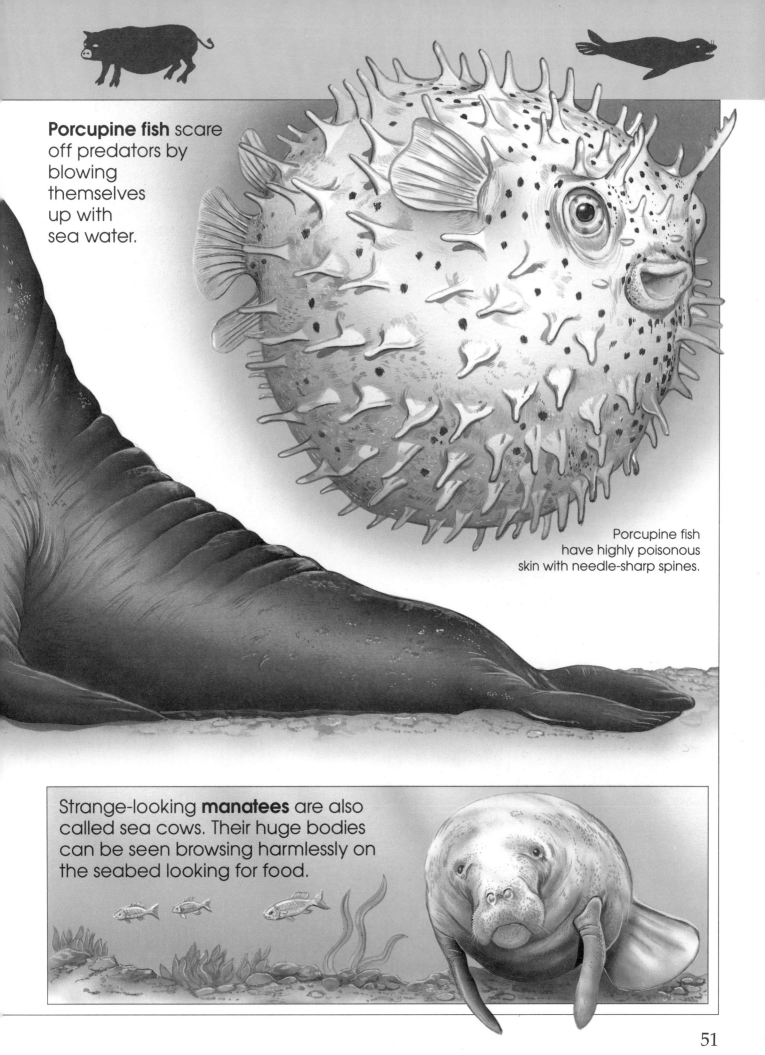

Porcupine fish scare off predators by blowing themselves up with sea water.

Porcupine fish have highly poisonous skin with needle-sharp spines.

Strange-looking **manatees** are also called sea cows. Their huge bodies can be seen browsing harmlessly on the seabed looking for food.

Some animals are very strange-looking to us. But these monsters are usually the shape they are for a reason.

Everything is made so that it is suited to where it lives so it can survive.

Chameleons can swivel their heads and eyes around independently from their bodies.

Jackson's chameleon is a lizard with three long horns on its head. It looks like the extinct dinosaur Triceratops.

Molochs look like bizarre prehistoric creatures. These spiny lizards live in the hot deserts of North America.

Animals do not usually have two heads, but sometimes they are born. This freak two-headed **kingsnake** was found in California, USA.

The strange-looking **hammerhead shark** is a ferocious hunter. It even attacks people.

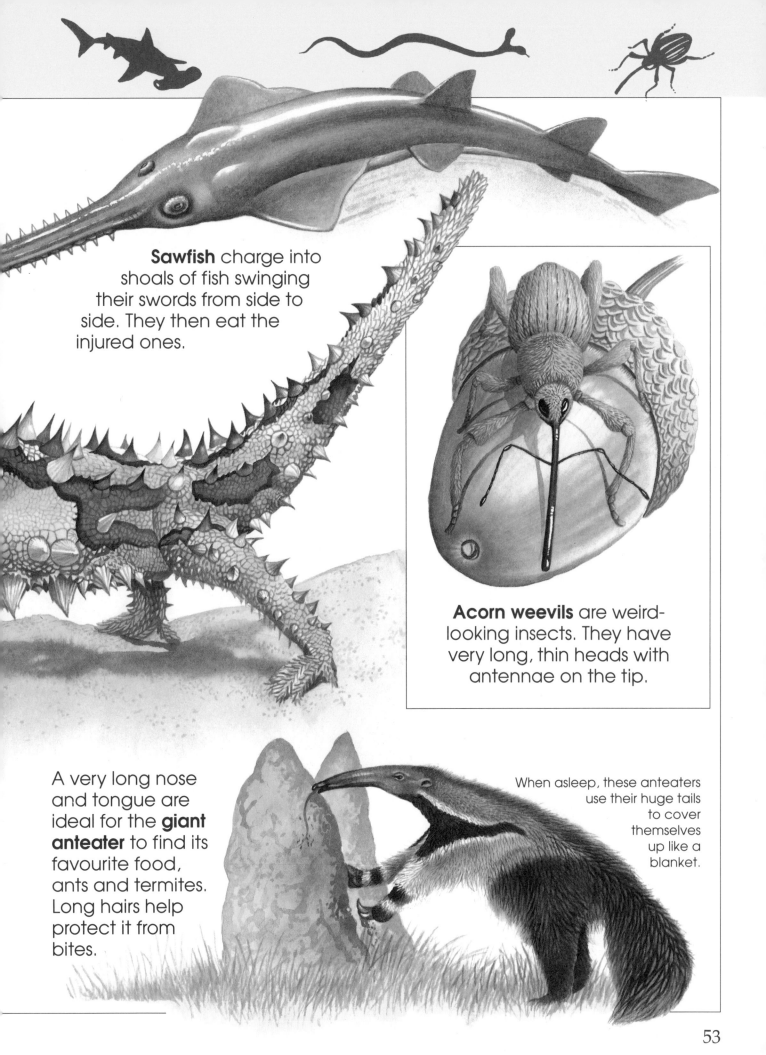

Sawfish charge into shoals of fish swinging their swords from side to side. They then eat the injured ones.

Acorn weevils are weird-looking insects. They have very long, thin heads with antennae on the tip.

A very long nose and tongue are ideal for the **giant anteater** to find its favourite food, ants and termites. Long hairs help protect it from bites.

When asleep, these anteaters use their huge tails to cover themselves up like a blanket.

53

Deadly monsters

Many animals protect themselves from attack by stinging or biting.

Some animals use poison to stun or kill their prey. Many of these deadly animals have ways of warning others to keep away!

A **black widow spider** traps its prey in a web and then sucks out its insides.

Long, brightly coloured spines cover the body of the beautiful but deadly **lion fish**. The sharp spines are coated with toxic mucus and cause terrible pain if touched.

The long trailing tentacles of the **Portuguese Man O'War jellyfish** are highly poisonous. Stinging cells shoot tiny barbed harpoons into anything that touches them.

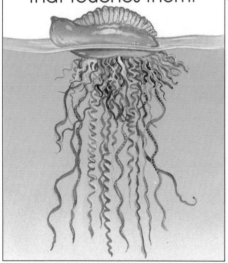

The bright colours of **poison dart frogs** warn predators to leave them alone.

People living in the rainforests of South America smear their blow-pipe darts with the frog's mucus (slime) to poison their prey.

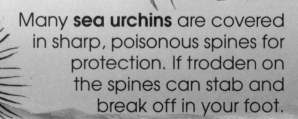

Many **sea urchins** are covered in sharp, poisonous spines for protection. If trodden on the spines can stab and break off in your foot.

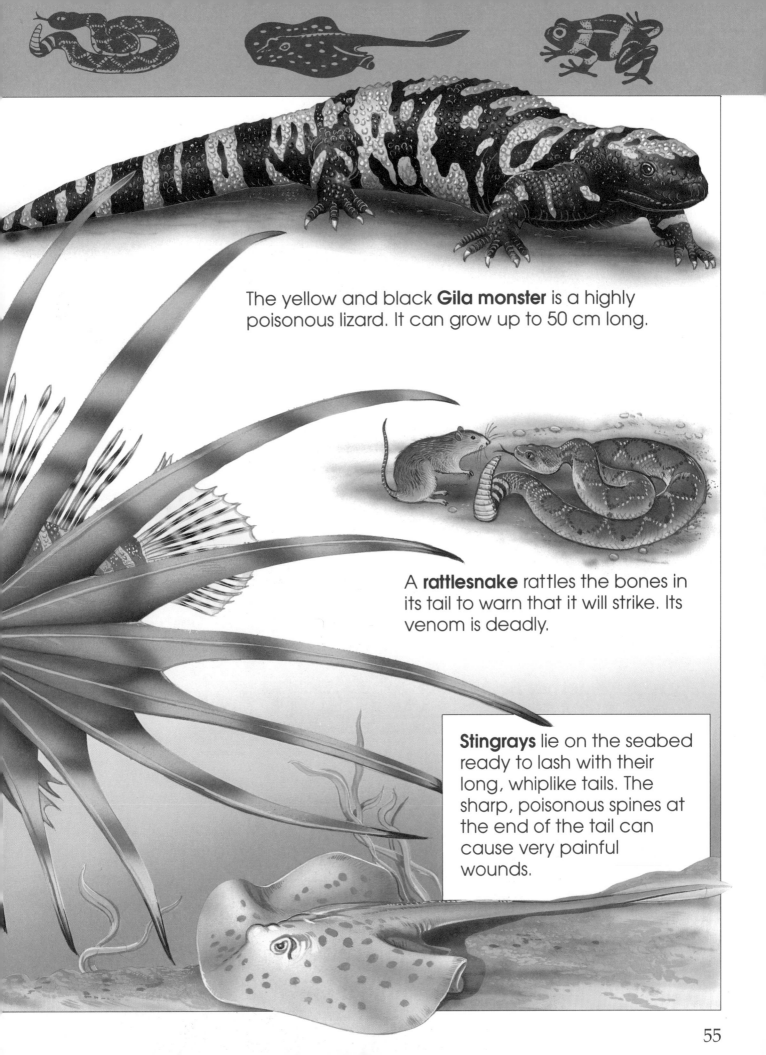

The yellow and black **Gila monster** is a highly poisonous lizard. It can grow up to 50 cm long.

A **rattlesnake** rattles the bones in its tail to warn that it will strike. Its venom is deadly.

Stingrays lie on the seabed ready to lash with their long, whiplike tails. The sharp, poisonous spines at the end of the tail can cause very painful wounds.

Masses of monsters

Some animals are only frightening and dangerous in large numbers.

Some, like bees, live together in groups to help each other. Others, like wolves, hunt in packs.

Some animals only group together in masses at certain times.

In some parts of the world, plagues of flying **locusts** can darken the sky, eating every green plant they land on.

Hornets live as a colony, nesting inside hollow trees. They use their huge jaws and deadly sting to hunt.

A colony of **army ants** marching through the forest will eat everything in its way - even small animals.

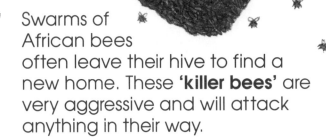

Millions of **mosquitoes** often breed together. The females must have a blood meal before they can lay their eggs. A person can lose nearly a litre of blood to these insects if they are not protected.

Swarms of African bees often leave their hive to find a new home. These **'killer bees'** are very aggressive and will attack anything in their way.

African wild dogs live in packs of up to 60. By circling their prey and dashing in and biting it, the victim is soon weakened and killed.

Hunting together in packs, **wolves** can catch and kill large animals. They usually attack the weak and sick, but rarely people.

Rare monsters

Many animals are becoming rare. Some have already become extinct and will never be seen again outside a museum.

People kill animals for their skin, fur, feathers and horns. We also destroy the places where they live.

The largest **false scorpion** in Europe lives under the bark of dead trees. It is now extremely rare and only found in ancient forests.

On Maria Island in the West Indies lives the world's rarest snake, the **St Lucia racer**. There are less than 100 left.

Racers are large, fast snakes which strike repeatedly with their heads when attacked, tearing the flesh.

Wildlife parks and zoos do important work trying to save animals from extinction. The last wild **Californian condor** was captured so it could breed under protection.

Trap door spiders in Southeast Asia are the rarest spiders. They use their jaws to dig holes, leaving a hinged lid at the entrance. When a victim comes near, the spider opens the lid, grabs its prey, and pulls it underground.

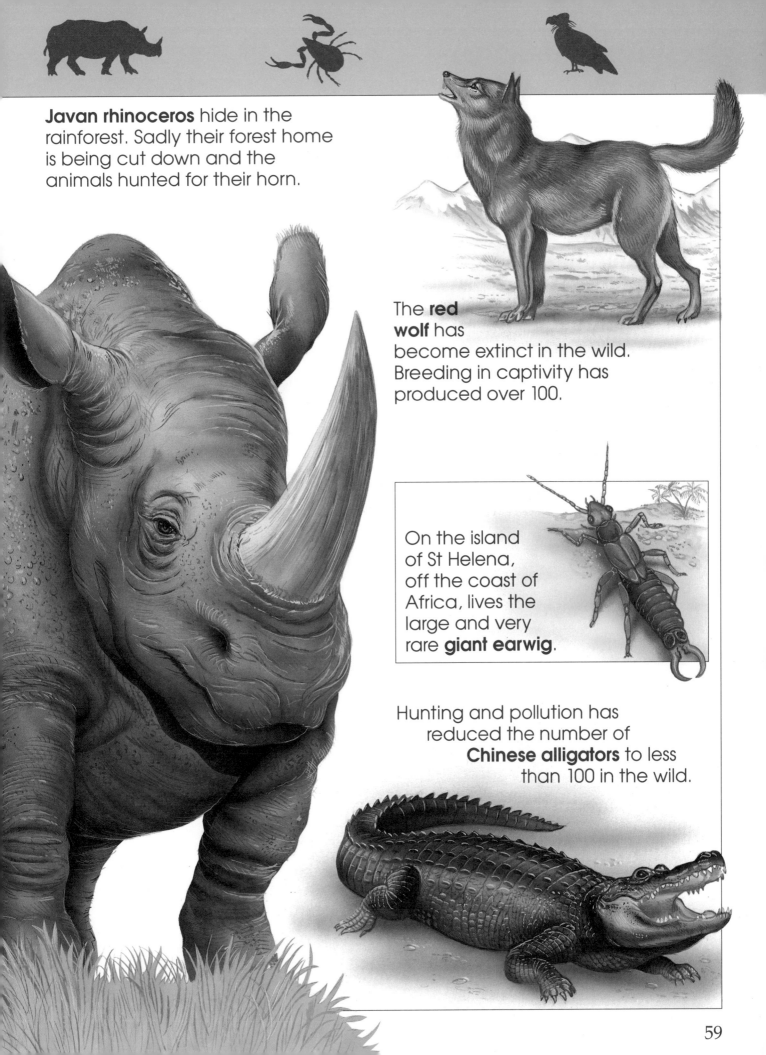

Javan rhinoceros hide in the rainforest. Sadly their forest home is being cut down and the animals hunted for their horn.

The **red wolf** has become extinct in the wild. Breeding in captivity has produced over 100.

On the island of St Helena, off the coast of Africa, lives the large and very rare **giant earwig**.

Hunting and pollution has reduced the number of **Chinese alligators** to less than 100 in the wild.

Imaginary monsters

Superstition and fear have made people dream up all kinds of strange and imaginary monsters.

Some of these unnatural creatures were invented from stories of unusual animals brought back by travellers.

Other mythical monsters are based on actual living, and extinct, animals.

Some imaginary monsters might be real, we just do not know for sure.

Every year, thousands of people watch the water on Loch Ness in Scotland, hoping to see the **Loch Ness Monster**. Some believe that the monster could be a surviving plesiosaur, a prehistoric sea creature.

The **hydra** is a nine-headed beast of Greek mythology. It was very difficult to kill as each time a head was cut off it grew two new ones.

Sailors' sightings of mermaids may have been **dugongs**. At a distance, female dugongs with their young look like women holding their babies in their arms.

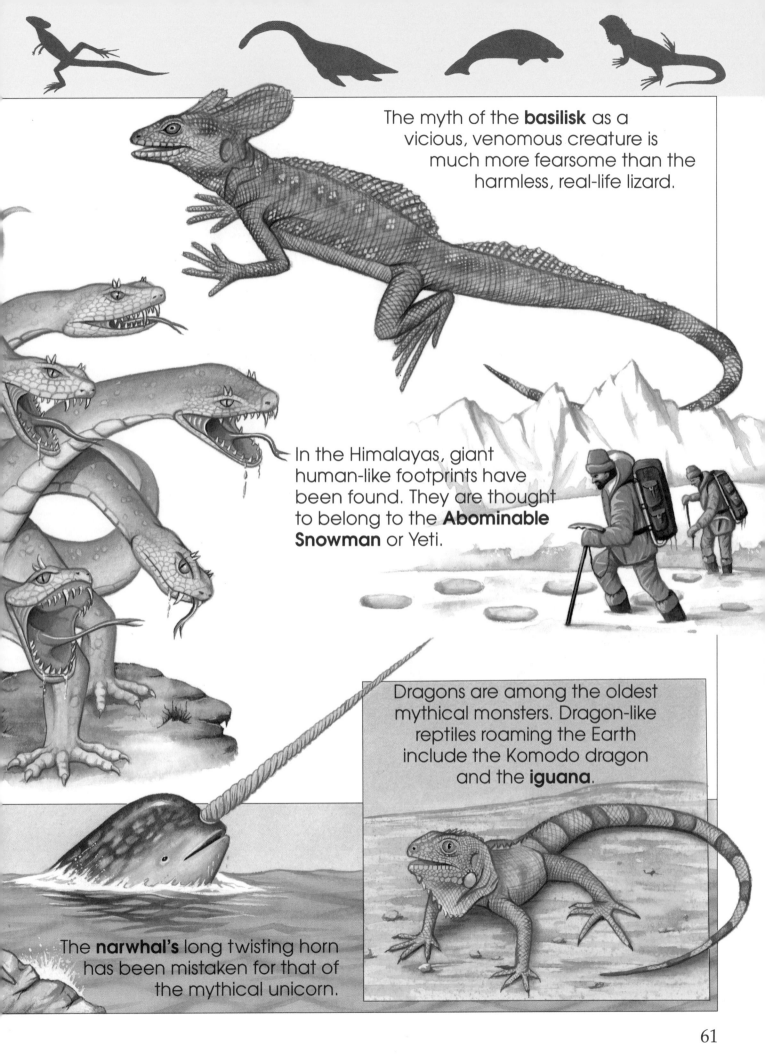

The myth of the **basilisk** as a vicious, venomous creature is much more fearsome than the harmless, real-life lizard.

In the Himalayas, giant human-like footprints have been found. They are thought to belong to the **Abominable Snowman** or Yeti.

Dragons are among the oldest mythical monsters. Dragon-like reptiles roaming the Earth include the Komodo dragon and the **iguana**.

The **narwhal's** long twisting horn has been mistaken for that of the mythical unicorn.

Millions of years ago, all kinds of strange monstrous animals roamed the Earth.

There were no people around when the dinosaurs ruled the world.

When people appeared they cut down forests and hunted animals. Some of the larger species were driven into extinction. Today, people still kill and threaten many animals.

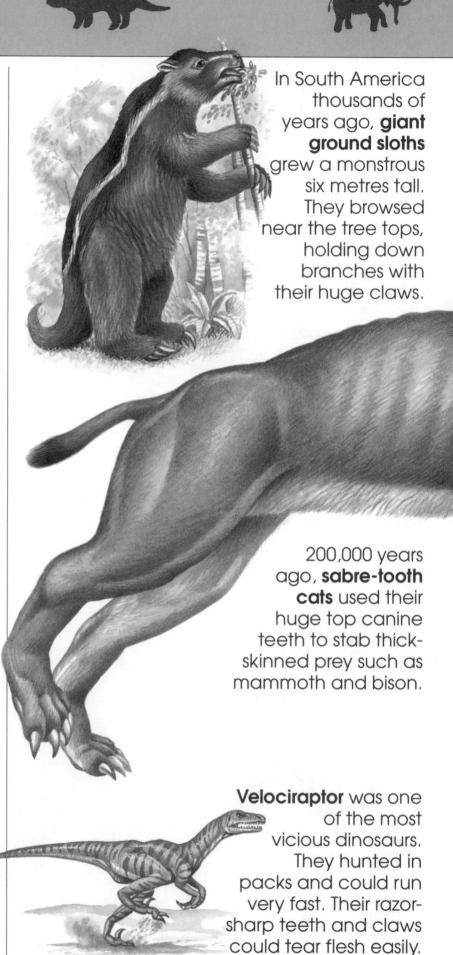

In South America thousands of years ago, **giant ground sloths** grew a monstrous six metres tall. They browsed near the tree tops, holding down branches with their huge claws.

200,000 years ago, **sabre-tooth cats** used their huge top canine teeth to stab thick-skinned prey such as mammoth and bison.

Velociraptor was one of the most vicious dinosaurs. They hunted in packs and could run very fast. Their razor-sharp teeth and claws could tear flesh easily.

Quetzalcoatlus' wings were made of skin like those of bats today.

97 million years ago, **quetzalcoatlus** soared through the air on wings spanning 12 metres.

Giant Irish deer grew antlers nearly four metres across. They died out 2,500 years ago.

Mammoths are one of the largest land mammals to have lived. They grew over four metres tall and had woolly coats and huge tusks.

The giant **moa** of New Zealand was the tallest bird that ever existed. It stood over three metres tall.

People destroyed the moa's habitat and hunted it, so that by 1800 it was extinct.

Hyaenodon must have been a fearsome hunter and scavenger. Its skull was 65 cm long and full of needle-sharp teeth.

Coral creatures

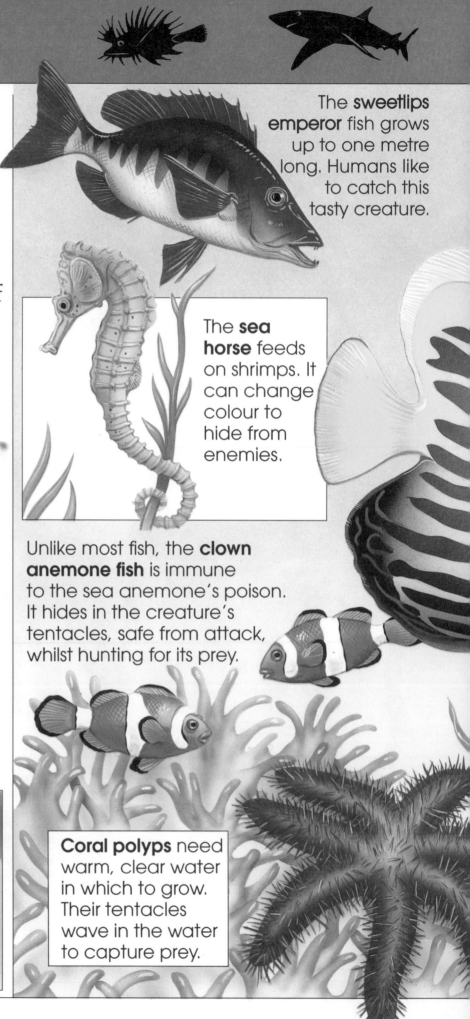

Coral reefs are made from millions of tiny creatures called coral polyps. When it dies, each polyp leaves behind a tiny limestone skeleton. There are thousands of types of polyp.

Many other creatures live on the reef. The shallow water and rocky crevices provide an ideal home.

The largest coral reef in the world is the **Great Barrier Reef** off the east coast of Queensland, Australia. It is over 2,000 km long.

The **sweetlips emperor** fish grows up to one metre long. Humans like to catch this tasty creature.

The **sea horse** feeds on shrimps. It can change colour to hide from enemies.

Unlike most fish, the **clown anemone fish** is immune to the sea anemone's poison. It hides in the creature's tentacles, safe from attack, whilst hunting for its prey.

Coral polyps need warm, clear water in which to grow. Their tentacles wave in the water to capture prey.

The **blue shark** cruises the reef, hunting for prey.

The **imperial angelfish** has bright stripes to match the colours of the coral.

A **lionfish** has bright stripes to warn other fish that its spines are poisonous.

Anemones use their tentacles to catch prey. Poisonous barbs kill the fish which are then pulled into the anemone's mouth.

The **stonefish** looks like a stone and hides in gaps in the reef. Any human who trod on its poisonous spines would die!

The **crown of thorns starfish** eats coral polyps. Usually, new polyps replace those eaten and the reef survives any damage.

Seashore creatures

Life on the shore can be very difficult for animals. As the tide comes in and goes out, their surroundings change from dry land to shallow sea.

Pounding waves throw animals around. The sand is always moving as the sea pushes and pulls it around. Seashore animals must be tough to survive.

Prawns feed among the seaweed. When the tide goes out, they swim into deeper water, but sometimes they are caught in rock pools.

The **scorpion fish** and other kinds of small fish feed among the stones in rock pools. They swim out with the tide.

The **masked crab** lives on sandy beaches. When the tide goes out, it burrows into the sand. The tips of its two antennae poke out of the sand and act as breathing tubes.

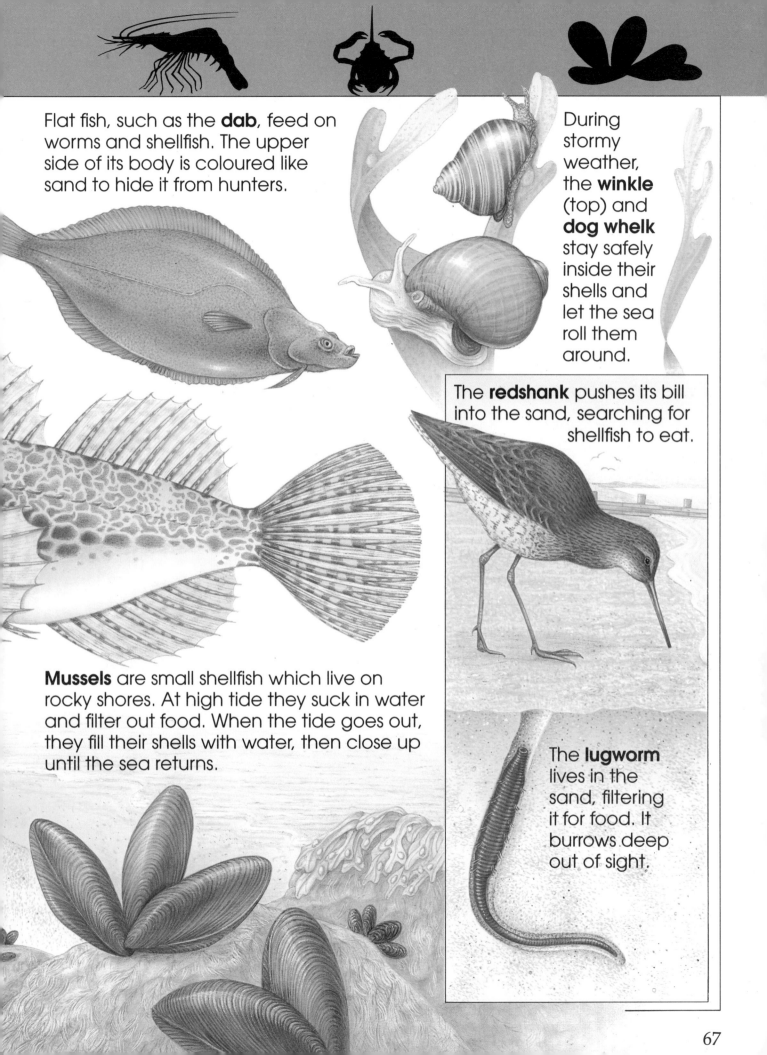

Flat fish, such as the **dab**, feed on worms and shellfish. The upper side of its body is coloured like sand to hide it from hunters.

During stormy weather, the **winkle** (top) and **dog whelk** stay safely inside their shells and let the sea roll them around.

The **redshank** pushes its bill into the sand, searching for shellfish to eat.

Mussels are small shellfish which live on rocky shores. At high tide they suck in water and filter out food. When the tide goes out, they fill their shells with water, then close up until the sea returns.

The **lugworm** lives in the sand, filtering it for food. It burrows deep out of sight.

Deep-sea creatures

Most sea creatures live near the surface, where the water is warm and sunlit. The light cannot travel very deep and the sea's currents rarely move the warm surface water down to the depths of the ocean.

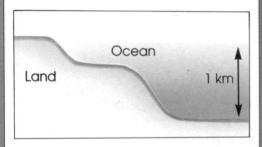

Ocean

Land

1 km

At depths of more than one kilometre, the sea is very cold and completely dark. Some very strange creatures live here. They feed on each other and on food which drifts down from above.

Sperm whales dive down for food.

The **giant squid** can grow to 20 metres long.

Deep-sea shrimps can glow to attract a mate.

The **deep-sea angler fish** has a long growth over its mouth which glows faintly. This attracts other fish, which are then swallowed whole!

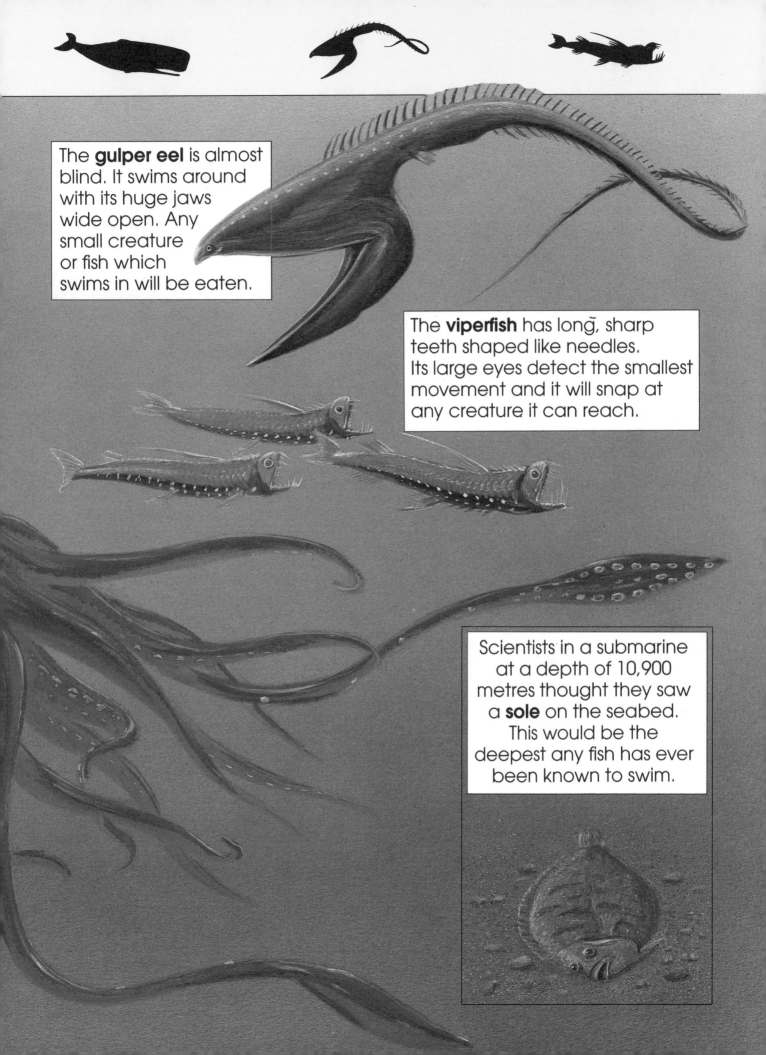

The **gulper eel** is almost blind. It swims around with its huge jaws wide open. Any small creature or fish which swims in will be eaten.

The **viperfish** has long, sharp teeth shaped like needles. Its large eyes detect the smallest movement and it will snap at any creature it can reach.

Scientists in a submarine at a depth of 10,900 metres thought they saw a **sole** on the seabed. This would be the deepest any fish has ever been known to swim.

Around both the North and South Poles, the weather is very cold. A layer of ice floats on top of the sea all year round.

Animals which live there must be able to keep warm. They may have thick fur, like the polar bear, or layers of fat under their skin, like the common seal.

Killer whales prey on any creatures they can catch. They will even push ice from underwater to knock penguins and seals into the sea.

Penguins are birds that live around the South Pole. They lay their eggs on the ice and hunt for fish in the sea.

The largest penguin is the **Emperor penguin** which grows to over one metre tall.

The smallest penguin is the **fairy penguin**, which is only 40 cm tall.

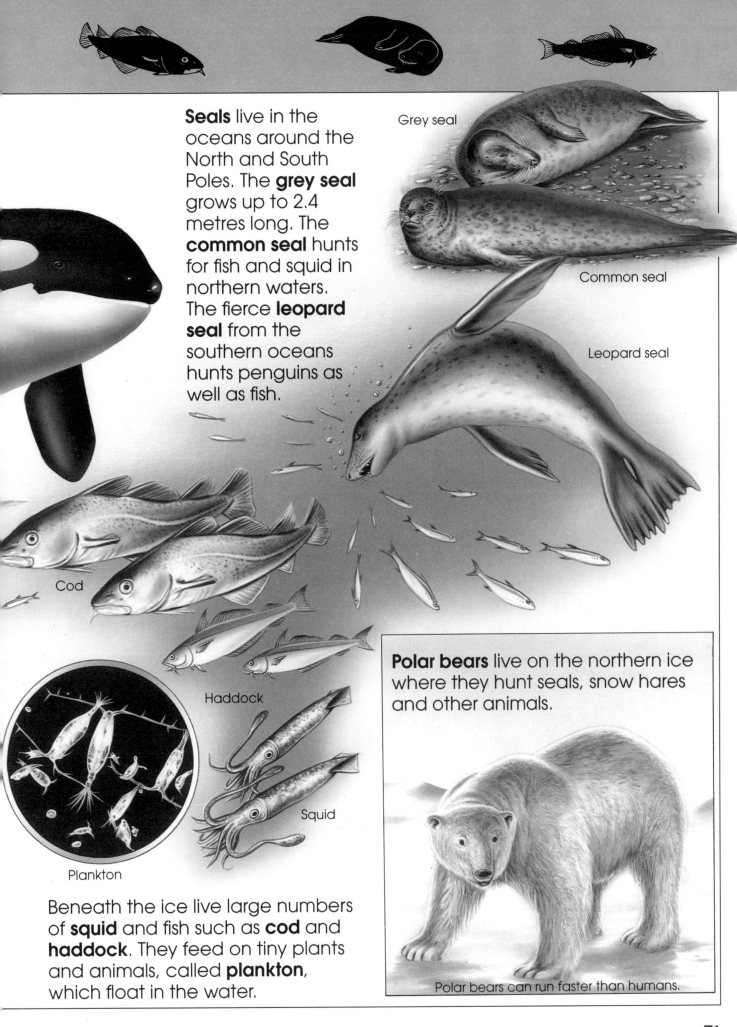

Seals live in the oceans around the North and South Poles. The **grey seal** grows up to 2.4 metres long. The **common seal** hunts for fish and squid in northern waters. The fierce **leopard seal** from the southern oceans hunts penguins as well as fish.

Grey seal

Common seal

Leopard seal

Cod

Haddock

Squid

Plankton

Beneath the ice live large numbers of **squid** and fish such as **cod** and **haddock**. They feed on tiny plants and animals, called **plankton**, which float in the water.

Polar bears live on the northern ice where they hunt seals, snow hares and other animals.

Polar bears can run faster than humans.

Microscopic creatures

The smallest living things in the sea are called plankton. They are so small that you could fit 40,000 of them on the end of your thumb.

Plankton can be either plants or animals. They are food for the larger sea animals.

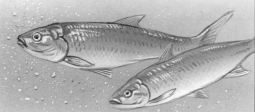

Large clouds of plankton drift in the surface waters of all seas.

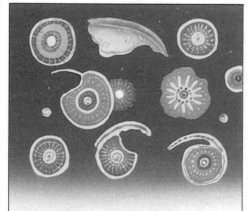

Phyto-plankton are microscopic plants. They use the sunlight's energy to grow like plants on land.

The smallest animals are made of a single body-cell. **Ceratium** moves by thrashing a long, whip-like 'arm'. It feeds on tiny plants.

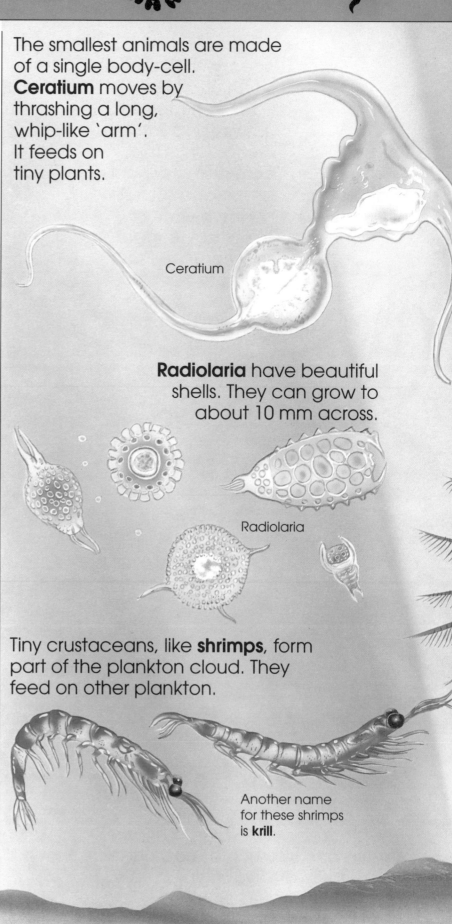

Ceratium

Radiolaria have beautiful shells. They can grow to about 10 mm across.

Radiolaria

Tiny crustaceans, like **shrimps**, form part of the plankton cloud. They feed on other plankton.

Another name for these shrimps is **krill**.

Some of the **plankton** are the young of much larger creatures. Because they drift with the ocean currents, these creatures can travel much further than they can as adults, allowing them to reach new homes.

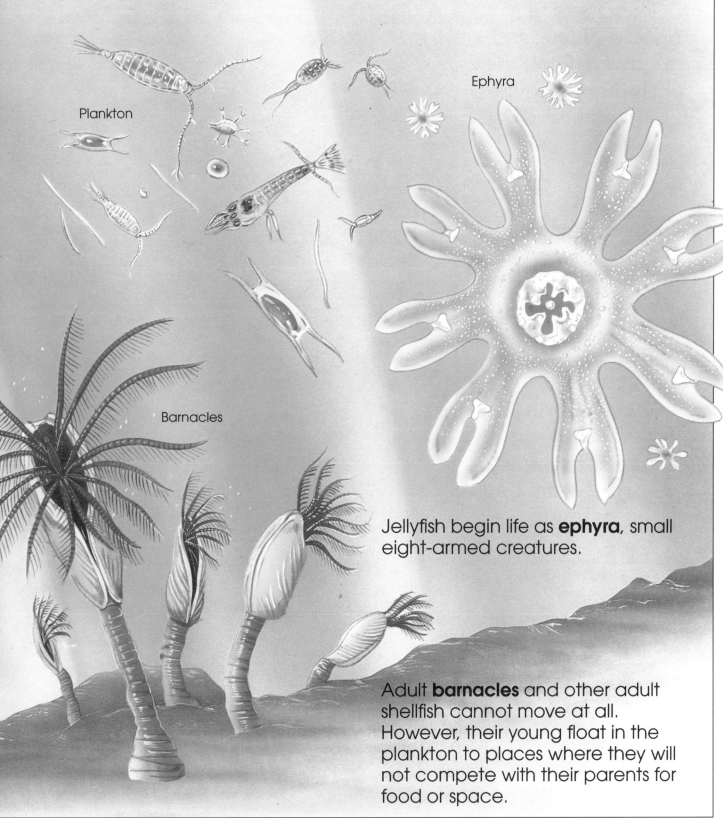

Plankton

Ephyra

Barnacles

Jellyfish begin life as **ephyra**, small eight-armed creatures.

Adult **barnacles** and other adult shellfish cannot move at all. However, their young float in the plankton to places where they will not compete with their parents for food or space.

Whales are mammals which have evolved to live in the sea. They have fins instead of legs and a powerful tail to push them through the water.

The **bowhead whale**'s head is six metres long. This is one-third of its length. The jaws are packed with baleen to filter food from the sea water.

The largest whales feed on plankton. They have special filters, called baleen, in their mouths which strain seawater and remove the tiny animals and plants to be eaten.

Like all mammals, whales breathe air, so they need to come to the surface from time to time.

The earliest known whale is **basiliosaurus**, which lived about 40 million years ago.

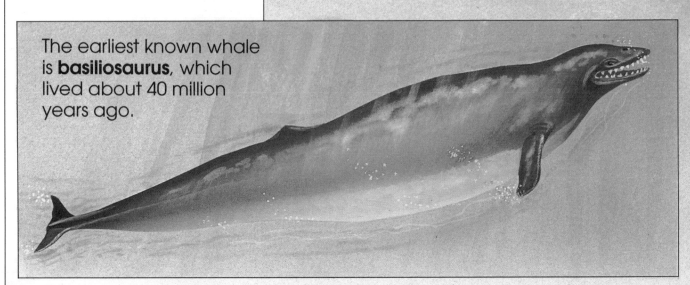

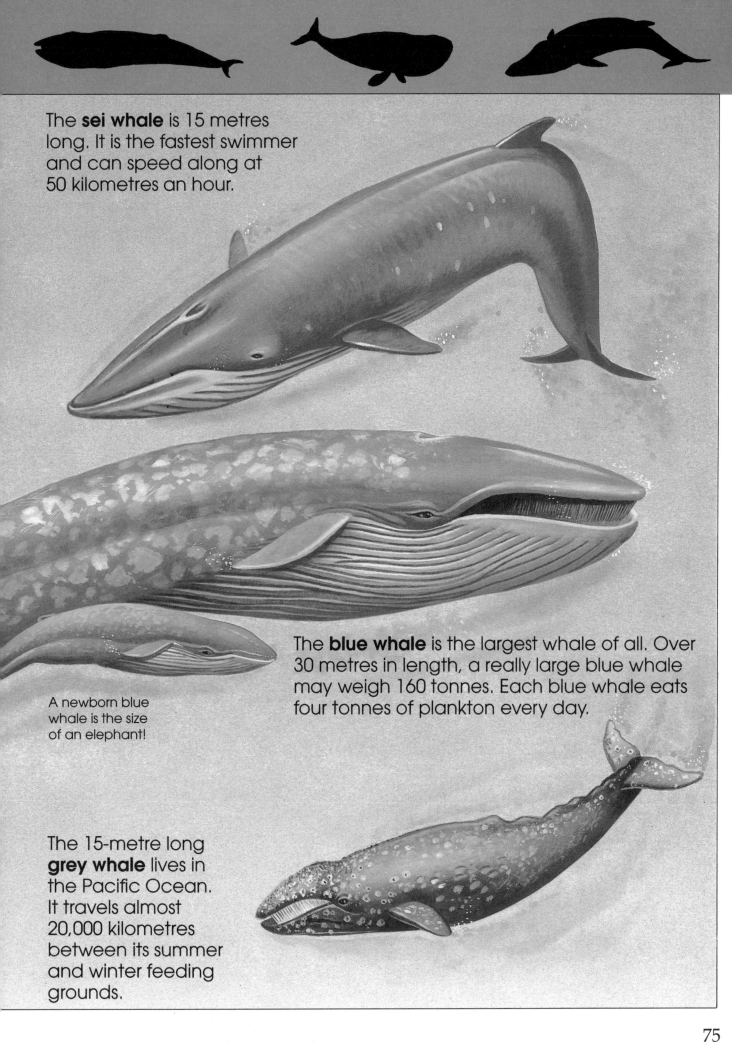

The **sei whale** is 15 metres long. It is the fastest swimmer and can speed along at 50 kilometres an hour.

A newborn blue whale is the size of an elephant!

The **blue whale** is the largest whale of all. Over 30 metres in length, a really large blue whale may weigh 160 tonnes. Each blue whale eats four tonnes of plankton every day.

The 15-metre long **grey whale** lives in the Pacific Ocean. It travels almost 20,000 kilometres between its summer and winter feeding grounds.

Seals are mammals which have evolved to live in the oceans.

Their legs have become flippers to help them swim, but they can still move on land.

Seals spend some of their time on shore, either caring for their babies or resting from hunting for fish.

Elephants seals were once hunted for the rich oil their bodies contained. At one time, only about 100 were still alive, but today there are over 50,000 of them.

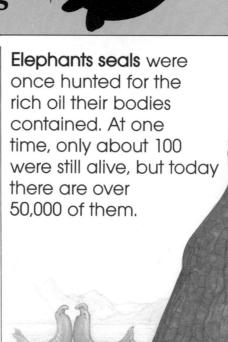

The **harp seal** hunts fish beneath the ocean surface. Thick layers of fat under its skin protect it from the icy water.

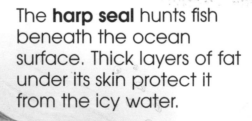

The **walrus** has two long tusks. It uses these to dig in mud for the shellfish it eats.

Male **hooded seals** have a large flap of skin on their heads. This is used to make a loud noise to frighten off rival seals.

Crabeater seals do not actually eat crabs, but feed on small shrimps, known as krill.

The **dugong** looks like a seal, but could be related to elephants. It lives in the Indian Ocean, and feeds on underwater plants.

Dolphins belong to a group of whales called toothed whales. They do not eat plankton but hunt squid and fish.

Dolphins are very intelligent creatures. They communicate with each other using different sounds arranged like words in a sentence.

Some dolphins are very rare. The **shepherd's beaked whale** is a recent discovery.

Dolphins are social animals. They live in family groups. If one dolphin is sick or injured, others will come to its rescue.

Dolphins are mammals. They breathe air and feed their babies with milk.

The **bouto** is a dolphin that lives in the Amazon river.

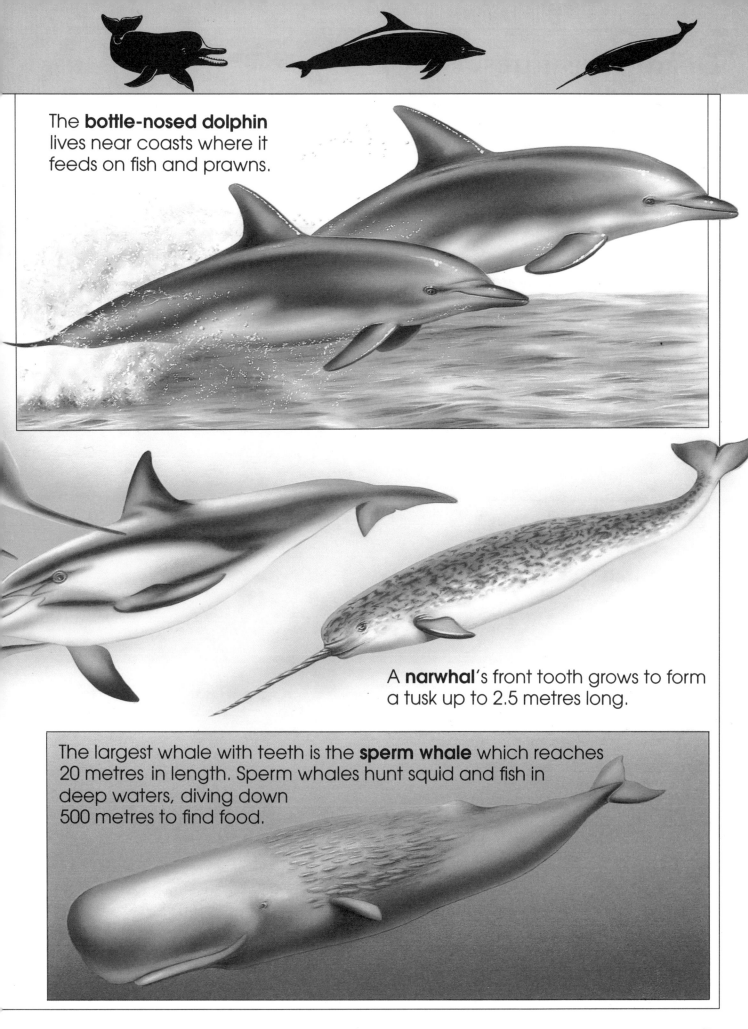

The **bottle-nosed dolphin** lives near coasts where it feeds on fish and prawns.

A **narwhal**'s front tooth grows to form a tusk up to 2.5 metres long.

The largest whale with teeth is the **sperm whale** which reaches 20 metres in length. Sperm whales hunt squid and fish in deep waters, diving down 500 metres to find food.

Sharks and rays are found in all seas. Their skeletons are made of soft cartilage instead of hard bone.

Sharks hunt other sea creatures, using their sharp teeth and strong muscles to overpower their prey.

The largest shark is the 18-metre long **whale shark**. Unlike most sharks, it does not hunt other animals. Instead, it feeds on plankton.

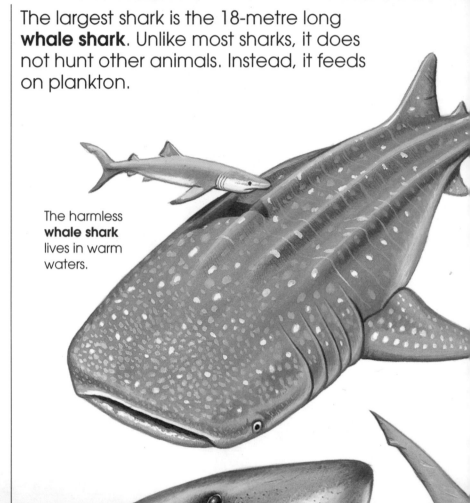

The harmless **whale shark** lives in warm waters.

The great white shark sometimes attacks people.

The largest hunting shark is the **great white shark**. It may grow to seven metres long and usually feeds on larger fish and other animals.

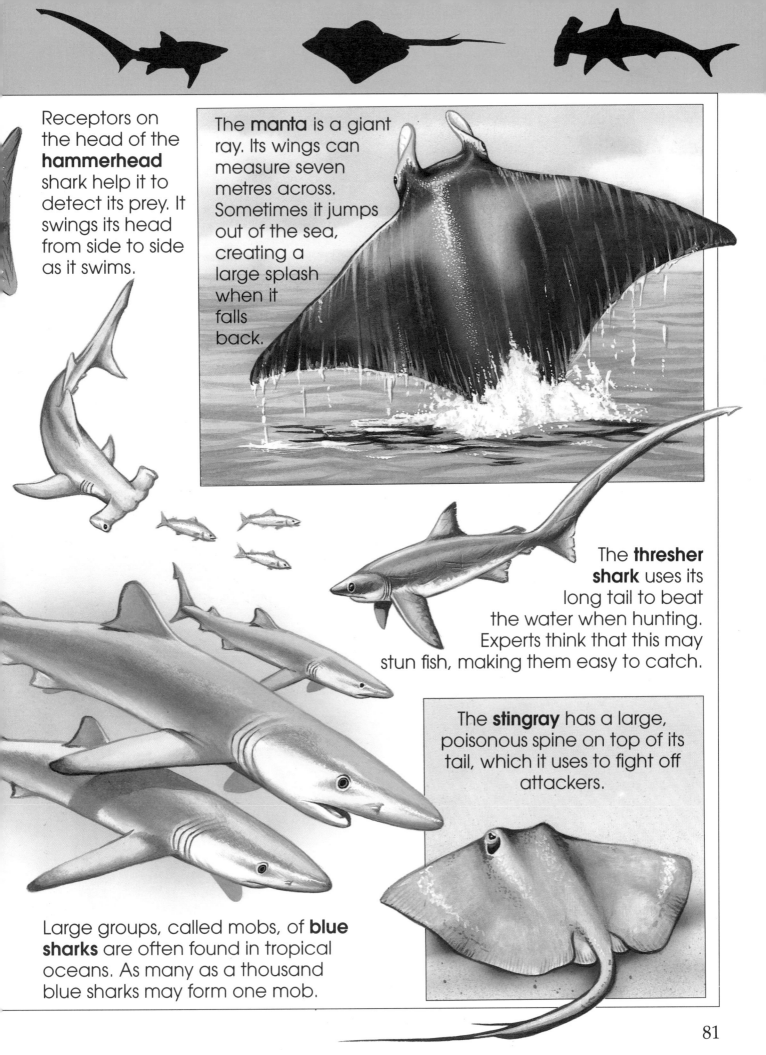

Receptors on the head of the **hammerhead** shark help it to detect its prey. It swings its head from side to side as it swims.

The **manta** is a giant ray. Its wings can measure seven metres across. Sometimes it jumps out of the sea, creating a large splash when it falls back.

The **thresher shark** uses its long tail to beat the water when hunting. Experts think that this may stun fish, making them easy to catch.

The **stingray** has a large, poisonous spine on top of its tail, which it uses to fight off attackers.

Large groups, called mobs, of **blue sharks** are often found in tropical oceans. As many as a thousand blue sharks may form one mob.

81

Flying creatures

Many birds live at sea feeding on fish or other sea creatures.

Most seabirds nest on islands, where their eggs and young are safe from attack.

Seabirds often make long journeys between their nesting sites and feeding grounds. Arctic terns travel between the Arctic and the Antarctic.

Herring gulls are very common. They feed on fish and shrimps, but will also fly inland to raid rubbish dumps and picnic areas.

The **great skua** is a large bird, over 50 cm long. It hunts other seabirds, as well as fish.

A **skimmer** finds fish by flying just above the surface of the sea, with its bill in the water. As soon as the bill strikes a fish, it is snapped up.

The largest seabird is the **wandering albatross**, which has wings 3.5 metres across. Long ago, sailors believed it was bad luck to kill an albatross.

Steamer ducks live around the coast. They cannot fly, but swim along the shore looking for shellfish, shrimps and crabs to eat.

Puffins nest on cliffs and rocky islands. The females lay just one egg each year.

Gannet fly around searching for fish in the water. They may dive from a height of 30 metres to catch their prey.

Reptiles are animals such as lizards. Most live on land.

A few types of reptile have evolved to live in the ocean, but they need to come to the surface often to breathe air.

Most sea reptiles lay their eggs on dry land. They may come ashore once a year to do this.

The **green turtle** has a tough shell to protect it from attack. It feeds on seaweed and jellyfish.

The **leatherback turtle** has no shell, but the skin on its back is very thick and tough.

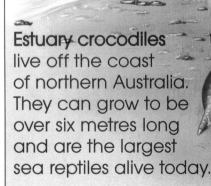

Estuary crocodiles live off the coast of northern Australia. They can grow to be over six metres long and are the largest sea reptiles alive today.

Ridley turtles crunch up shellfish with their strong jaws.

The **banded sea snake** lives in the Pacific Ocean where it hunts fish. It is one of the most poisonous snakes in the world.

The **hawksbill turtle** is very rare. Not long ago, it was hunted for its shell. This was used to make things such as ornate boxes and spectacle frames.

Marine iguanas live around the remote Galapagos islands in the Pacific Ocean. They dive into the ocean to feed on seaweed.

Marine iguanas come ashore to bask in the sun.

Strange creatures

There are many fish in the oceans that look strange to us, but they are actually very well adapted to their surroundings.

Thousands of fish have evolved to live in different places - on coral reefs, in icy waters, near the surface of the sea, or on the sea-bed.

Flying fish are able to leap out of the water and glide through the air, using their fins as wings. It is thought that the fish 'fly' in this way to escape hunters.

When danger threatens, the **porcupine fish** gulps huge amounts of water and swells up to four times its usual size. The stiff spines stick out to make the fish look like a spiky football.

The **four-eyed fish** swims at the surface with each of its two eyes half in and half out of the water. The fish looks for insect prey on the surface, while watching for danger under the sea.

The **swordfish** has a bony upper jaw which can be over one metre long and shaped like a sword. Nobody knows what the sword is used for.

The **sailfish** is the fastest fish in the sea. It can reach speeds of 110 kilometres per hour.

The **coelacanth** lives in the deep waters of the Indian Ocean. Before it was caught in 1938, the coelacanth was known only from fossils dating back 60 million years. Scientists thought it had been extinct ever since.

Porcupine fish

The **sea dragon** is only 40 cm long. It swims near seaweed where it can hide easily.

Millions of years ago, strange creatures lived in the oceans.

Scientists know about these creatures because they have found fossils of their bones buried in ancient rocks.

Many of these giant sea animals lived at the same time as the dinosaurs.

Kronosaurus had the largest head of any hunter in the sea. It was almost three metres long and was armed with lots of sharp teeth.

Cryptocleidus had strong flippers to propel it through the water. It caught small fish in its long jaws armed with sharp teeth.

Archelon was the largest turtle. It was nearly four metres long and lived about 70 million years ago.

Ichthyosaurus looked like a dolphin or large fish, but was really a reptile. Ichthyosaurus could not come on shore to lay eggs like most reptiles, so it gave birth to live young.

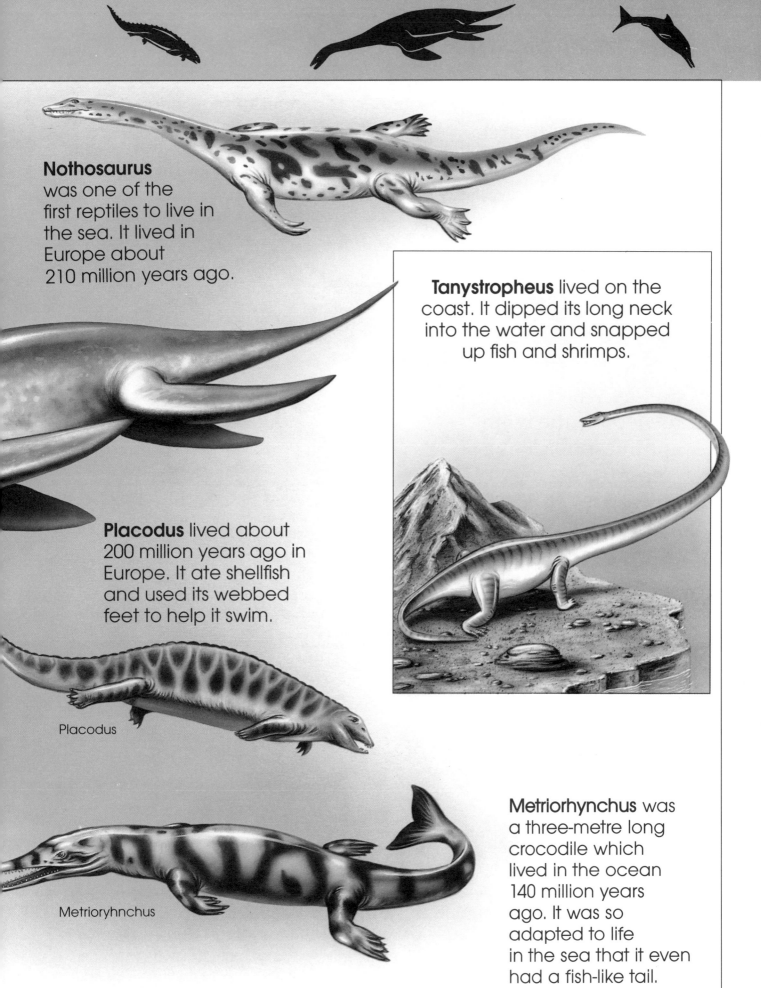

Nothosaurus was one of the first reptiles to live in the sea. It lived in Europe about 210 million years ago.

Tanystropheus lived on the coast. It dipped its long neck into the water and snapped up fish and shrimps.

Placodus lived about 200 million years ago in Europe. It ate shellfish and used its webbed feet to help it swim.

Placodus

Metrioryhnchus

Metriorhynchus was a three-metre long crocodile which lived in the ocean 140 million years ago. It was so adapted to life in the sea that it even had a fish-like tail.

Because the oceans are so vast, there are many areas which have never been explored properly.

Sailors who have travelled off the main shipping routes have reported seeing strange and curious creatures. As nobody has ever caught one of these mysterious creatures, scientists do not believe they really exist.

The type of **sea monster** most often seen has a small head and a long neck held upright. Witnesses say they see a large body under the water with four large fins which move the creature slowly along.

This sea monster looks like a prehistoric sea animal, **elasmosaurus**, which was about 10 metres long.

The four-metre long **megamouth shark** was not discovered until the 1980s. Nobody knew about it until one was accidentally caught in a net. This proved that large sea creatures can exist without anybody knowing about them.

Manatees swim slowly in shallow coastal waters, feeding on water plants.

Long ago, sailors believed in **mermaids**. Today, scientists know that what they probably saw were seal-like creatures called **manatees**.

The **sea serpent** is supposed to be a gigantic, snake-like creature up to 30 metres long. Many people have reported seeing them.

A giant turtle-like creature was seen in 1877 by the crew of *HMS Osborne*. The creature was about 20 metres long and swam quickly.

Europe

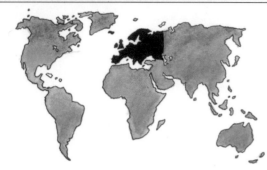

Europe is the second smallest continent in the world. About 700 million people live there, so it is very crowded compared to other regions.

Europe has water to the north, south and west. To the east it borders the continent of Asia.

The Ural Mountains separate Europe from Asia.

There are more than 40 countries in Europe. The continent stretches from inside the Arctic Circle down to the Mediterranean Sea.

Each country has its own government, capital city, languages and customs.

Key facts

Size: 10,521,000 sq km (7% of the world's land surface)
Smallest country: Vatican City (0.44 sq km)
Largest country: Russia (4,551,000 sq km of it is in Europe)
Longest river: Volga (3531 km)
Highest mountain: Mount Elbrus (5633 m) in the Caucasus mountain range

Countries

Fifteen European countries are members of the EU, or the European Union. The members work together to make laws in areas such as farming, industry and finance.

The flag of the EU

The group of countries in the west of the European continent is sometimes known as Western Europe.

Many countries in the east of Europe are changing. The former Soviet Union has now divided into fifteen separate republics.

Landscape

Europe's landscape is very varied. In the far north you can see lots of forests and lakes. In central parts there are meadows and low hills. The south has some high mountain ranges and wide plains.

Western Europe's highest mountain range is the Alps, which stretches across the top of Italy. Alpine peaks are snowy all year. The Alps are very popular for skiing holidays.

Yassoo! Greek

¡Hola! Spanish

Halloj! Danish

Zdras-vuytya! Russian

Economy

There are lots of industries in Europe. Goods are imported and exported through the many seaports. Farming of all kinds is also important.

Europe has many busy seaports

Main industries

Fishing — Steel
Timber — Engineering
Farming — Mining
Textiles

Weather

In Scandinavia it is cold much of the time. In Eastern Europe the winters are very cold, but the summers are warm. In Western Europe the summers are warm, the winters are cool and rain falls throughout the year.

Map key

1 Albania
2 Andorra
3 Austria
4 Belarus
5 Belgium
6 Bosnia & Herzegovina
7 Bulgaria
8 Croatia
9 Czech Republic
10 Denmark
11 Estonia
12 Finland
13 France
14 Germany
15 Gibraltar
16 Greece
17 Hungary
18 Iceland
19 Ireland
20 Italy
21 Latvia
22 Liechtenstein
23 Lithuania
24 Luxembourg
25 Macedonia
26 Malta
27 Moldova
28 Monaco
29 Netherlands
30 Norway
31 Poland
32 Portugal
33 Romania
34 Russia
(34) Kaliningrad
35 San Marino
36 Slovakia
37 Slovenia
38 Spain
39 Sweden
40 Switzerland
41 Ukraine
42 United Kingdom
43 Vatican City
44 Yugoslavia

Map of Europe

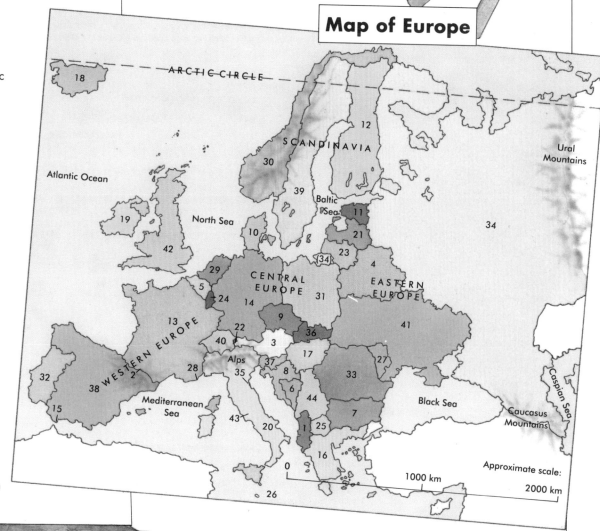

United Kingdom

The United Kingdom lies off Europe's north-west coast. It is made up of four countries.

Key facts

Size: 244,046 sq km
Population: More than 58 million
Currency: Pound sterling
Main language: English
Also called: Britain, UK

England, Scotland, Northern Ireland and Wales make up the UK.

English flag

Scottish flag

Welsh flag

Northern Irish flag

A London bus

Capital city: London. About 6.4 million people live here. London is the centre of business and government.

Landscape: The highest mountains are in Wales and Scotland. The tallest is Ben Nevis (1343 m) in Scotland. The longest river is the Severn (754 km). It flows from Wales into England.

Industries

Chemicals

Electronics

Textiles

Heavy machinery

Oil

Ben Nevis

Places to visit: There are lots of historical sites, ancient cities and towns. Britain is famous for its royal palaces and stately homes.

The Tower of London, Britain's most popular tourist attraction

France

France is one of the largest countries on the European continent.

Key facts

Size: 547,026 sq km
Population: Over 58 million
Currency: French franc
Main language: French

Capital city: Paris. This is a world centre of fashion and art. It has many famous art galleries and museums.

The Eiffel Tower is in Paris. It is made of iron and stands 300 m high. You can travel to the top by lift.

Eiffel Tower

Landscape: France has many different kinds of scenery, with spectacular mountains, pretty river valleys and sunny beaches. Mont Blanc, on the Italian border, is the highest mountain (4807 m). The longest river is the Loire (1050 km).

Grapes are grown for wine

Industries

Farming

Wine

Tourism

Fashion

Vehicles

Chemicals

Places to visit: You can ski in the Alps, swim in the Mediterranean or visit many historic châteaux. Euro Disney is near Paris.

The royal château at Versailles

Spain

Spain is in south-west Europe. It is the third largest country on the continent.

Madrid

Key facts

Size: 504,782 sq km
Population: Over 39 million
Currency: Peseta
Main language: Spanish

The Royal Palace

Capital city: Madrid. This is a famous centre of culture with many theatres, cinemas, opera houses, museums and galleries.

Landscape: Spain is a mountainous country. In the centre there is a vast, high plateau. The highest mountain is Mt Mulhacen (3487 m). The longest river is the Tagus (1007 km).

The Sierra Nevada mountains

Places to visit: There are many historic cities and palaces built by the Moors, who invaded from Africa in AD 711. In the south there are sunny beaches.

Industries

Tourism
Wine
Farming
Vehicles
Chemicals
Electronics

The Alhambra, a Moorish palace near Granada

Germany

Germany borders nine other countries. In 1990, East and West Germany joined to become one country.

Berlin

Key facts

Size: 356,755 sq km
Population: About 82 million
Currency: Deutsche Mark
Main language: German
Full name: Federal Republic of Germany

Capital city: Berlin. This city was once divided by a high wall mounted with guns. Today, people can go wherever they like in the city.

The Brandenburg Gate, Berlin

Black Forest pinewoods

Landscape: There are many different kinds of scenery. The beautiful Rhine river valley and the Black Forest are very famous. The Zugspitze (2963 m) is the highest mountain. The longest river is the Elbe (1165 km).

Industries

Chemicals
Vehicles
Engineering
Coal
Shipbuilding

Neuschwanstein Castle, Bavaria

Places to visit: There are historic cities and ancient castles in the regions of Bavaria and Saxony. In the north there are sandy beaches.

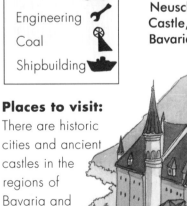

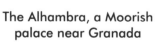

Norway

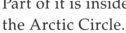

Norway lies along the coast of Scandinavia. Part of it is inside the Arctic Circle.

Oslo

Key facts

Size: 324,219 sq km
Population: Over 4 million
Currency: Norwegian krone
Language: Norwegian

Capital city: Oslo. This is one of the world's largest cities, but only 500,000 people live here. You can visit many ancient Viking burial mounds and settlement sites in Norway.

Landscape: Norway has a long coastline, famous for its deep inlets called fjords. It also has over 150,000 islands. Mountains and moorland cover three-quarters of the country. The Glittertind is the highest mountain (2470 m). The longest river is the Glama (600 km).

A Norwegian fjord

Places to visit: The Norwegian mountains are famous for winter sports. There are about 10,000 ski jumps in the country, as well as lots of forest trails.

Industries

Oil
Paper-making
Timber
Fishing

Cross-country skiing in Norway

Sweden

Sweden is the largest Scandinavian country. It has a long coastline and many islands.

Stockholm

Key facts

Size: 449,964 sq km
Population: Over 8 million
Currency: Swedish krona
Main language: Swedish

Capital city: Stockholm. The city is built on a string of islands. It is the home of the Royal Palace and many other historic buildings.

The Royal Palace

Landscape: Over half of Sweden is covered with forest. There are about 96,000 lakes in the south and centre of the country. Lapland (northern Sweden) is inside the Arctic Circle. Mount Kebnekaise (2111 m) is the highest peak in Sweden.

Places to visit: Sweden has thousands of islands which are ideal for boating and fishing. You can find out about Viking longboats in the Nordic Museum, Stockholm.

Industries

Timber
Vehicles
Electronics
Minerals
Chemicals

A Viking longboat

Denmark

Denmark is the smallest Scandinavian country. It is made up of a peninsula and about 400 islands.

Copenhagen

Key facts

Size: 43,069 sq km
Population: Over 5 million
Currency: Danish krone
Main Language: Danish

Capital city: Copenhagen. This is a city with many old buildings, fountains and pretty squares. The well-known statue of

The Little Mermaid

the Little Mermaid sits on a rock in Copenhagen harbour. The story of the mermaid was written by a famous Dane, Hans Christian Andersen.

Landscape: Denmark has mainly low-lying countryside with forests and lakes. There are many beautiful sandy beaches and about 500 islands. Yding Skovhoj is the highest mountain (173 m).

The longest river is the Guden (158 km).

Places to visit: Copenhagen has palaces, castles and a Viking museum. At Legoland Park everything is made of Lego, including full-sized working trains and lots of miniature buildings.

Industries

Farming
Tourism
Textiles
Electronics
Oil

A Legoland train

The Netherlands

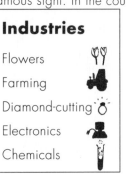

The Netherlands is one of the flattest European countries. Two-fifths is below sea-level.

Amsterdam

Key facts

Size: 40,844 sq km
Population: Over 15 million
Currency: Guilder
Main language: Dutch
Also called: Holland

Capital city: Amsterdam. This city is built on canals and is sometimes called 'the Venice of the North'. It has about a thousand bridges and many attractive seventeenth-century houses.

Amsterdam

Landscape: The Netherlands is very flat and is criss-crossed by rivers and canals. In the past, large areas of land were reclaimed from the sea. Sea-dams, called dykes, were built and the sea water was drained away. The highest point of land is only 322 m.

Places to visit: The tulip fields are a world-famous sight. In the countryside there are lots of

Industries

Flowers
Farming
Diamond-cutting
Electronics
Chemicals

pretty old towns and villages, country houses and castles. Windmills are still used in parts of the country.

Tulips are exported to many parts of the world

Italy

Italy is in southern Europe. The Mediterranean islands of Sicily and Sardinia are part of this country.

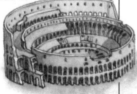

Key facts

Size: 301,225 sq km
Population: Over 57 million
Currency: Lira
Main language: Italian

Capital city: Rome. This was once the capital of the ancient Roman empire. It has lots of Roman remains, including the ruins of the Colosseum. Here, huge audiences watched as gladiators fought and Christians were thrown to the lions.

The Colosseum

In Rome there is a tiny separate country called Vatican City. This is the home of the Pope, the head of the Roman Catholic Church.

Landscape: There are spectacular mountains and beautiful lakes in the north. In central and southern regions you can see plains and smaller mountains. Italy has several live volcanoes, including Etna, Vesuvius and Stromboli. Mont Blanc is the highest mountain (4807 m). The Po is the longest river (652 km).

Stromboli

Industries

Farming
Vehicles
Electronics
Fashion

Places to visit: Italy has many historic cities, such as Venice, which is built on a lagoon. The easiest way to travel around Venice is by gondola. Some of the world's greatest artists have lived in Italy. You can see their work in art galleries and museums.

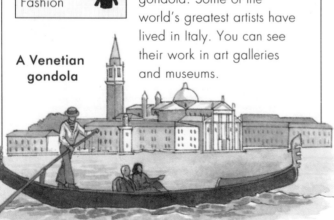

A Venetian gondola

Greece

Greece juts out into the Mediterranean Sea. About one-fifth of the country is made up of small islands.

Key facts

Size: 131,957 sq km
Population: Over 10 million
Currency: Drachma
Main language: Greek

Capital city: Athens. This is one of the world's oldest cities. On the top of the Acropolis ridge, you can see the ruins of the Parthenon. This Greek temple is 2400 years old.

The Parthenon, in Athens

Landscape: Mainland Greece has plains and forests in the south and is mountainous in the north. Mount Olympus is the highest mountain (2917 m). The Greek islands vary in size and landscape. Crete is the largest of these. The longest river in Greece is the Aliakmon (297 km).

Mount Olympus, legendary home of the ancient Greek gods

Industries

Tourism
Fishing
Farming

Places to visit: There are lots of ancient sites. Many of them are linked with stories from Greek mythology. For instance, the Palace of Knossos, on Crete, is the legendary home of the Minotaur monster.

The Minotaur

Poland

Poland is in Central Europe. It shares its borders with four other countries. Its coastline is on the Baltic Sea.

Key facts

Size: 312,677 sq km
Population: Over 38 million
Currency: Zloty
Main language: Polish

Capital city: Warsaw. The old city of Warsaw was destroyed in World War Two. The 'Old Town' area has been rebuilt in the style of the old buildings.

Warsaw 'Old Town'

Landscape: There are many lakes and wooded hills in northern Poland, and beach resorts along the Baltic coast. Rysy Peak (2503 m) is the highest point in the mountainous south. The longest river is the Vistula (1069 km).

Industries

Farming
Coalmining
Shipbuilding
Timber

A northern lake

Places to visit: There are lots of museums and art galleries in Warsaw. There are several National Parks where rare forest creatures live, such as lynxes and moose.

A rare lynx

Russia

Russia is the largest country in the world. About a quarter lies in Europe. The rest is in Asia.

Key facts

Size: 17,075,400 sq km
Population: About 148 million
Currency: Rouble
Main language: Russian

Capital city: Moscow. The famous Kremlin building is in the centre of the city. It was once a fortress occupied by tsars (Russian emperors) who ruled for centuries.

St Basil's Cathedral, Moscow's famous landmark

Landscape: Russia is the world's largest country. It has some of the largest lakes and forests and longest rivers in the world. Mount Elbrus (5633 m) is the highest mountain in Europe. The longest river is the Volga (3530 m).

Industries

Engineering
Farming
Oil
Minerals
Coal mining

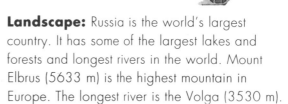

Lake Baykal is the world's deepest lake at 1940 m

Places to visit: Russia has many old cities, all with long and exciting histories. The world's longest railway, the Trans-Siberian, runs across the country from Moscow to Vladivostok.

The Trans-Siberian railway

Main industries:

 Forestry  **Steel**

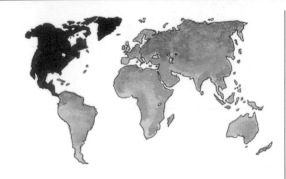

North America is the third largest continent in the world. It stretches from the frozen Arctic Circle down to the sunny Gulf of Mexico. It is so wide that there are eight different time zones.

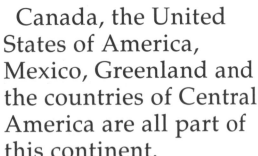

The frozen north

Canada, the United States of America, Mexico, Greenland and the countries of Central America are all part of this continent.

The islands of Hawaii, Bermuda and the West Indies lie off the mainland.

The tropical south

Key facts

Size: 23,400,000 sq km
Largest country: Canada (second largest in the world) 9,976,139 sq km
Longest river: Mississippi-Missouri (6212 km)
Highest mountain: Mount McKinley (6194 m)

Landscape

The North American landscape is very varied. There are huge forests, ice-covered wastelands, scorching deserts and wide grassy plains.

In the west, mountains run from Alaska down to Mexico. They are called the Cordillera, and include the Rocky Mountains. The Appalachian mountains run down the eastern side.

The Rocky Mountains

A vast plain stretches about 4800 km from the Gulf of Mexico to northern Canada. The Great Plains and the Mississippi-Missouri River are in this region. Much of the world's maize is grown here.

The most northern parts of the continent border the icy Arctic Ocean. This area is called tundra. Here, the land just beneath the surface is permanently frozen.

Weather

Temperatures vary from -60°C in an Arctic winter to 50°C in summer in Death Valley, California, one of the world's hottest places. Every year in North America, there are about 550 tornadoes, mostly in the central states of the USA. Tornado winds can spin at up to 650 km/hr.

A tornado

People

Long ago, North America was populated only by native American people, sometimes called Amerindians. Over the centuries, settlers came from Europe and slaves were brought from Africa. Now, most of the population is descended from these people.

For many centuries, the Canadian Arctic has been the home of the Inuit people.

Many people from the West Indies are descended from Africans captured and brought over to the country as slaves.

The Statue of Liberty in New York City Harbour was the first sight many immigrants had of North America

Economy

The continent of North America has many natural resources, such as oil, minerals and timber.

The USA is the world's richest country. It has many different industries.

Timber products, such as paper, come from the northern areas

Cities

The USA has many cities. New York City is the largest, with a population of over 17 million.

Although Canada is the biggest country in North America, it has a small population. Its major cities are all in the south of the country, where the climate is milder than the Arctic north.

Mexico City, in Mexico, is one of the most overcrowded cities in the world.

Map of North America

Approximate scale: 0   1000 km   2000 km

Bering Strait
Arctic Ocean
Greenland (Denmark)
CANADA
Hudson Bay
Rocky Mountains
Great Lakes
Toronto
USA
Pacific Ocean
MEXICO
New York City
Atlantic Ocean
Mexico City
Gulf of Mexico
1
2
WEST INDIES
Hawaiian Islands
CENTRAL AMERICA
4
8
5 6 7
Carribean Sea

Map key

1 Bermuda
2 Bahamas
3 Cuba
4 Jamaica
5 Haiti
6 Dominican Republic
7 Puerto Rico

USA

The United States of America stretches from the Atlantic Ocean to the Pacific. It includes Alaska in the north and the Hawaiian islands in the Pacific Ocean.

Washington DC

Key facts

Size: 9,372,614 sq km
Population: Over 265 million
Currency: US dollar
Main language: English

Capital city: Washington DC. This is the centre of government. The President lives here in the White House.

The White House

The US flag is called the 'Stars and Stripes'. It has thirteen red and white stripes that stand for the thirteen states that first made up the USA. The country now has fifty states, shown by the fifty stars.

Landscape: As well as mountain ranges, vast plains and deserts, there is the deep land gorge, the Grand Canyon, in Arizona. Mount McKinley is the highest point (6194 m). The Mississippi-Missouri (6212 km) is the longest river in the USA.

Grand Canyon

Places to visit: The USA has many historic sites, big cities and beach resorts. Famous places include Hollywood in California, Disney World in Florida, and many National Parks.

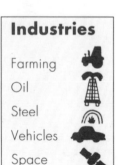

Industries

Farming
Oil
Steel
Vehicles
Space

The famous Hollywood sign

Canada

Canada is the largest country in North America. Its northern part is inside the Arctic Circle.

Ottowa

Key facts

Size: 9,976,139 sq km
Population: About 29 million
Currency: Canadian dollar
Main languages: English and French

Capital city: Ottawa. Canada is divided into ten provinces and two territories. Ottawa is in the province of Ontario.

CN Tower

The CN Tower, the world's tallest free-standing structure (553 m high), is in Toronto, the largest city in Canada.

Landscape: Nearly half of Canada is covered by forest. The Great Lakes, the world's largest group of freshwater lakes, are on the border with the USA. The Rocky Mountains are in the west. In the centre, there are vast plains, called prairies. The highest mountain is Mount Logan (5951 m). The Mackenzie is the longest river (4241 km).

The Rocky Mountains

A totem pole

Industries

Farming
Forestry
Vehicles

Places to visit: You can see ancient totem poles in Stanley Park, Vancouver. Canada has lots of National Park areas, where bears and wolves live. The world-famous Niagara Falls is a spectacular sight.

Mexico

Mexico lies south of the USA and north of South America.

Mexico City

Key facts

Size: 1,792,547 sq km
Population: Over 92 million
Currency: Peso
Main language: Spanish

Capital city: Mexico City. Almost one-fifth of the population lives here. There are modern buildings next to ancient Aztec ruins.

Mexico once belonged to Spain. You can still see many Spanish-style buildings and churches.

A Spanish-style church

Landscape: More than half the country is over 1000 m high. Central Mexico is a plateau surrounded by volcanic mountains. There are also deserts and swamps. Mount Orizaba (5700 m) is the highest mountain. The longest river is the Rio Grande (2090 km), which flows along the USA border.

Industries

Coffee
Oil
Minerals
Crafts

Places to visit: Aztec, Mayan and Toltec people once ruled Mexico. You can still see the remains of cities and temples they built.

A Mayan temple

Jamaica

Jamaica is an island in the Caribbean Sea, south of Cuba.

Kingston

Key facts

Size: 10,991 sq km
Population: Over 2 million
Currency: Jamaican dollar
Main language: English

Capital city: Kingston. Built by a deep, sheltered harbour, this city was once ruled by a pirate, Captain Morgan, and his Buccaneers.

Landscape: Jamaica is a tropical island with lush rainforests, pretty waterfalls and dazzling white beaches. It is actually the tip of an undersea mountain range. Blue Mountain Peak (2256 m) is the highest mountain on the island.

Captain Morgan

Places to visit: As well as beaches, there are wildlife parks and bird sanctuaries where some of the world's most exotic birds can be seen. There are working sugar and banana plantations.

Industries

Tourism
Minerals
Farming

A Jamaican beach

South America

South America is the world's fourth largest continent. It stretches from the border of Central America to the tip of Chile.

Early settlers came from Europe

There are 13 South American countries, each with its own distinctive type of landscape and culture.

For centuries the continent was populated only by native peoples. Europeans did not arrive until 1499. Now, many of the people are descended from these Spanish or Portuguese settlers.

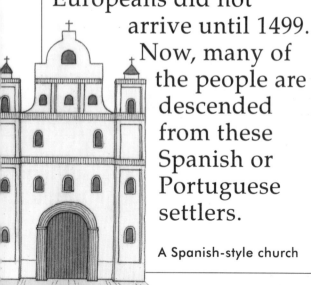

A Spanish-style church

Landscape

There are lots of different landscapes, including high mountains, hot and cold deserts, rainforests and plains.

The world's longest mountain range is the Andes, which runs all the way down the western side. Some of its mountains are live volcanoes. There are also regular earthquakes in this area.

Between the highland areas there are vast lowlands. Much of these areas are covered by dense rainforests. There are also grasslands, such as the Argentinian pampas.

There are some live volcanoes in the Andes mountain range

South America has many dense rainforests

People

Many large South American cities are on the eastern coast. Outside the cities, most people live on small farms, growing just enough food to feed themselves.

There are still a few Amerindians (native Americans) living in forest settlements deep in the Amazon river basin. They hunt animals, gather fruit and grow crops to eat.

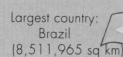

Amazon butterflies

The Amazon

The Amazon River carries more fresh water than any other. It flows across South America from the Andes to the Atlantic and drains more than 7 million sq km of land, much of it rainforest. It is one of the world's richest wildlife areas, with many extraordinary creatures such as hummingbirds, sloths, jaguars and piranha fish.

A hummingbird

A jaguar

Weather

In rainforest areas, it is warm and humid all the time and it rains almost daily.

The warmest part of South America is in northern Argentina. The coldest place is Tierra Del Fuego, which faces Antarctica at the southern tip of the continent.

The world's driest place is the Atacama Desert in Chile. Until 1971 it had not rained there for 400 years.

Industries

Coffee
Forestry
Cacao
Oil
Farming
Minerals

Map of South America

Approximate scale: 0   1000 km   2000 km

Caracas
VENEZUELA
Orinoco River
COLOMBIA
2
3
4
1
PERU
Amazon River
EQUATOR
BRAZIL
Lima
La Paz
Brasília
BOLIVIA
Pacific Ocean
CHILE
6
São Paulo
Paraná River
Santiago
5
Buenos Aires
Atlantic Ocean
ARGENTINA
Falkland Islands (UK).
Tierra del Fuego
(Chile) (Argentina)

Map key

1 Equador
2 Guyana
3 Surinam
4 French Guiana
5 Uruguay
6 Paraguay

Brazil

Brazil covers almost half of South America. It is the fifth largest country in the world.

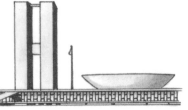
Brasilia

Key facts

Size: 8,511,965 sq km
Population: Over 157 million
Currency: Real
Main language: Portuguese

Capital city: Brasilia. This city was begun in the 1950s. It is famous for its futuristic architecture.

Brasilia's futuristic buildings

Landscape: Brazil has over 3 million sq km of rainforest. The mighty Amazon River (6437 km) runs through it, carrying more water than any other river in the world. Pica da Neblina (3014 m) is the highest mountain in Brazil.

Flesh-eating piranha fish live in the Amazon River

Industries

Coffee
Sugar cane
Timber
Iron
Precious gems

Places to visit: The Amazon rainforest has many thousands of animal and plant species. It is also the home of the Amazon Indians. Ecologists are trying to save the forest from destruction.

Rainforest birds

Argentina

Argentina lies to the east of the Andes Mountains, facing the Atlantic Ocean.

Buenos Aires

Key facts

Size: 2,766,889 sq km
Population: Over 35 million
Currency: Peso
Main language: Spanish

Capital city: Buenos Aires. This is one of the largest cities in the southern half of the world. It is the birthplace of the famous tango dance.

Dancing the tango

Landscape: The scenery includes hot desert, the Andes mountain range and the cold wilderness of the Patagonia desert in the south. Mount Aconcagua (6960 m) is the highest point. The longest river is the Paraná (4880 km).

Argentinian grassland, called pampas

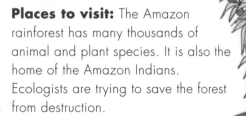

Places to visit: There are historic cities, beach resorts and wildlife parks in Argentina. The Andes is home to the spectacular and rare bird, the condor.

Industries

Farming
Textiles
Steel
Chemicals

A condor

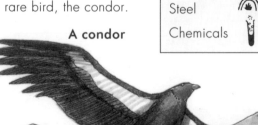

Peru

Peru is on the Pacific coast of South America. The Andes mountains run down the centre.

Lima

Key facts

Size: 1,285,216 sq km
Population: Over 24 million
Currency: New Sol
Main languages: Spanish, Quechua

Capital city: Lima. This city was founded by the Spaniard, Francisco Pizarro, in 1535. He attacked and conquered Peru in the 1500s in search of its legendary treasure.

Francisco Pizarro

Landscape: Peru is a country of deserts, mountains and rainforests, some of it still unexplored. The source of the Amazon River is in the Peruvian Andes. The highest point is Mount Huascarán (6768 m). The Ucayli is the longest river (1465 km).

Industries	
Farming	
Coffee	
Cotton	
Fishing	
Minerals	

The Andes mountains

Places to visit: Peru was once ruled by the Inca people. They built fabulous palaces, towers and temples covered in gold. You can visit the ruins of their cities, such as Cuzco and Machu Picchu.

Machu Picchu

Venezuela

Venezuela is on the north coast of South America. This is where Christopher Columbus first set foot on the American mainland.

Caracas

Key facts

Size: 912,050 sq km
Population: Over 22 million
Currency: Bolívar
Main language: Spanish

Capital city: Caracas. The national hero, Simon Bolívar, is buried here. He helped to free Venezuela from the Spanish. Many buildings and streets are named after him.

Simon Bolívar

Landscape: There are lowland and highland areas. One of the lowland areas is a dense alligator-infested forest around the Orinoco River. Some of the highlands are still unexplored. Mount Bolívar is the highest point (5007 m). The Orinoco (2736 m) is the longest river.

Industries	
Fruit	
Coffee	
Minerals	
Tourism	

The Venezuelan landscape

Places to visit: Venezuela has some of the most spectacular scenery in the world. the world's highest waterfall, Angel Falls (979 m) is in the Canaima National Park.

Angel Falls

Africa

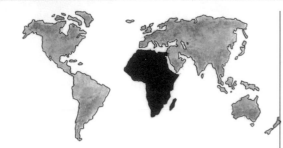

Africa is the second largest continent in the world. It is only 13 km to the south of Europe, across the Strait of Gibraltar. A strip of land called the Isthmus of Suez separates the continent from Asia.

There are 670 million people in Africa, but they are spread thinly throughout more than 50 countries.

Nairobi, Kenya

Large parts of Africa are uninhabited because the climate is harsh and the terrain makes travel difficult. There are mountains, rainforests, deserts and grassland, called savannah.

African desert

Key facts

Size: 30,262,000 sq km
Population: 670 million
Largest country: Sudan
Smallest country: Seychelles
Highest mountain: Mount Kilimanjaro (5895 m)
Longest river: Nile (6670 km)

Mount Kilimanjaro

Landscape

Much of Africa is on a high plateau. Around this high, flat tableland there are narrow coastal plains. The highest mountains are in East Africa.

The Sahara Desert crosses the northern part of Africa. It is the biggest desert in the world, spreading out over a huge area almost as large as the USA! Some parts are sandy, but much of it is rocky wasteland.

In central Africa, there are dense tropical rainforests. In southern Africa there are savannah and desert areas.

The River Nile is the longest river in the world. It flows north to the Mediterranean Sea.

The River Nile

Animals

Africa is very rich in wildlife. Many of the large mammals live on the wide grassy plains of the savannah.

Some species of animals are in danger of dying out. To save them, large areas have been made into reserves and national parks, where hunting is illegal.

African savannah

Weather

The Equator crosses Africa. Here there are hot, humid rainforests where it rains almost every day.

African rainforest

People

In the north, many people speak Arabic and follow the Muslim religion.

Pygmy people live in the rainforests of Congo and Zaïre.

In South Africa, black people make up two-thirds of the population. For many years they had few rights but now they can vote in their new democracy.

Economy

Many Africans are farmers. They work on the land growing crops such as peanuts and cocoa beans (used for making chocolate).

A major industry is mining. Africa is rich in minerals such as gold, silver, tin and copper. It has large stores of oil and natural gas.

A farmer harvesting his crop

Map of Africa

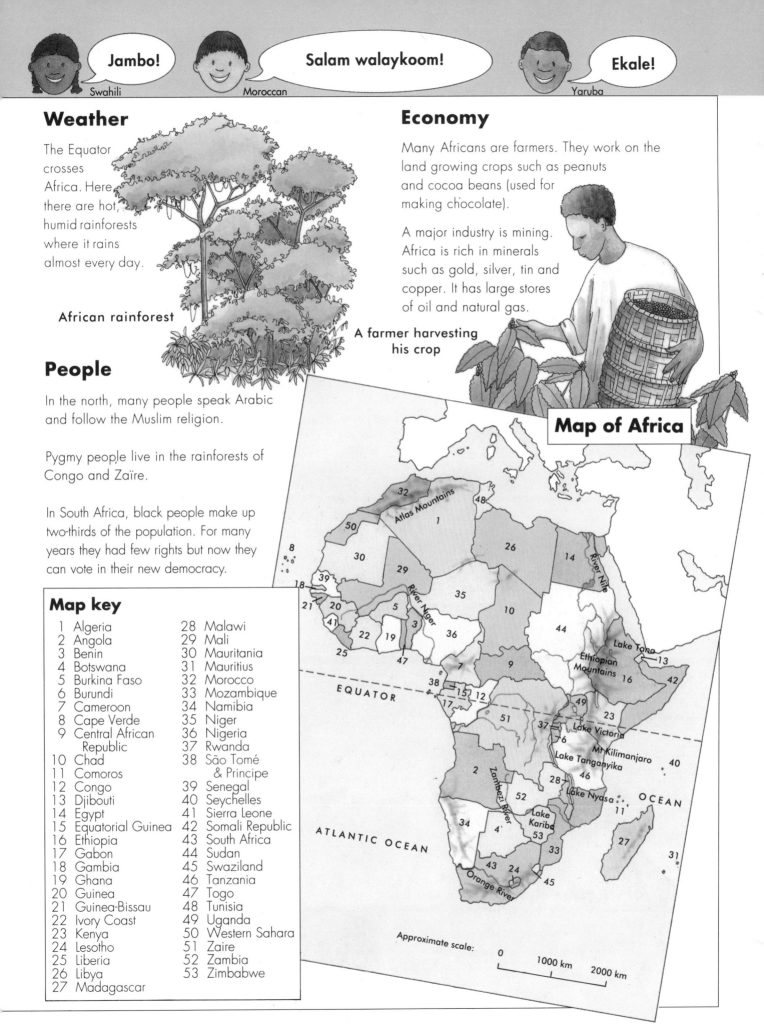

Map key

1	Algeria	28	Malawi
2	Angola	29	Mali
3	Benin	30	Mauritania
4	Botswana	31	Mauritius
5	Burkina Faso	32	Morocco
6	Burundi	33	Mozambique
7	Cameroon	34	Namibia
8	Cape Verde	35	Niger
9	Central African Republic	36	Nigeria
		37	Rwanda
10	Chad	38	São Tomé & Principe
11	Comoros		
12	Congo	39	Senegal
13	Djibouti	40	Seychelles
14	Egypt	41	Sierra Leone
15	Equatorial Guinea	42	Somali Republic
16	Ethiopia	43	South Africa
17	Gabon	44	Sudan
18	Gambia	45	Swaziland
19	Ghana	46	Tanzania
20	Guinea	47	Togo
21	Guinea-Bissau	48	Tunisia
22	Ivory Coast	49	Uganda
23	Kenya	50	Western Sahara
24	Lesotho	51	Zaire
25	Liberia	52	Zambia
26	Libya	53	Zimbabwe
27	Madagascar		

Approximate scale:

0   1000 km   2000 km

South Africa

South Africa is at the southernmost tip of the African continent.

Key facts
Size: 1,221,037 sq km
Population: Over 42 million
Currency: Rand
Main languages: English, Afrikaans

Capital cities: South Africa has three capital cities called Pretoria, Bloemfontein and Cape Town. Each plays a different part in the government of the country.

Table Mountain, near Cape Town

Landscape: South Africa has a huge high plateau bordered by mountains. On the plateau there are wide grassy plains called the 'veld'. The long coastline has lots of beautiful beaches. The highest point is Champagne Castle in the Drakensberg (3375m). The River Orange (2100 km) is the longest river.

Industries
Mining
Precious gems
Farming

South Africa is famous for its diamond mines

Places to visit: There are several famous wildlife reserves. You can see eagles, elephants, giraffes and lions living in their natural habitat.

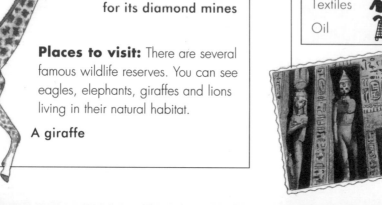

A giraffe

Egypt

Egypt is in the north-eastern corner of Africa. Its northern shore is on the Mediterranean.

Key facts
Size: 1,001,449 sq km
Population: Over 61 million
Currency: Egyptian pound
Main language: Arabic

Capital city: Cairo. This is a centre of historic monuments and unique historical sites.

The Ancient Egyptian civilization began about 5000 years ago. The Pyramids at Giza were built as tombs for the pharoahs the kings who ruled at that time.

The pyramids and Sphinx at Giza, just outside Cairo

Landscape:
The country is divided by the great River Nile. A belt of green fertile land runs along the river and spreads out around its delta (river mouth). The rest of Egypt is sandy desert. The highest mountain is Jabal Katrinah (2637 m). The River Nile is the world's longest river (6670 km).

Farming the Nile delta

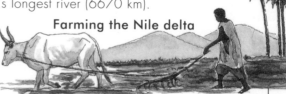

Industries
Tourism
Textiles
Oil

Places to visit: Some pharoahs were buried in the Valley of the Kings. You can see their tomb treasures on display. There are huge temples at Luxor and Abu Simbel. Around the Red Sea there are beaches and spectacular coral reefs.

The great temple of Abu Simbel

Nigeria

Nigeria's coast is on the Gulf of Guinea in western Africa.

Key facts

Size: 923,768 sq km
Population: Over 104 million
Currency: Naira
Main language: The official language is English but there are over 250 local languages

Capital city: In 1991 Abuja became the new capital city, in place of Lagos.

Many people live in villages. The main groups of people are the Hausa, Ibo and Yoruba.

A village market

Landscape: There are lagoons, beaches and mangrove swamps along the coast. Inland, there are rainforests where the trees can grow as high as 30 m. An area of grassland with scattered trees, called the savannah, lies in the south.

Coastal mangrove swamp

Places to visit: Many ancient cultures flourished in Nigeria. There are several historic cities, such as Kano, famous for its festival of horsemanship. There are wildlife parks and spectacular scenery.

Industries

Oil
Cacao
Palm oil
Minerals

A Yoruba festival mask and drummer

Tanzania

Tanzania lies in eastern Africa on the Indian Ocean. It includes the islands of Zanzibar and Pemba.

Key facts

Size: 945,087 sq km
Population: About 29 million
Currency: Tanzanian shilling
Main languages: English, Swahili

Capital city: Dodoma. Dar es Salaam is the largest city and main port.

There are about 120 groups of people in Tanzania including the wandering Masai, the tallest people in the world.

Masai women

Landscape: Most of Tanzania consists of a high plateau. Savannah and bush cover about half the country. There are huge inland lakes. Mount Kilimanjaro (5895 m), in Tanzania, is the highest mountain in Africa. The longest river is the Rufiji.

An inland lake

Industries

Farming
Cotton
Coffee
Minerals

Places to visit: Some of the world's finest wildlife parks are here, including the Serengeti Plain and the Ngorongoro volcano.

Lake Manyara is famous for its tree-climbing lions

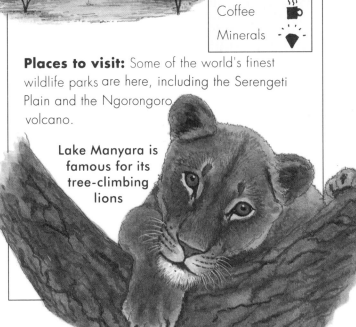

Shalom! — Hebrew

A-salam alekum! — Dhivehi (Maldives)

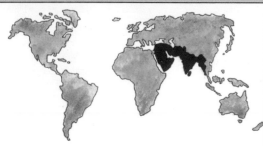

This area stretches about 5000 km from the Mediterranean Sea to the Bay of Bengal. It includes Middle Eastern countries such as Saudi Arabia and the south Asian countries of Pakistan, Afghanistan, India and Bangladesh. The island of Sri Lanka and the mountainous countries of Bhutan and Nepal are also in this vast area.

The landscape varies from barren desert to the Himalayas, the highest mountains in the world.

Middle Eastern desert

The mountains of Nepal

Key facts

Size: 11,450,000 sq km
Population: About 1330 million
Longest river: Ganges (4667 km)
Highest mountain: Mount Everest (8848 m)
Largest country: India (3,287,590 sq km)
Smallest country: Maldives (298 sq km)

Landscape

The landscape of Western and Southern Asia includes high mountains, wide plains, deserts and rainforests.

Mountains run all the way from Turkey to Afghanistan and dry, scrubby grassland stretches from Pakistan to Syria.

Desert covers most of Saudi Arabia and the surrounding lands.

Weather

The mountainous northern areas of the Middle East have hot summers and freezing winters. Farther south, it is hot all year round.

In India and Bangladesh, the farmers rely on the monsoon for their crops to grow. The monsoon is a season of heavy rain that falls between June and October.

Middle Eastern desert and mountains in Afghanistan

Monsoon rainfall in Southern Asia

Marhabah assalamu aleikum! — Arabic

Namaste! — Hindi

Min ga la baa! — Burmese

People

There are many different cultures in this area. Here are some examples:

In the Middle East, many people follow the Muslim faith. They pray every day facing the holy city of Mecca, centre of their religion.

Many Indians are Hindus. They worship several gods, the chief of which is called Brahman. Some Indians follow the Sikh faith. Many Sikhs live in the Punjab region.

To Hindus, cows are sacred animals and are allowed to graze wherever they like

Economy

The countries around the Persian Gulf, in the Middle East, have vast oil reserves. They depend on the money they make from selling this oil around the world.

Throughout Southern Asia many different crops are grown, including wheat, millet, rice and cotton. India and Sri Lanka are among the world's biggest tea producers.

Tea-picking

Main industries

Oil	🛢	Farming	🚜
Mining	⛏	Textiles	👕

Map of Western & Southern Asia

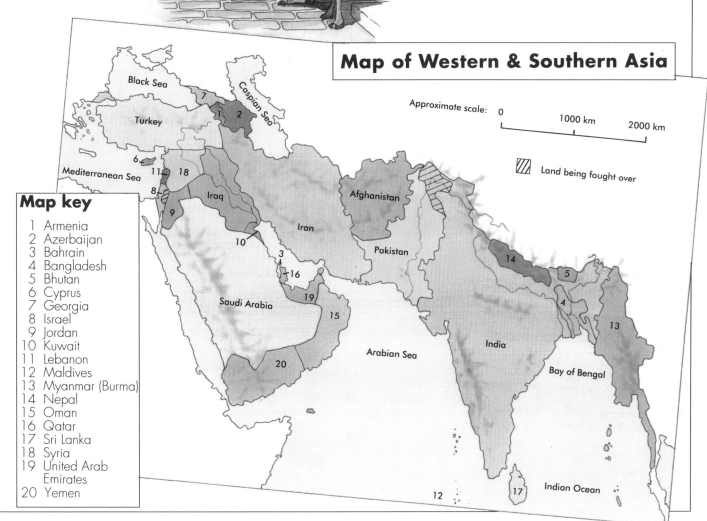

Approximate scale: 0   1000 km   2000 km

▨ Land being fought over

Map key

1 Armenia
2 Azerbaijan
3 Bahrain
4 Bangladesh
5 Bhutan
6 Cyprus
7 Georgia
8 Israel
9 Jordan
10 Kuwait
11 Lebanon
12 Maldives
13 Myanmar (Burma)
14 Nepal
15 Oman
16 Qatar
17 Sri Lanka
18 Syria
19 United Arab Emirates
20 Yemen

Black Sea
Caspian Sea
Turkey
Mediterranean Sea
Iraq
Afghanistan
Iran
Pakistan
Saudi Arabia
India
Arabian Sea
Bay of Bengal
Indian Ocean

Israel

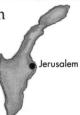

Israel is on the Mediterranean coast. The modern country of Israel was founded in 1948.

Jerusalem

Key facts

Size: 20,770 sq km
Population: About 5 million
Currency: Shekel
Main languages: Hebrew, Arabic

Capital city: Jerusalem. This ancient holy city is about 4000 years old. It is a centre of Judaism, Christianity and Islam. There are many important historic sites from the Bible and the Islamic holy book, the Koran.

Jerusalem

Landscape: The hills of Galilee are in the north of Israel, and there is desert in the south. In between, there are fertile plains. The longest river is the Jordan (1060 km), which flows into the Dead Sea. This sea is so salty that if you swim in it you cannot sink. Mount Meiron (1208 m) is the highest point.

The Dead Sea

Places to visit: The history of this area goes back to about 2000 BC. There are many religious sites including the Wailing Wall, the Church of the Holy Sepulchre, the Mount of Olives and the Dome of the Rock. The town of Beersheba stands on the spot where Abraham is supposed to have pitched his tent 3800 years ago.

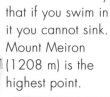

Industries
Engineering
Electronics
Chemicals
Textiles
Fruit

The Tomb of Absalom on the Mount of Olives

Saudi Arabia

Saudi Arabia covers about four-fifths of the Arabian peninsula. It is more than four times as big as France.

Riyadh

Key facts

Size: 2,149,690 sq km
Population: Over 18 million
Currency: Saudi Riyal
Main language: Arabic

Capital city: Riyadh. This modern city is built on an ancient site. It is the home of the ruling Royal Family.

The Bedouin people wander the desert in search of grazing for their animals

Landscape:
Much of the country is barren desert scattered with oases. The Rub Al-Khali ('Empty Quarter'), in the south, is the largest sand desert in the world. The highest point is in the Asir Range (3133 m). There are no rivers in Saudi Arabia!

Giant sand dunes in the 'Empty Quarter'

Places to visit: Only Muslims are allowed to visit the sacred cities of Mecca and Medina. The Prophet Muhammad was born in Mecca and Muslims pray towards it, wherever they are in the world. Other ancient sites include camel markets, potteries and salt mines dating back 5000 years.

Industries
Oil
Natural gas
Farming

The sacred city of Mecca

Iran

Iran is in Western Asia, east of the Mediterranean Sea. It borders the Caspian Sea.

Key facts

Size: 1,648,000 sq km
Population: About 62 million
Currency: Rial
Main language: Persian (Farsi)

Capital city: Tehran. The old city gates are in the old part of Tehran. It has one of the world's largest bazaars, where you can buy everything from carpets to silver and exotic spices.

A holy mosque

Landscape: Most of the cities are near the Caspian Sea, where the land is fertile. The rest of Iran is barren desert where much of Iran's oil is found. There are mountains in the western part of the country. The highest point is Mount Demavend (5604m).

Oil wells in the desert

Industries

Oil
Farming
Crafts

Places to visit: Iran was once called Persia. It was on the Silk Route, an important trail for merchants bringing silk and spices from the east. There are many ancient cities, museums and remains of the Roman and Persian Empires.

The Bakhtiari people spend the summer in the Zagros Mountains and the winter in the lowland areas of Iran

India

India is in Southern Asia between the Arabian Sea and the Bay of Bengal.

Key facts

Size: 3,287,590 sq km
Population: Over 950 million
Currency: Rupee
Main languages: Hindi, Urdu, Gujarati

Capital city: New Delhi. This modern city stands beside Old Delhi, where there are many ancient streets, temples, mosques and bazaars. The biggest city in India is Bombay. More than 10 million people live there.

Old Delhi

India is the seventh largest country in the world, with the second biggest population after China.

Landscape: India is separated from the rest of Asia by the Himalayan mountain range in the north. In the north, many people live on the huge river plains of the Ganges and the Brahmaputra. Kanchenjunga (8598 m) is the world's second highest mountain. The Brahmaputra (2900 km) is the longest river.

Ganges

Industries

Farming
Chemicals
Electronics
Oil

Places to visit: There are many temples and palaces from the days when maharajahs ruled India. The most famous monument is the Taj Mahal.

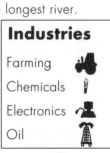

The Taj Mahal

Ni hao! Cantonese

Haere-mai! Maori

This vast area includes China and its neighbouring countries. Over one-fifth of the world's population lives in China. Asian Russia (to the east of the Ural Mountains) is in this region.

Indonesian island

Malaysia and Indonesia (a group of thousands of islands) stretch down towards Australasia. This region includes Australia, the world's smallest continent, and New Zealand.

Chinese junks in the Pacific

Key facts about Northern & Eastern Asia

Size: About 32,115,000 sq km
Largest country: Russia (about 12,524,000 sq km in Asia)
Longest river: Chang (Yangtze) (6300 km)
Highest mountain: Mount Everest (8848 m)

Key facts about Australasia

Size: About 8,400,000 sq km
Largest country: Australia (7,686,848 sq km)
Longest river: Murray (2589 km)
Highest mountain: Mount Wilhelm (4509m)

Landscape

Asian Russia has vast plains, with mountains in the far east and south. There is tundra in the Himalayas, with grassland and desert in central China.

Tropical rainforest stretches from southern China down through Malaysia, Indonesia and New Guinea. Some of this forest is still unexplored.

An erupting volcano

Part of this area is in the 'Pacific Ring of Fire'. It is called this because it has so many active volcanoes.

Much of Australia is dry grassland, with few trees. Australians call this the 'outback' or 'bush'. There are also low mountain ranges, rainforests and deserts.

Weather

In the Himalayan mountains it is cold all year round. Farther south the weather is warm all the time. The monsoon season brings heavy rainfall to South-East Asia. Hurricanes (also called typhoons) often blow in this area. They are giant, spinning masses of wind and rain, sometimes stretching as wide as 500 km across.

Hurricanes can blow at over 150 km/h

Economy

Eastern Asia is mainly farmland. Much of the world's rice is grown here. Rubber is also exported from here, all around the world. The rubber is made from milky sap, called latex, drained from trees.

Australia and New Zealand are important sheep-farming centres. In both countries, there are far more sheep than people. The sheep's wool and meat are exported to countries around the world.

Japan is one of the most powerful industrial countries in the world. It is famous for its electronic goods, such as computers and music systems. Japanese cars are exported all around the world.

Main industries

Farming
Mining
Oil
Shipbuilding
Forestry
Sheep

Map of Northern & Eastern Asia & Australasia

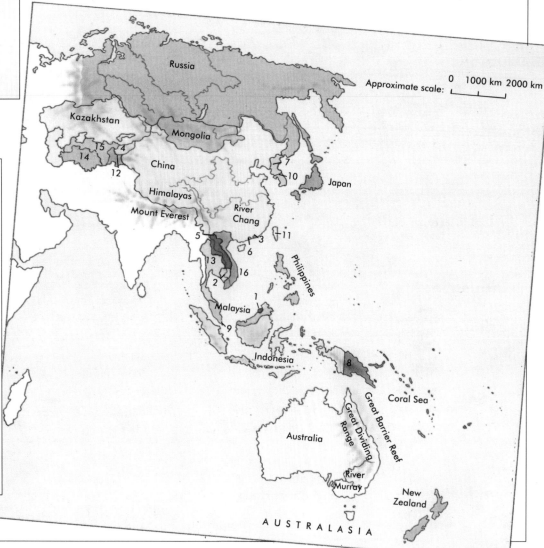

Map key

1. Brunei
2. Cambodia
3. Hong Kong
4. Kyrgyzstan
5. Laos
6. Macao
7. North Korea
8. Papua New Guinea
9. Singapore
10. South Korea
11. Taiwan
12. Tajikistan
13. Thailand
14. Turkmenistan
15. Uzbekistan
16. Vietnam

Japan

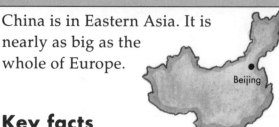

Japan is a chain of islands off the east coast of Asia, in the Pacific Ocean.

Tokyo

Key facts

Size: 377,708 sq km
Population: About 125 million
Currency: Yen
Main language: Japanese

Capital city: Tokyo is one of the world's most crowded cities. The Imperial Palace, where the present Emperor still lives, is here.

The Imperial Palace

Japan has many islands. The four main ones are called Kyushu, Shikoku, Honshu and Hokkaido.

Landscape:

Two-thirds of Japan is mountainous. The only flat land is along the coast. There are over 200 volcanoes, half of them active. The highest point in Japan is Mount Fuji (3776 m). The Shinano-gawa (367 km) is the longest river.

Mount Fuji

Industries

Vehicles
Electronics
Farming
Shipbuilding

Places to visit: There are many temples dedicated to the god Buddha, historic sites and ancient palaces. If you visit Japan you are likely to see traditional crafts, and rituals such as the tea ceremony.

A Japanese temple

China

China is in Eastern Asia. It is nearly as big as the whole of Europe.

Beijing

Key facts

Size: 9,596,961 sq km
Population: Over 1,220 million (about a fifth of the world's people)
Currency: Renminbi
Main language: Mandarin Chinese

Capital city: Beijing.
There are beautiful palaces and gardens to see. The Forbidden City is in the middle of Beijing. This was once the home of the Chinese emperors.

The Forbidden City

Landscape: There is a high plateau in the west, with flat lands in the east and several very long rivers. Mountains take up about a third of the country. Mount Everest (8848 m), on the border of China and Nepal, is the world's highest mountain. The Chang (5530 km) is the longest river.

Mount Everest

Places to visit: The Great Wall of China runs from east to west for about 6400 km. It is the only structure on Earth visible from space. The ancient tomb of emperor Quin Shihuangdi is at Xi'an. It was guarded by thousands of life-sized clay warriors, called the 'terracotta army'

Industries

Farming
Minerals
Chemicals

The Great Wall of China

New Zealand

New Zealand is in the Pacific. It is made up of two main islands, North Island and South Island.

Wellington

Key facts

Size: 268,676 sq km
Population: Over 3 million
Currency: New Zealand dollar
Main languages: English, Maori

Capital city: Wellington. Most people live in this city and the surrounding area. Wellington has a magnificent harbour and many old buildings.

Landscape: Much of the land is mountainous, with rivers and plains. In parts of North Island there are volcanoes, hot water geysers and pools of boiling mud. The highest point is Mount Cook (3764 m). The Waikato (425 km) is the longest river.

Industries

Minerals
Farming
Wool

A geyser spouting hot water

Places to visit: There is lots of spectacular scenery, including rainforests and glaciers. The Maoris were the first settlers in this country. Rotorua is the centre of Maori culture. Many kinds of animals and birds, such as the kiwi, are found only in New Zealand.

Maori dancers

Australia

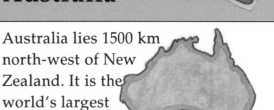

Australia lies 1500 km north-west of New Zealand. It is the world's largest island.

Canberra

Key facts

Size: 7,686,848 sq km
Population: Over 18 million
Currency: Australian dollar
Main language: English

Capital city: Canberra. Most of the population lives along the eastern and south-eastern coastline. Australia is made up of six states and two territories, each with its own capital.

Sydney Opera House

Landscape: In the middle of Australia, there are several large deserts and dry grasslands. The Great Barrier Reef stretches 2012 km along the north-east coast. The highest point in Australia is Mount Kosciusko (2230 m). The Murray (2589 km) is the longest river.

Ayers Rock, a famous landmark near Alice Springs

Industries

Farming
Minerals
Iron
Engineering

Places to visit: The original settlers in Australia were the Aborigines. Some of their cave paintings and historic sites date back to prehistoric times. There are wildlife parks where you can see koalas, kangaroos and other animals found only in Australia. The beaches are world-famous.

In the second century BC, a Greek man called Antipater of Sidon decided to write about seven of the most marvellous structures that existed at the time. These became known as the Seven Wonders of the Ancient World.

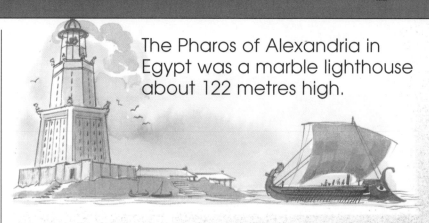

The Pharos of Alexandria in Egypt was a marble lighthouse about 122 metres high.

The pyramids of Giza in Egypt were the tombs of Ancient Egyptian kings and queens. They were buried with all the things they thought they might need in their next life, such as food, furniture and jewels.

The statue of Zeus, King of the Greek gods, was carved from ivory and marble. It was 12 metres tall and built at Olympia, Greece.

The Ancient Greeks built temples to worship gods and goddesses. The Temple of Artemis, in Ephesus, Turkey, was built to worship the goddess of hunting and fertility.

King Mausolus decided to build himself the grandest tomb in the world at Halicarnassus, Turkey. A new word was invented to describe the tomb – mausoleum, after Mausolus.

The Colossus of Rhodes was a huge bronze statue of the Sun god, Helios. It was 37 metres high, and stood on the Mediterranean island of Rhodes.

The biggest pyramid at Giza is about 146 metres high, and is made of over two million blocks of stone.

King Nebuchadnezzar built the beautiful Hanging Gardens of Babylon in Mesopotamia for his wife. Stone terraces were shaped like pyramids and filled with colourful plants.

Building Wonders

Amazing buildings are found all over the world. There are wonderful castles and palaces, strange houses, and very unusual shops!

In Houston, US, a shop has been designed to look as though it is falling down!

Neuschwanstein Castle

In Germany in 1869, King Ludwig of Bavaria began building himself a fairytale castle with lots of towers and turrets.

Imagine a huge building made completely of glass. Crystal Palace was built in London, UK in 1851. Its great iron frame contained 300,000 pieces of glass.

In Beijing, China, the Emperor lived in his own private city, with palaces, lakes and gardens. Ordinary people were not allowed in, so it was called the Forbidden City.

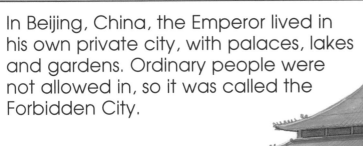

The Biosphere, in the Arizona desert, US, was like a huge greenhouse, containing different habitats, each with plants and animals.

The Palace of Versailles in France is 580 metres long and is the biggest palace in the world. It was built for King Louis XIV in 1682.

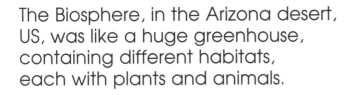

The Biosphere experiment was set up to see if people could survive on what they could grow within the building. Volunteers had to stay inside for two years.

One of the strangest houses in the world is in California, US. Its owner, Sarah Winchester, was afraid of ghosts and believed that they would harm her unless she kept doing building work on the house. Work went on for 38 years!

The house started with 18 rooms and ended with 160!

It has weird features such as staircases which lead nowhere.

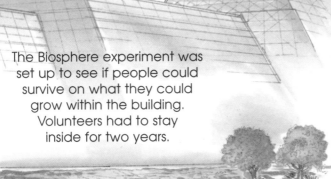

Mountains are made when rocks under the Earth's surface move. Sometimes molten rock rises up inside the Earth and pushes the land into a dome shape.

Some mountains are volcanoes. A volcano is a hole in the Earth's surface. Hot molten rock (lava) inside the Earth shoots out of the hole when the volcano erupts.

Ayers Rock in Australia is the biggest rock in the world. It is 2.5 kilometres long and 348 metres high.

From the rocky desert of Monument Valley in Utah, US, strange towering chunks of rock rise to 300 metres. Water, wind and temperature changes have worn away the surrounding rock to make shapes that look like ruined castles or crumbling skyscrapers.

The largest active volcano is Mauna Loa, in Hawaii. An active volcano is one that still erupts. Mauna Loa last erupted in 1984.

One of the biggest and most terrifying volcanic eruptions was when Krakatoa in Indonesia exploded in 1883. Rock shot 25 kilometres into the air, and dust fell over 5000 kilometres away.

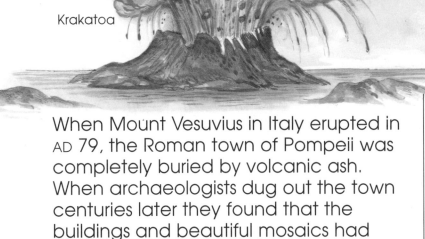

Krakatoa

When Mount Vesuvius in Italy erupted in AD 79, the Roman town of Pompeii was completely buried by volcanic ash. When archaeologists dug out the town centuries later they found that the buildings and beautiful mosaics had been preserved by the lava.

The highest mountain in the world is Mount Everest, in the Himalayan mountains. It is 8848 metres high. The first people to climb to the top were Edmund Hillary and Sherpa Tenzing Norgay, in 1953.

The longest range of mountains is the Andes in South America. It stretches for about 7600 kilometres.

Towering Wonders

Many tall buildings are built with a frame made from steel and concrete. Others are built around a huge hollow concrete tube.

Builders dig deep into the ground to make a support for the building, called the foundations.

The world's most famous tower looks as if it will fall over! The Leaning Tower of Pisa, in Italy, was finished in 1350. It is 56 metres high. Because the soft ground has sunk under the tower, it leans over 4 metres to one side.

Alexandre-Gustave Eiffel built the world's tallest tower for the Paris Exhibition of 1889.

The Eiffel Tower, Paris, France is 300 metres high, made of iron girders held together by rivets.

Built in 1931, the Empire State Building in New York City, US, appeared in a famous film. Using trick photography, a fierce giant ape called King Kong was shown clinging to the top of the 381-metre skyscraper.

Lighthouses warn ships where there is danger from underwater rocks. The tallest lighthouse in Britain is Bishop Rock, near the Scilly Isles. It is 49 metres high.

The tallest tower in the world today is the CN Tower in Toronto, Canada. It is 553.34 metres high. From its revolving restaurant you can see for 120 kilometres.

More than 62,000 tonnes of earth was excavated for the CN Tower's foundations.

The Chrysler Building, New York, US, is one of the world's most beautiful skyscrapers. Some of its design was based on a rising sun and parts of a Chrysler car!

Since ancient times, people have sculpted images of humans and gods. Some are carved from stone or wood, or cast from metal. Many of them are enormous.

In Ancient Britain, people carved giant figures and animals into chalky hillsides. The 'Long Man' at Wilmington, East Sussex is 68 metres long – the largest hill carving in Britain.

An enormous statue of Jesus overlooks Rio de Janeiro in Brazil. The sculptor, Paul Landowski, built the 40-metre tall concrete statue in 1931.

On Easter Island in the South Pacific Ocean, hundreds of strange stone figures were discovered. Archaeologists think they were carved some time between AD 1000 and 1600.

In 1257 BC, an Egyptian pharaoh decided to build a great temple at Abu Simbel. It had four 20-metre tall statues of the pharaoh, Ramesses II, at the entrance.

The tallest statue in the world stands in Tokyo, Japan. This bronze statue of Buddha is 120 metres tall and weighs 1000 tonnes.

One man turned a mountainside into a sculpture! Gutzon Borglum carved the heads of four American presidents on Mount Rushmore in South Dakota, US. It took him 14 years.

In 1501, the artist Michelangelo carved a beautiful lifelike marble statue of David, who killed the giant Goliath in the Bible story. It was sculpted out of a huge marble block which a sculptor had worked on years before, but had abandoned. Michelangelo designed his sculpture to fit into the chiselled marble block. The statue is over twice life-size.

A waterfall is formed when a river wears away the soft rock beneath a layer of hard rock to form a step.

Geysers are caused when water is heated by hot rocks under the ground. Steam pressure builds up and forces a jet of hot water out of a hole in the ground.

The highest waterfall in the world is the Angel Falls in Venezuela. It drops 979 metres.

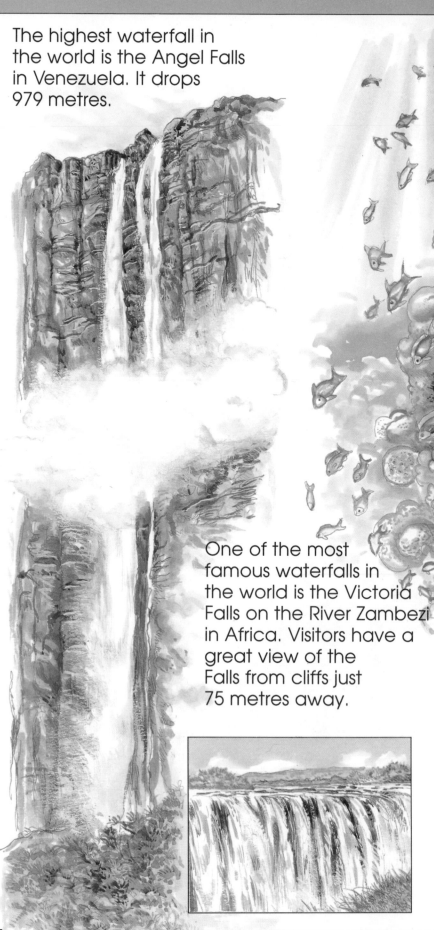

One of the most famous waterfalls in the world is the Victoria Falls on the River Zambezi in Africa. Visitors have a great view of the Falls from cliffs just 75 metres away.

The Great Barrier Reef off Queensland in Australia is the biggest coral reef in the world. It is a rock-like mass built up from tiny sea creatures called corals and their skeletons.

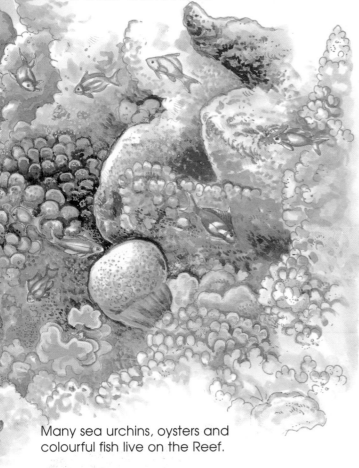

Many sea urchins, oysters and colourful fish live on the Reef.

On his way to California, US, in 1933, a sailor saw the highest ever recorded wave during a hurricane. It was 34 metres tall.

The tallest ever geyser shot out hot, black water and huge rocks to a height of 460 metres. The Waimangu Geyser in New Zealand used to erupt about every three days, but has been quiet since 1904.

Today, the tallest geyser is in Yellowstone National Park in Wyoming, US. Known as the Steamboat Geyser, its eruptions reach heights of up to 115 metres.

The strongest sea currents in the world reach a speed of 30 kilometres per hour in the Nakwakto Rapids, British Columbia in Canada.

Tunnelling Wonders

Tunnels carry roads and railways beneath cities, through mountains and under the sea. Some tunnels supply water, and others take away sewage.

Tunnels may be cut out of rock by huge boring machines. Some tunnels are built in sections and then buried.

Tunnels allow canals to pass through hills. Up until the mid-1900s, canal boats were guided through tunnels by men called 'leggers'.

The Channel Tunnel is the world's longest tunnel under the sea. It travels 50 kilometres under the English Channel from England to France.

The Channel Tunnel was dug out by enormous machines with 100 cutters and 200 teeth. They chewed through the rock and passed it backwards to be taken away on trains.

It took 24 years for engineers to build the world's longest rail tunnel. The Seikan Tunnel in Japan is 53.85 kilometres long. It joins two islands by passing 100 metres below the sea-bed.

The tunnels of the gold mine at Carletonville in South Africa are 3581 metres under the ground, making it the deepest mine in the world. Every day, over 11,000 miners dig out the gold.

In Switzerland, the St. Gotthard Tunnel burrows through mountains called the Alps. Measuring 16.32 kilometres, this is the longest road tunnel in the world.

Deep under the city, the tube trains of the London Underground in England rumble through 171 kilometres of tunnels. This is the biggest underground railway in the world.

Entertaining Wonders

Throughout history, people have created magnificent structures for entertainments.

Sydney Opera House overlooks Sydney harbour in Australia. It is shaped like a series of shells and is covered in tiles which catch the light. There are five separate halls inside.

Las Vegas, US, has lots of buildings decorated with neon lights.

The Romans built the Colosseum in Rome, Italy. It was a huge sporting arena. Up to 50,000 people would come to watch gladiators fight.

Walt Disney World in Florida, US, is the biggest amusement park in the world. It takes five days to look round all of it!

The longest roller coaster ride in the world is at Lightwater Valley Theme Park in Yorkshire, UK. It is over 2 kilometres long.

In Ancient Greece, open-air theatres were very popular. At Epidaurus theatre, 14,000 people could watch a play. Actors on stage could be heard even if you sat right at the top.

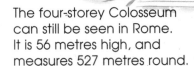

The four-storey Colosseum can still be seen in Rome. It is 56 metres high, and measures 527 metres round.

The biggest football stadium in the world is in Rio de Janeiro in Brazil. It can hold a crowd of 205,000 people.

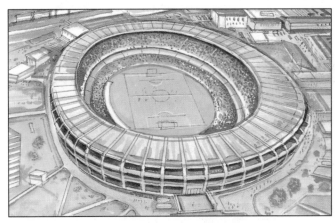

The Superdome in New Orleans, US, is the largest indoor stadium in the world. In Toronto, Canada, SkyDome Stadium, pictured below, has the biggest moving roof in the world. It is rolled back in summer.

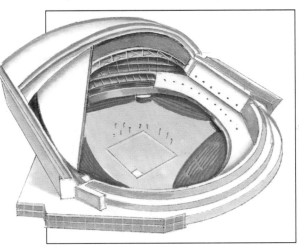

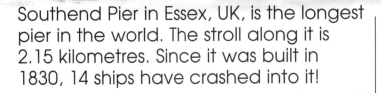

Southend Pier in Essex, UK, is the longest pier in the world. The stroll along it is 2.15 kilometres. Since it was built in 1830, 14 ships have crashed into it!

Caves are formed when rainwater gradually wears away rock, and streams work their way underground. The streams form tunnels which slowly grow into caves.

In the Cueva de Nerja, Málaga, Spain, hangs a 59-metre stalactite – the longest in the world. The tallest stalagmite in the world is in the Krásnohorská cave in Slovakia. It is 32 metres tall.

In Kentucky, US, explorers have found the biggest collection of connected caves in the world. The Mammoth Cave system covers 560 kilometres.

The deepest cave in the world is at Réseau Jean Bernard in France. It is 1602 metres deep.

Stalagmites and stalactites are formed in limestone caves by continually dripping water containing calcite, which gradually collects on the rock. Stalactites grow down from the roof, like icicles. The water which drips off them forms stalagmites which build upwards. Eventually, the two may meet!

Since the sixteenth century, people in Knaresborough, UK, have hung objects at the Dropping Well. Dripping water gradually turns the objects to stone. This happens in the same way as stalactites are formed.

The biggest underwater cave is in Mexico. Divers have explored 39,480 metres of passages in the Nohoch Na Chich caves.

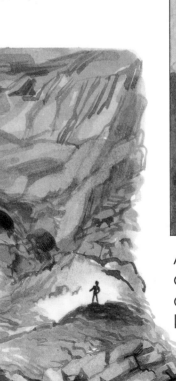

At 700 metres long and 300 metres wide, with a roof at least 70 metres high, the biggest cave in the world is the Sarawak Chamber, Lubang Nasib Bagus, in Sarawak, Malaysia.

There have been many religions in the history of the world. Since ancient times people have believed in one or many gods.

Often impressive structures have been built as places of worship.

In the Far East, Buddhists build tower-shaped temples called pagodas. This wooden Japanese pagoda in Kyoto was built in the seventh century.

In Wiltshire, UK, the massive stones of ancient Stonehenge stand in a circle. Nobody really knows what they were for, but they may have been used for religious ceremonies. Stonehenge could be over 4,000 years old.

The Buddhist Temple of Borobudur in Indonesia is built in huge layers of steps. There are 72 bell-shaped shrines on them, each containing a statue of the Buddha. It is the largest Buddhist temple in the world.

Angkor Wat is the biggest place of worship in the world. It is a Hindu temple in Cambodia built in the twelfth century. The carved stone towers and passageways cover 1.62 square kilometres.

The architect Antoni Gaudí started work on the Cathedral of the Sagrada Familia (Barcelona, Spain) in 1883, but it remains unfinished. Its fantastic spires are over 106 metres tall.

In Moscow, Russia, the towers of St. Basil's Cathedral look as though they are topped with many different coloured sweets!

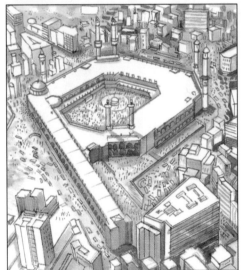

The Great Mosque at Mecca in Saudi Arabia is visited by many Muslim pilgrims. This vast mosque was built in the seventh century. At the centre of its huge open courtyard is a holy shrine.

The Golden Temple at Amritsar in India is the most holy shrine of the Sikh religion. This beautiful golden building glistens in the sunlight. Inside, it is richly decorated with elaborate paintings and gold.

Artists have created exciting works of art in many different forms, from painting and sculpture to textiles and glass.

The oldest artistic wonders date back to 30,000 BC, when Palaeolithic people created cave pictures using mineral powder.

One of the earliest ways to decorate walls was by mosaic. Using tiny pieces of glass, stone or marble, artists put together colourful pictures like amazing jigsaw puzzles.

The first cartoon strip in the world was embroidered in wool in the eleventh century! The Bayeux Tapestry tells the story of how the French conquered England in 1066. It is 70 metres long.

A battle scene from the Bayeux Tapestry.

This mosaic of the Empress Theodora is in a church in Ravenna, Italy. It was made in the sixth century AD.

Pablo Picasso produced more works of art during his life than any other artist. When Picasso died at the age of 92 in 1973, he had created around 148,000 pieces. His cubist paintings show several views of an object at the same time.

Stained glass windows in Christian churches were used to teach people about the Bible. This window in Cologne Cathedral in Germany tells the story of Jonah and the whale.

The most famous painting in the world is probably the *Mona Lisa*, which was painted by the Italian artist, Leonardo da Vinci, in about 1503.

It is said that music was played at every sitting for the portrait, so that the mysterious smile would not fade from the model's face.

Wherever the weather is very hot, dry or cold, the landscape displays incredible features. Canyons or gorges are valleys with steep rock walls.

The biggest glacier in the world is the Lambert Glacier in Antarctica, which is over 700 kilometres long. The fastest-moving glacier is in Alaska, and can move about 20 metres a day.

The Vicos Gorge in Greece is 1,100 metres wide and 900 metres deep.

A glacier is a huge, slow-moving river of ice.

The biggest gorge in the world is the Grand Canyon, Arizona, US. It is about 16 kilometres wide and 446 kilometres long.

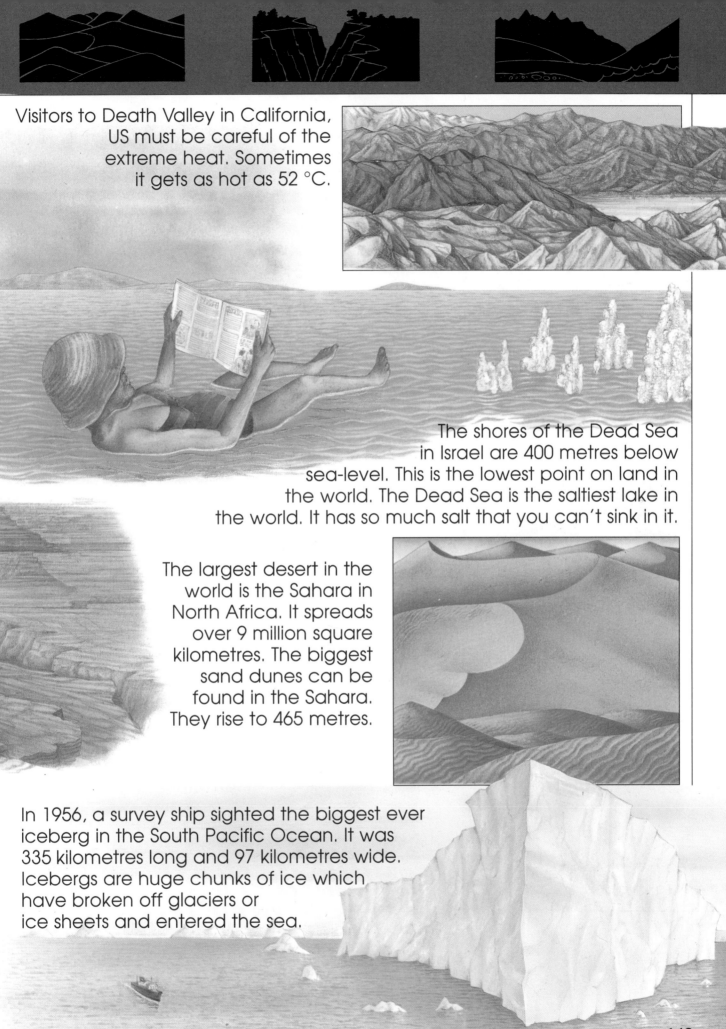

Visitors to Death Valley in California, US must be careful of the extreme heat. Sometimes it gets as hot as 52 °C.

The shores of the Dead Sea in Israel are 400 metres below sea-level. This is the lowest point on land in the world. The Dead Sea is the saltiest lake in the world. It has so much salt that you can't sink in it.

The largest desert in the world is the Sahara in North Africa. It spreads over 9 million square kilometres. The biggest sand dunes can be found in the Sahara. They rise to 465 metres.

In 1956, a survey ship sighted the biggest ever iceberg in the South Pacific Ocean. It was 335 kilometres long and 97 kilometres wide. Icebergs are huge chunks of ice which have broken off glaciers or ice sheets and entered the sea.

143

Engineering Wonders

Engineering is work that uses scientific knowledge for designing and building machines, vehicles, buildings, roads and structures such as bridges, dams and walls.

Aqueducts were first built in ancient times to carry water over a distance into towns. The Romans built the longest, which ran to the city of Carthage in Tunisia from springs 141 kilometres away.

Work on Britain's longest wall was started by the Romans in AD 122. Hadrian's Wall took only four years to build, and snaked 118 kilometres across northern England.

The most concrete ever used to build a dam was poured into the huge Grand Coulee Dam in Washington State, US. It is 1272 metres long and 167 metres high.

In the US, trains trundle 19 kilometres along the longest railway viaduct in the world. The viaduct crosses the Great Salt Lake in Utah.

Suspension bridges hang from cables between two towers. The Humber Estuary Bridge in Humberside, UK, is the longest in the world. The distance between its towers is 1410 metres.

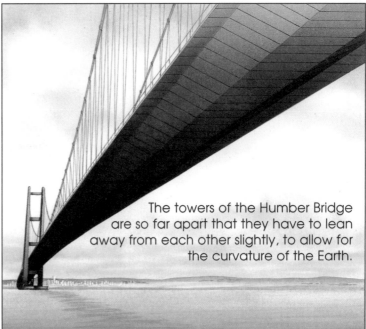

The towers of the Humber Bridge are so far apart that they have to lean away from each other slightly, to allow for the curvature of the Earth.

Sydney Harbour Bridge in Australia is the widest bridge in the world. At 48.8 metres wide, it carries two railway tracks, eight lanes of road, a cycle path and a footway.

The longest wall in the world can be seen from Space! The Great Wall of China stretches 3460 kilometres along a mountain range. The wall was built to keep invaders out of China. Builders worked for over a hundred years to finish it in about 210 BC.

Phenomenal Wonders

A phenomenon is any remarkable occurrence. Natural phenomena are those which occur in nature.

A comet is a rocky object which travels around the Sun and can periodically be seen from Earth. Halley's Comet was first recorded in 240 BC.

A waterspout is a tornado which has formed over water, and created a tall spinning column of watery mist. The highest waterspout reached 1528 metres off New South Wales, Australia, in 1898.

A mirage is the illusion of a distant object or a sheet of water. It is caused by atmospheric conditions in hot weather.

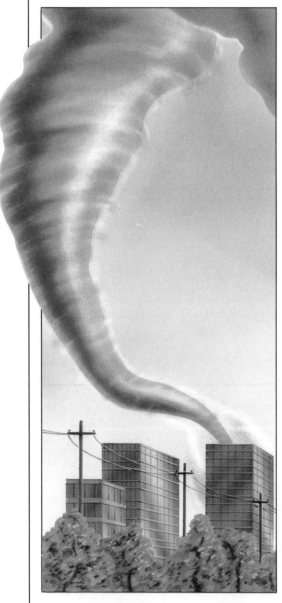

A tornado looks like a tube reaching out of a cloud. Its spiralling winds may reach 500 kilometres per hour.

A solar eclipse is when the Moon passes between the Sun and the Earth. The longest solar eclipse in recent times was in 1715, and lasted four minutes.

Meteorites are broken bits of comets or asteroids which fall to Earth. The biggest one ever found was 2.7 metres long and weighed 59 tonnes. It was found in Namibia, Africa, in 1920.

Hailstones form when water droplets in storm clouds freeze and fall to Earth. The heaviest hailstones fell in Bangladesh in 1986. They weighed a kilogramme and killed 92 people.

The northern lights, or aurora borealis, are different coloured bands of light that move across the sky in the polar region. They are caused by particles from the Sun reaching the Earth's magnetic field.

St. Elmo's fire is a luminous area which may appear around objects such as church spires, ships' masts, or aircraft wings. It is caused by electricity in the atmosphere.

Earthquakes

An earthquake happens when the surface of the Earth moves suddenly, and without warning. Buildings collapse and people are often buried alive.

We live on the Earth's crust. This is divided into huge plates which glide around very slowly. The most severe earthquakes take place near the edges of these plates.

The size of an earthquake depends on the amount of **pressure** that has been built up along the plates. It can be a small rumble or be so strong it brings down buildings, bridges and roads.

Pacific plate

North American plate

Blue lines show plates moving together

Red lines show plates moving apart

South American plate

Eurasian plate

African plate

Pacific plate

Indian plate

Antarctic plate

In the middle of the oceans, **plates** move apart and new rock is formed to fill the gaps. This movement causes earthquakes but we do not feel these because they are so far from land.

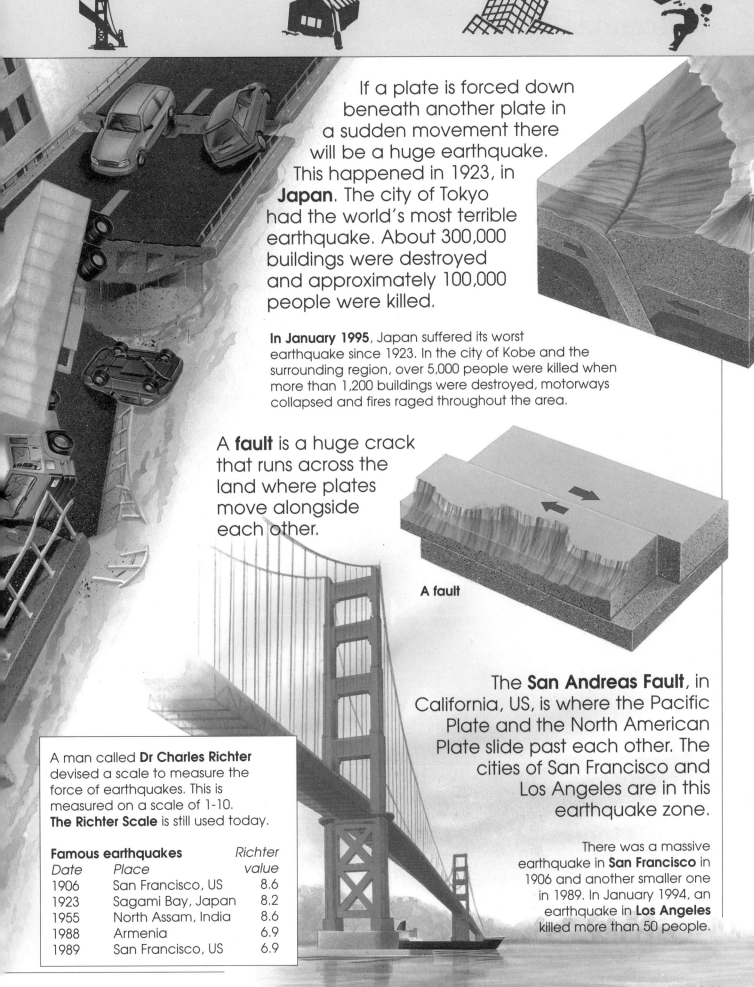

If a plate is forced down beneath another plate in a sudden movement there will be a huge earthquake. This happened in 1923, in **Japan**. The city of Tokyo had the world's most terrible earthquake. About 300,000 buildings were destroyed and approximately 100,000 people were killed.

In January 1995, Japan suffered its worst earthquake since 1923. In the city of Kobe and the surrounding region, over 5,000 people were killed when more than 1,200 buildings were destroyed, motorways collapsed and fires raged throughout the area.

A **fault** is a huge crack that runs across the land where plates move alongside each other.

A fault

The **San Andreas Fault**, in California, US, is where the Pacific Plate and the North American Plate slide past each other. The cities of San Francisco and Los Angeles are in this earthquake zone.

There was a massive earthquake in **San Francisco** in 1906 and another smaller one in 1989. In January 1994, an earthquake in **Los Angeles** killed more than 50 people.

A man called **Dr Charles Richter** devised a scale to measure the force of earthquakes. This is measured on a scale of 1-10. **The Richter Scale** is still used today.

Famous earthquakes		Richter
Date	Place	value
1906	San Francisco, US	8.6
1923	Sagami Bay, Japan	8.2
1955	North Assam, India	8.6
1988	Armenia	6.9
1989	San Francisco, US	6.9

149

Volcanoes

A volcano is a hole in the Earth's crust. When a volcano erupts, hot molten rock from inside the Earth pours out of the hole on to the surface.

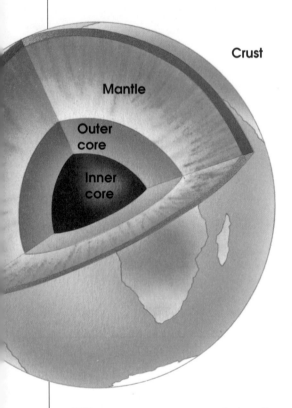

Crust

Mantle

Outer core

Inner core

There are two kinds of volcanic eruptions. Some volcanoes explode without warning, and others erupt slowly and quietly, usually allowing time for people to escape.

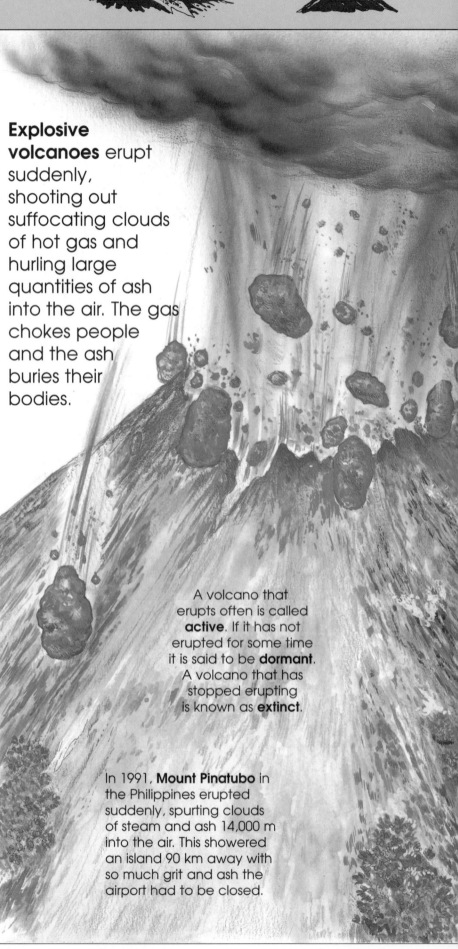

Explosive volcanoes erupt suddenly, shooting out suffocating clouds of hot gas and hurling large quantities of ash into the air. The gas chokes people and the ash buries their bodies.

A volcano that erupts often is called **active**. If it has not erupted for some time it is said to be **dormant**. A volcano that has stopped erupting is known as **extinct**.

In 1991, **Mount Pinatubo** in the Philippines erupted suddenly, spurting clouds of steam and ash 14,000 m into the air. This showered an island 90 km away with so much grit and ash the airport had to be closed.

In the Pacific Ocean there is a string of volcanic islands which form the US state of **Hawaii**. The volcanoes were caused by a hot spot in the Earth's mantle.

In 1883, the volcanic island of **Krakatoa** erupted with such force that a pillar of steam 11,000 m high shot up into the sky. The air was filled with fumes, hot cinders and black dust that blotted out the sun. The heat from the island could be felt over 3 km away.

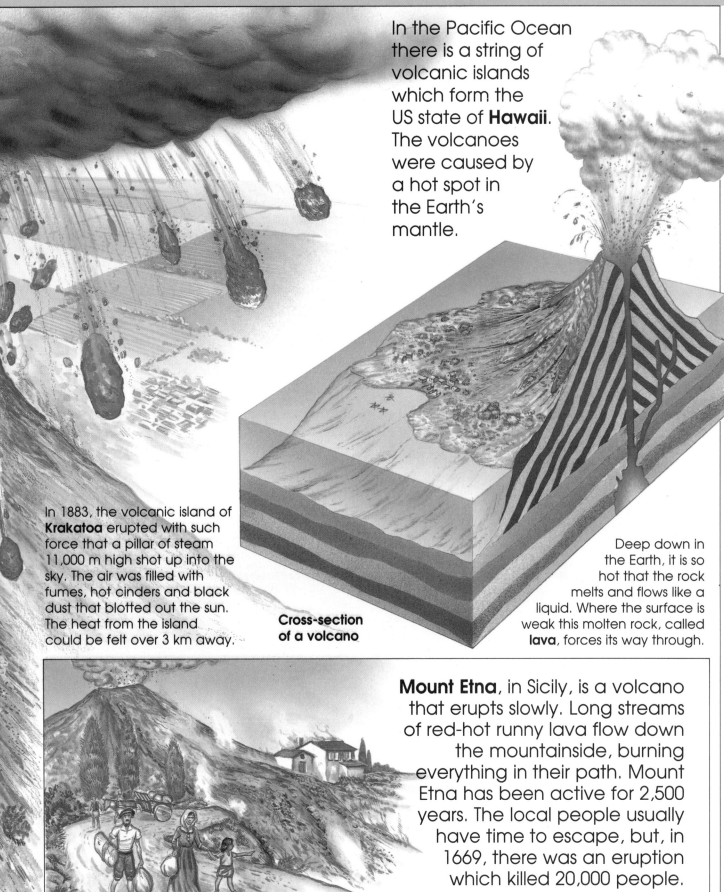

Cross-section of a volcano

Deep down in the Earth, it is so hot that the rock melts and flows like a liquid. Where the surface is weak this molten rock, called **lava**, forces its way through.

Mount Etna, in Sicily, is a volcano that erupts slowly. Long streams of red-hot runny lava flow down the mountainside, burning everything in their path. Mount Etna has been active for 2,500 years. The local people usually have time to escape, but, in 1669, there was an eruption which killed 20,000 people.

151

Thunder and lightning

Many natural disasters are caused by weather, especially storms. Every day about 45,000 thunderstorms happen somewhere in the world.

A thunderstorm is caused when warm, moist air rises very quickly, forming thunderclouds.

Electrical charges build up inside the clouds. These charges cause flashes inside the clouds, between one cloud and another, or between a cloud and the ground as lightning.

Light travels nearly one million times faster than sound so lightning is seen before thunder is heard.

A flash of **lightning** carries enough electrical energy to light a small city for several weeks. It causes heat five times that of the sun. This makes the air expand and makes a crash of **thunder**.

The safest place to be in a thunderstorm is inside a car, or in a building. Never stand under a tree or hold a metal umbrella.

Thunderstorms sometimes contain **hailstones**. In April 1986, hailstones weighing up to 1 kg killed 92 people in Bangladesh.

In 1959, **Colonel William Rankin** bailed out of his aircraft which had been battered by a thunderstorm in Virginia, USA. As he parachuted down, he was sucked into the heart of the storm. For 40 minutes he was pelted by hailstones, deafened by thunder, and blinded by lightning, but he survived.

Sheet lightning lights up the whole sky.

Forked lightning may reach the ground.

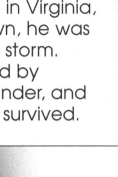

Many buildings have **lightning conductors**. These carry the electricity down into the ground so the building is not damaged. The **Empire State Building** in New York City, USA, is struck by lightning 500 times a year but is protected by a conductor.

In December 1963, 81 people were killed when a **Boeing 707 jet airliner** was struck by lightning in Maryland, USA.

Hurricanes and tornadoes

Hurricanes are the most violent large storms. They form over the warm oceans during the hottest months of the year.

The high winds of a hurricane become more powerful as they reach land. Some can release the same energy as a volcanic eruption and cause terrible destruction.

A tornado is a smaller storm than a hurricane, but it can have even stronger winds.

In the Atlantic Ocean the storms are called **hurricanes**; in the Indian Ocean they are known as **cyclones**, and in the Western Pacific they have the name **typhoon**.

In 1992, **Hurricane Andrew** swept across southern USA. Winds of over 200 km/h made 200,000 people homeless and caused $20,000 million worth of damage in Florida alone. It was the costliest natural disaster in the history of the US.

Warm air

Cold air

A **hurricane** starts when warm, wet air over the sea rises and forms enormous columns of cloud full of water vapour. Cold air rushes in below the rising warm air and begins to spiral around at up to 300 km/h.

Every hurricane is given a **name** to identify it. The names are chosen in alphabetical order, alternating between male and female names for each new storm. **Hurricane Gilbert** was the most powerful hurricane this century.

In 1991, a cyclone disaster killed almost 139,000 people in **Bangladesh**. Winds of 230 km/h caused floods over 1,300 sq km. Ten million people were made homeless, and four million risked death from starvation.

A **tornado** is a funnel-shaped cloud which descends from storm clouds to the ground, sucking up dust and debris as it moves. Tornadoes can tear trees out of the ground and make buildings explode.

About 200 tornadoes a year are recorded across the US. They are a major hazard in the Mississippi Valley, which is sometimes known as **Tornado Alley**.

Tornado Alley

Mexico

Caribbean

In May 1986, in **China**, it was reported that 13 schoolchildren had been sucked up into a tornado and carried 19 km before being dropped gently to the ground again.

A flood is an overflow of water. This can result from heavy rainfall, high tides, overflowing rivers or a sudden melting of snow.

Throughout history floods have caused more death and destruction than any other natural disaster on this planet.

The Bible story of **Noah** tells of a great flood that destroyed every living thing, except the family and animals on the ark.

In 1993, there was severe flooding in the **Mid-west US**. The Mississippi and Missouri rivers burst their banks along a stretch of 800 km, killing over 40 people and submerging 40,000 sq km of land. The president announced it to be a major disaster area.

In **1994-5**, there were more floods across the world than there have been for many years.

Northern Italy had the most ferocious rainstorms of the century. Over 100 people died.

In **Northern Spain** houses were flooded, and a bridge collapsed.

Greece suffered from heavy flooding.

In **Egypt**, floods killed hundreds and caused damage of £1.7 billion.

In **Africa**, flash floods hit drought areas. The cocoa crops of West and Central Africa were destroyed.

In **Germany**, the River Rhine became three times deeper than normal and flooded the city of Cologne.

In **China**, freak rainstorms made thousands of people homeless.

Huge seas washed away roads in Victoria, **Australia**.

In **India**, 192 people died, and 40,000 people were made homeless after rainfall caused by a cyclone.

The Huang River is known as 'China's Sorrow' because it has caused the world's worst floods. In 1887, in the city of **Zhengzhou**, over one million people died, either by drowning or from the terrible disease and starvation which followed.

Low-lying land near the sea is at risk from floods at high tide. The Dutch have built many **dykes** to protect their land below sea level.

In January 1995, 250,000 people fled their homes in the Netherlands as the worst floods in nearly sixty years swept across large areas of Europe. The country's dykes were threatened and some were close to collapse.

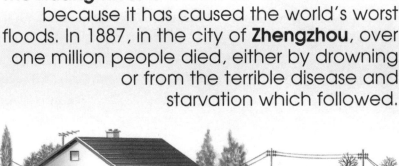

Bangladesh, in Asia, suffers from terrible floods when cyclones sweep in from the Bay of Bengal, causing high tides and heavy rain. Nearly all of Bangladesh is on the floodplain of the Ganges and Brahmaputra rivers.

The **Thames Barrier** was built across the River Thames in London, UK, to prevent the surges of the tide from flooding the city.

Torrential rainfall and earthquakes often trigger off landslides, which can cause terrible destruction.

Avalanches often happen after prolonged snowfalls. They can be caused by the slightest noise.

In the Alps, during **World War I**, 10,000 soldiers lost their lives in one day in a series of snow slides.

An **avalanche** is a mass of loosened snow and earth which slips down a mountainside, growing in size as it travels.

In January, 1718, the Swiss village of **Leukerbad** was engulfed by a huge avalanche. Over 50 houses disappeared, and 52 villagers were buried under a blanket of snow.

Avalanches are a danger in any mountainous area with bare slopes and heavy snow. Where slopes have been cleared of trees for skiing or farming, walls and snow fences are built to break up any avalanche that might develop.

In **winter sports areas**, snow patrols keep a special watch and give warnings of possible avalanches to ski resorts. All roads and ski fields are closed at any sign of danger.

In 1970, on **Mount Huascaran**, Peru, an earthquake caused a gigantic **rock** and **mudslide**. It covered 14 km in less than four minutes and wiped out towns and villages in its path. A dam burst, rivers flooded and 186,000 buildings were destroyed. It was estimated that 20,000 people died and 200,000 were made homeless.

Soil and rock on mountains and hills can creep, slide, flow or fall. **Creeps** happen on hillsides, usually very slowly. **Slides** can travel between 5 cm a year and 3 m a second. Slides on mountains can remove large sections of rock.

Rock slide

Earth flow

Soil creep

Rock fall

Mud flow

A drought is a shortage of rain. In parts of the world where there are long periods of dry weather, droughts are common.

This means that trees and crops die, and so there is a shortage of food.

If the drought continues for a long time there is a famine in the land and many people die of starvation.

In 1770, millions of Indians died of hunger when **drought** ruined their harvests. In 1877, nearly ten million Chinese lives were lost in a famine. In the twentieth century, thousands of Africans have died of starvation when crops were ruined and cattle starved to death.

The plains of Oklahoma and Texas, in the US, were once covered in lush grass. Then the farmers ploughed them up to plant wheat. In 1930, a drought killed all the crops, and strong winds blew away the top soil. Nothing could be grown there, and the area was called **The Dust Bowl**. Later the land was reclaimed and today is no longer a desert.

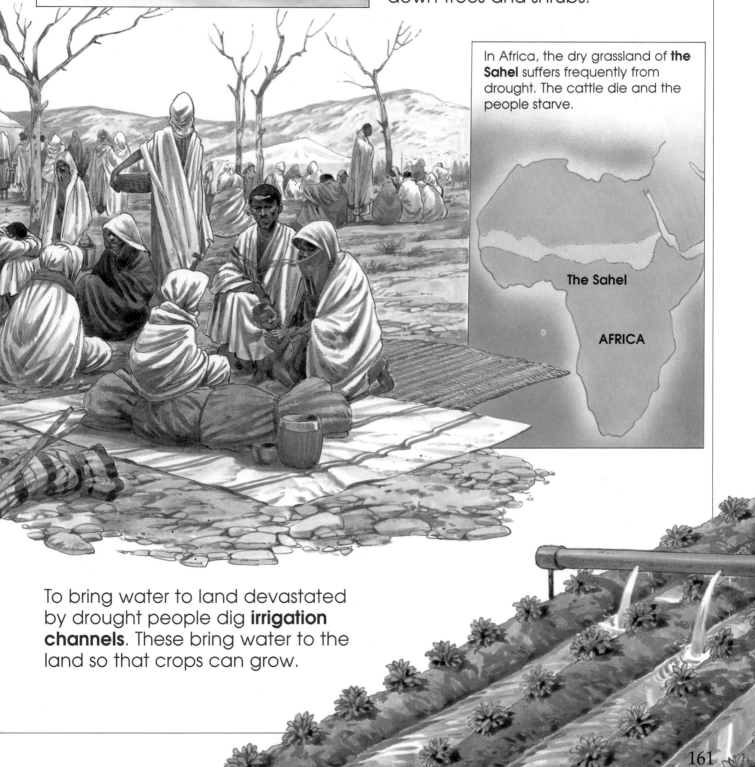

During droughts up to 100 sq km of land may become desert every day.

When plants die the soil is exposed to the wind, and may easily be blown away. Green grasslands can soon turn into deserts. This is called **desertification**. It is worst in areas where people overgraze land with their large herds of cattle, or cut down trees and shrubs.

In Africa, the dry grassland of **the Sahel** suffers frequently from drought. The cattle die and the people starve.

The Sahel

AFRICA

To bring water to land devastated by drought people dig **irrigation channels**. These bring water to the land so that crops can grow.

Forest fires

When droughts cause plants to dry up, they can catch fire easily.

In January 1994, high temperatures and hot winds fanned the worst **bush fires** ever known in **Australia**. Over 130 fires raged around Sydney and the coast of New South Wales, destroying hundreds of homes. The heat was so intense it caused windows to melt and houses to explode. Over 7,500 firefighters battled with the blaze which stretched for 960 km and burned over 400,000 hectares of land. Miraculously, only four people died.

Lightning from a storm or a lighted cigarette can start a fire that destroys thousands of square kilometres of forest.

In the autumn of 1993, a series of bush fires raged across **California**, on the west coast of the US. Many rich and famous Hollywood stars watched as their homes went up in flames.

In some large forests there are tall **look-out towers** where foresters can spot the first signs of fire. Observers in helicopters fly over the fire and note its size. Then they quickly transport firefighters and equipment to the scene of the fire to fight the blaze.

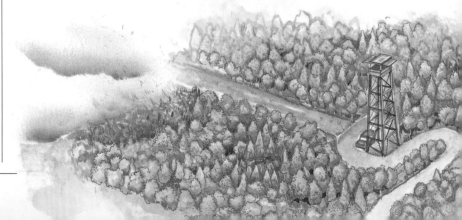

During the 1994 bush fires in Australia, most of the wildlife which lived in the surrounding national parks was wiped out, including entire colonies of **koalas**. The animals that did manage to flee had no food or shelter.

Some scientists feel that fire is nature's way of renewing the land. In 1988, fires raged through **Yellowstone Park**, in the US. Many people wanted the fires put out, but as there was no property in danger they were allowed to burn. After the fires were over, the vegetation grew again very quickly.

The main tree in Yellowstone Park is the **Lodgepole pine**. The cones on this tree depend on fire because they need a minimum temperature of 45°C to open and so release their seeds.

Ice ages are periods when great sheets of ice extend far beyond the land and sea they cover today.

The Earth has experienced many ice ages, some lasting for over 100 million years.

During an ice age, sheets of ice cover large parts of the world and the level of the sea is much lower than it is now.

Ice sheets and **glaciers** erode or wear away the land they move over. The ice drags pieces of rock from the land beneath it. These rocks can be carried for kilometres before they are dropped.

This glacier is moving slowly down the valley.

The ice sheets that covered much of North America and Europe during the last ice age were up to 3,000 m thick. The ice covering the continent of **Antarctica** today is even thicker.

The most recent ice age started two million years ago. During that time there were periods called **glacials** when the ice sheets were expanding, and times called **interglacials** when they became smaller. We may now be living in an interglacial period. If world temperatures fall, the ice sheets could grow again.

Woolly mammoths lived on Earth during the recent ice age, and became extinct about 10,000 years ago.

When the glacier melts it leaves a valley in the land.

The **fjords**, or deep sea inlets along the coast of Scandinavia were made by glaciers during the last ice age.

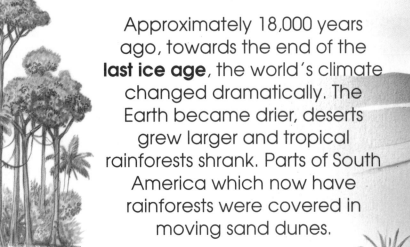

Approximately 18,000 years ago, towards the end of the **last ice age**, the world's climate changed dramatically. The Earth became drier, deserts grew larger and tropical rainforests shrank. Parts of South America which now have rainforests were covered in moving sand dunes.

165

The sea has always held many dangers for sailors and other voyagers. High winds during storms create huge waves in mid-ocean. These can drive ships off their course, or wreck them on rocks and seashores.

In April 1912, the *Titanic*, the most luxurious ocean liner of its time, set sail from Southampton, England, on her maiden voyage to New York City, USA. One night the ship collided with an enormous **iceberg**, which caused water to flood in below decks. About 1,500 people were left stranded on the liner which quickly sank beneath the waves. It was one of the worst shipping disasters of all time.

Waterspouts, tidal waves, icebergs and pack ice are hazards which can cause great loss of life.

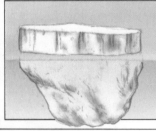

Icebergs from **Antarctica** are low, flat-topped and cover a large area.

Icebergs in the **north Atlantic** are tall, jagged, and mostly hidden beneath the waves.

A **waterspout** is a column of rising water which forms when a tornado descends over the sea. Waterspouts are often seen off the coast of the Gulf of Mexico and over the Atlantic Ocean, near Florida, USA. They suck up huge amounts of sea water into a great black cloud. Boats floating on the sea can be sucked up too.

Pack ice in the Arctic Ocean and around Antarctica can trap or crush ships. Some of the vessels used by the polar explorers were lost in this way. Nowadays, specially built **ice-breakers** can force their way through.

50m

The **biggest wave** ever recorded in the open sea was seen from a ship during a storm in 1933. It was estimated to be 34 m high.

34m

The huge volcanic eruption of **Krakatoa**, in August 1883, caused enormous waves, called **tsunamis**, to form in the sea. These swept towards the shores of Java and Sumatra, sucking up more water as they travelled. The gigantic waves, more than 50 m high, crashed down on the coast, destroying 300 villages and drowning 36,000 people.

A plague is a very contagious disease which spreads quickly, killing many people.

Many diseases can spread rapidly if people do not take special care to stop this happening. Any illness that causes many members of a community to be ill at the same time is called an epidemic.

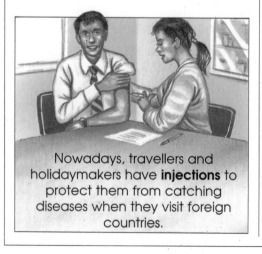

Nowadays, travellers and holidaymakers have **injections** to protect them from catching diseases when they visit foreign countries.

Between 1334 and 1351, a terrible epidemic, **the Black Death**, swept across Asia and Europe, killing millions of people. The disease was a form of **bubonic plague** and was spread by black rats which boarded trading ships. It was the fleas that lived on the rats which carried the plague, but unfortunately no-one realised this at the time.

Another insect which carries disease is the mosquito. **Malaria** is passed on by the bite of a mosquito which lives in tropical and sub-tropical areas.

Although there are medicines which can keep malaria at bay, no one has found a cure for it. Millions still die from the disease each year.

Leprosy is a disease which can be infectious. It occurs mainly in tropical and subtropical regions. It is a terrible disease which causes disfigurement.

The disease can now be treated, but in the past, **lepers** were sent away from the community to live together in **leper colonies**.

In 1994, **plague** broke out in **India**. This, too, was spread by fleas, carried by rats. Nowadays, the disease can be treated with medicine called **antibiotics** if it is detected early enough.

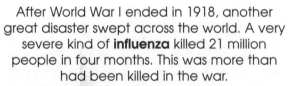

After World War I ended in 1918, another great disaster swept across the world. A very severe kind of **influenza** killed 21 million people in four months. This was more than had been killed in the war.

Epidemics of **cholera** are common in Asia. Between 1898 and 1907, 370,000 people in India died of this disease, which is often caused by drinking dirty water.

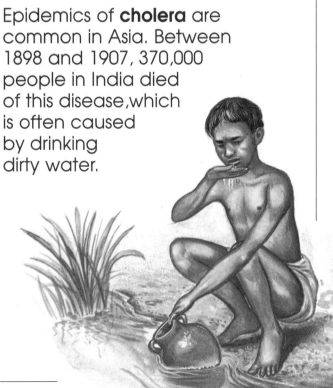

169

Plant and animal pests

Throughout history natural disasters have been caused by insect or animal pests, which destroy the crops on which humans live.

Some of these disasters are caused by people changing the creatures' habitats, by farming the land or by introducing new animals into areas where they were previously unknown.

One of the worst pests in Africa is the **quelea bird**. These small brown birds live together in large flocks and can destroy crops. Sometimes two million pairs can be found in an area of about 50 hectares.

In 1889, a swarm of locusts seen flying over the **Red Sea** was roughly 5,000 sq km in size.

Locusts are giant grasshoppers which can fly long distances and travel in vast swarms. When they land, they devour the crops for miles around, causing great destruction and often widespread famine.

In the 1840s, there was a terrible disease, or **blight**, on the potato crops in Ireland. As many people lived only on these vegetables, there was a terrible shortage of food, known as the **Potato Famine**.

Dutch Elm disease has killed thousands of elm trees throughout the world. It is spread by the **European elm bark beetle**. Young trees can die within two months.

The Colorado beetle, or potato bug, is an insect pest that feeds on the leaves of potato plants in western North America. Originally, the insect fed on a wild plant which grows in the Rocky Mountains. But since potato plants were introduced into the US, it has preferred to eat those instead.

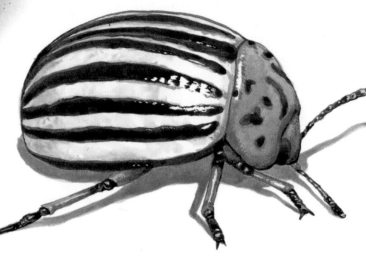

In the nineteenth century, English settlers took **rabbits** to Australia with them. Some of these eventually escaped to the outback, where they started a colony of wild rabbits, which was to become one of Australia's greatest pests. They ate farmers' crops, turned grassland into desert and their warrens caused the ground to collapse.

In the 1930s, the **cane toad** was introduced into Queensland, Australia, in order to control beetles. Now the toads are a pest!

171

Over the past hundred years, industry and modern technology have changed the world. Because of these changes, many new forms of pollution now affect our planet.

Many nations have begun to act to combat pollution. But we still need stricter laws to stop any further damage.

Oil tankers spill vast amounts of crude oil into the sea, poisoning everything that lives there. These are called **oil slicks**.

Many factories and power plants produce **toxic waste**. This is released into the environment and poisons rivers and lakes. The creatures that live in and around these waterways die or grow deformed.

The burning of forests increases the carbon dioxide in the air, and means that there are fewer trees to absorb this gas.

Heat radiation reflected by greenhouse gases

Heat lost by radiation

Heat radiation from the Sun

Atmosphere

As we pollute the atmosphere by burning fossil fuels, we also poison our rain, sleet and snow. **Acid rain** has killed forests and freshwater fish in many parts of the world. It also eats away at stone buildings and corrodes anything made of steel.

If we do not stop pollution, scientists think the average world **temperature** will rise dramatically over the next 50 years. This could cause the polar **ice-caps** to melt, flooding large areas of the world. Other areas would have terrible droughts.

Low-lying parts of London could be flooded if the average world temperature rose.

We burn the **fossil fuels** in factories, cars and power plants. These cause pollution and increase the amount of **carbon dioxide** in the air. This gas keeps heat in the **atmosphere** around the Earth. We call this **global warming**. The Sun's rays are trapped within the atmosphere just as they are in a greenhouse. So, the warming of the planet is called the **greenhouse effect**.

Some aerosols and refrigerators give off chemicals called CFCs into the atmosphere. These are damaging the **ozone layer**, which protects us from the Sun's dangerous **ultra-violet** rays. The use of CFCs has now been banned.

Danger from space

Some scientists believe that, 65 million years ago, a meteorite fell to Earth from space.

They think that the effects of the crash damaged our planet so badly that the dinosaurs became extinct.

If a similar collision happened today, it could threaten the human race.

Every year the Earth attracts more than a million tonnes of new material from space. These are called **meteors**. Most meteors disintegrate before they reach the ground, but sometimes the core survives and is called a **meteorite**.

If, as some scientists think, a large meteorite did hit the Earth millions of years ago, it would have thrown up a huge cloud of dust. This would have lowered the temperature and eventually killed most of the plant and animal life.

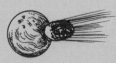

In **Arizona**, USA, there is a gigantic crater in the ground, caused by a meteor measuring about 30 m across. It must have been travelling at a speed of about 50,000 km/h because the meteor struck the ground with such force it made a crater nearly 200 m deep and 1.2 km wide.

Small meteors often break up into fragments as they travel through the atmosphere, causing streaks of light that flash across the sky. We call these **shooting stars**.

In July 1994, 21 giant particles of rock and ice from the comet **Shoemaker-Levy 9**, collided with the planet **Jupiter**. One of the fragments created a giant fire-ball and Earth-sized hole in the planet's atmosphere. The US government has given scientists fifty million dollars to create an early warning system to predict such a thing happening to the Earth.

Warriors were men or women who fought bravely. Often they were not paid to fight, but fought because they believed they were right.

Warriors did not win all of the time. Some of the most famous warriors are those who lost, but who fought with great courage.

Byrhtnoth was an English earl. In 991, he and all his men died fighting a Viking force near Maldon in Essex. They fought so bravely that a poem, called 'The Battle of Maldon', was written about their heroic struggle.

Shaka was the king of the Zulu, a large tribe in South Africa. In 1816 Shaka trained the Zulu warriors in new battle tactics. By 1850 the Zulus had defeated all neighbouring tribes. In 1879 the Zulus wiped out a British regiment before being defeated by the British at Rorke's Drift and Kambula.

Warriors used different types of **weapons**. Early warriors used clubs and rocks, while more modern warriors used rifles and cannons.

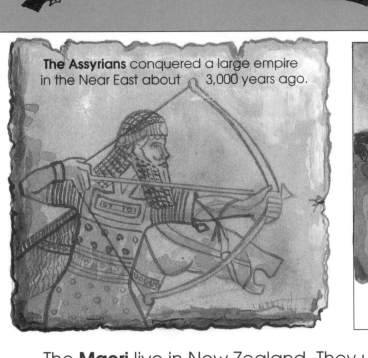

The Assyrians conquered a large empire in the Near East about 3,000 years ago.

Ashanti warriors fought in the dense forests of West Africa about 100 years ago.

The **Maori** live in New Zealand. They used to live in great tribes which fought wars with each other, and later, with European settlers. Sometimes whole tribes were killed in battle as they refused to surrender. Although the Europeans accepted the Maori as equals in 1840, wars continued for many years.

In 336 BC Alexander the Great became King of Macedonia (in northern Greece). He was only 20 years old. Within 13 years he had become the most powerful ruler in the world.

He defeated armies larger than his own using clever new tactics and weapons.

Alexander's horse was called **Bucephalus**. According to legend Alexander, who was only 12 years old at the time, was the only person who could control him. When Bucephalus died Alexander named a town in India, Bucephala, in honour of him.

The Battle of Gaugamela in 331 BC was Alexander's greatest victory. He defeated a Persian army of 150,000 men with his army of only 35,000 Macedonians. The battle was won when Alexander led a cavalry charge which scattered the Persian infantry.

The cavalry led the attacks in battle. They were used to open gaps in the enemy army. The horsemen would charge forward, followed by the infantry.

King Darius, was Alexander's biggest enemy. He became ruler of the Persian Empire in 336 BC after murdering the previous three rulers. Darius was a successful warrior who defeated many enemies, but he lost two major battles to Alexander. In 330 BC Darius was murdered by his cousin.

Infantry in Alexander's army used a very long spear called a **sarissa**. Each sarissa was 4.5 metres long.

In 323 BC Alexander's Empire was the largest in the world at that time. He wanted to join all the kingdoms he had conquered to form one country. After Alexander died, his generals divided the empire between themselves. Within 150 years the empire no longer existed.

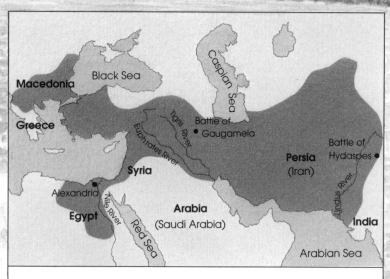

The Empire of Alexander the Great

Alexander reached **India** in 326 BC. He defeated a local king, Porus, at the Battle of the Hydaspes (modern day Jhelum) and added new territories to his empire.

Attila the Hun

Attila was the king of the Huns, a warlike tribe feared in Europe and Asia. He became sole King in 444 after murdering his elder brother, Breda, who was joint King at the time.

Attila organised the Huns into a powerful army. By conquering neighbouring kingdoms he built up a large empire. Soon, he became known as 'the scourge of God'.

In 453 Attila died suddenly after a feast on his wedding day. He was buried with his treasure. The slaves who buried him were all killed to keep the location secret. Without Attila's leadership, the Huns were easily defeated by their enemies.

The Huns came from central Asia in about 370 and settled in what is now Hungary. Attila led his tribe in wars that ranged across Greece, southern Russia, Germany and France.

The Huns loved gold - during one raid into Greece they stole over 1,000 kg!

Attila arrived in Italy in 452 and captured many cities. Pope Leo I persuaded him to spare Rome from attack.

Venice is a city in northern Italy surrounded by the sea. It was founded by Romans fleeing from Attila. The escaping Romans were safe on the islands of Venice as the Huns did not have a navy.

Horses were the Huns' most important possession. They used them to look after their large herds of cattle and sheep. They also fought on horseback, using spears and bows to attack their enemies.

Hun warriors scarred their faces with knives to make themselves look fierce to frighten their enemies.

The Huns used the **lasso** as a weapon. One Hun would catch an enemy with a lasso, allowing another warrior to kill the captive.

The Roman Empire began around 753 BC and lasted over 1,000 years until AD 476. It covered all the lands around the Mediterranean, and much of Europe.

These lands were conquered and policed by the Roman Army. The Romans defeated many enemies because of their superior weapons and tactics.

The Romans were excellent builders as well as warriors. They made roads to move their armies from one place to another, and built forts and walls to keep out invaders. **Hadrian's Wall**, in northern England, was built to keep enemies from invading England from Scotland.

The legionary was the most important type of Roman warrior. Legionaries wore strong suits of armour and fought on foot. They were grouped together in a century, made up of 80 legionaries led by an officer known as a centurion.

Roman legionaries marched and fought together in a large group of 5,200 legionaries, called a **legion**.

Horatius was a legendary early Roman warrior. In about 670 BC a large Etruscan army (from northern Italy) attacked Rome. The bridge leading to Rome across the River Tiber had to be cut down to stop the Etruscan invasion. Horatius fought the Etruscans single-handed to give the Romans time to cut down the bridge. Rome was saved and Horatius survived to be declared a hero.

182

Mark Antony was a famous general. He fell in love with Cleopatra, the Queen of Egypt, and gave her land belonging to Rome. This led to a civil war with the Roman authorities which Mark Antony lost. Later, he took his own life.

Legionaries arranged themselves in special formations when attacking the enemy. The 'tortoise' protected legionaries from arrows and spears. The 'wedge' was used to smash through enemy ranks.

The tortoise formation

A bronze eagle was the symbol of a legion and it was carried into battle. Romans thought it was an insult to the Gods if the eagle were captured by the enemy.

The Roman Empire was very large and had many enemies. There were tribes fighting their Roman conquerors, and armies from other empires trying to invade Rome.

The **Celts** were divided into many different tribes, who lived right across Europe from Scotland to Serbia. They were often a war-like people, who rode chariots into battle and sometimes sang as they fought. After a battle, the Celts would cut off the heads of their dead enemies and hold a feast to celebrate.

Vercingetorix was the Celtic leader of Gaul (modern day France). He fought against the Roman general Julius Caesar in 52 BC. After several battles, Vercingetorix was captured and beheaded.

Hannibal was a famous nobleman from Carthage (in modern day Tunisia). He was one of Rome's most dangerous enemies. In 218 BC he led his army, along with 38 elephants, from Spain through France and across the Alps into Italy. He won many battles there, including the defeat of 50,000 Romans at Cannae. He never reached Rome and was forced to return to Carthage.

Spartacus was a slave who escaped from a gladiator school in 73 BC. Thousands of other slaves ran away to join him. Spartacus led them through Italy, stealing and burning everything they could find. He was defeated and died in battle at Lucania in 71 BC. The 6,000 prisoners captured by the Romans were all crucified.

Boudicca was Queen of the Iceni, a tribe from East Anglia, in England. In AD 61 she led her tribe in revolt after she and her daughters had been ill-treated by the Romans, who had also increased the taxes. Boudicca's Celtic warriors destroyed Colchester, London and St Albans before being beaten by the Romans. Rather than surrender, she poisoned herself.

Arminius was a German chief. In AD 9 he and his warriors trapped three Roman legions in a swampy forest and killed them all.

Masada was a fortress in Palestine held by 1,000 Jewish rebels in AD 72-73. After a two-year siege by 15,000 Romans, all but seven of the Jews, including the children, committed suicide rather than surrender.

Cuchulainn was the great warrior hero of Ulster. His story is told in a poem called 'The Cattle Raid of Cooley' which was written around the year 500. In the poem, Cuchulainn is described as being very strong and having a terrible temper.

Ireland was never conquered by the Romans. Instead, Ireland remained a land ruled by Celtic chiefs.

Although there was a High King of Ireland most tribes continued to fight each other.

Irish kings and chiefs often lived in well defended **strongholds**. The remains of the Rock of Cashel in County Tipperary are a good example of an ancient Irish stronghold. The rock was home to the kings of Munster.

Brian Boru was the greatest High King of Ireland, reigning from 1002 to 1014. He fought to free Ireland from Viking invaders. He was murdered by a fleeing band of Vikings after finally defeating the Viking army at Clontarf.

Women are important characters in Irish mythology. The legendary **Queen Maeve** of Connaught led an army against Ulster, and fought against Cuchulainn.

Fionn mac Cumhaill was the legendary hero of Leinster. According to the stories told about him, he led a band of brave young warriors who loved to hunt. These warriors were known as the Fianna. The Fianna rebelled against Cairbre, High King of Ireland, in an argument about hunting lands. The Fianna were destroyed in the following battle.

Strongbow was the nickname of Richard Fitzgilbert, a Norman lord. He came to Ireland in 1170 to help Dermot MacMurrogh, King of Leinster, become High King. After Dermot's death, Strongbow grabbed his lands for himself. Soon, other Norman and English knights came to Ireland and took over much of the country.

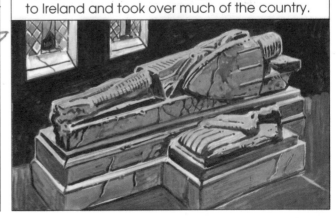

Vikings

The Vikings came from Norway, Denmark and Sweden. They raided northern Europe and even travelled to North America and Italy.

A carved head from a Viking ship

The Vikings were also merchants, trading with Arabs and people from Asia. They sold furs, ivory and slaves and bought silk, spices and gold.

Weapons were made by skilled craftspeople. Axes and swords were favourite weapons. Valuable swords were passed from father to son. They were given frightening names such as 'blood-sucker' or 'man-killer'!

Raids were carried out by warriors in longships. As many as 100 longships would take part in a single raid. The Vikings would land, capture as much money, food, cattle and valuables as possible and sail away again.

Longships were narrow boats which could be up to 30 metres in length. They were not very heavy and were very quick through the water as they had oars as well as a large sail. Some longships had dragon heads carved on to them to make them look fiercer.

Sweyn Forkbeard was the greatest Viking of his time. He built a large empire based around the North Sea. He was King of Denmark and Norway, and in 1013 he became King of England.

The Vikings started to settle in the places that they had raided in the past. There were **settlements** in northern England, northern France and southern Ireland. Remains of these settlements can still be seen in York, in England, and Dublin, in Ireland.

Eric Bloodaxe became King of Northumberland, in England, in 948. He had been forced to flee from Norway after murdering two of his brothers to become sole King of Norway. Eric was driven out of England in 948, and again in 954. He was killed later that year on returning to England.

Viking warriors believed that when they died they would go to **Valhalla**, the banquet hall of the gods. Viking chiefs and famous warriors would often be buried with their boats and their favourite possessions when they died. Sometimes the body would be placed on the deck of the boat and burned.

189

Genghis Khan

Genghis Khan united all the Mongol tribes of central Asia and created the largest land empire the world has ever seen.

His empire relied upon ferocious mounted warriors and a reign of terror, which left cities burnt to the ground and millions of people dead.

Each warrior had two bows, 100 arrows, a lance and a sword. Arrows came in several designs. Some were specially shaped to travel long distances, others to pierce metal armour. One type of arrow was fitted with a whistle to frighten enemy troops.

Genghis Khan's real name was **Temujin**. He was born in 1167, the son of a minor tribal chief. His father was poisoned by a neighbouring tribe, and Temujin became leader himself. He acted very bravely in battle and at a meeting of the Mongol tribes in 1206 he was given the title 'Genghis Khan', which means 'Great Ruler'.

Genghis Khan was also the ruler of the **Merkit**, **Tartar**, **Kirghiz** and **Naiman** tribes.

The Mongols were a very ruthless tribe. When they captured a city they would put women, young children and the craftsmen who made weapons to one side. Then they would kill everybody else. When the city of **Merv** was captured, about 700,000 people were killed.

The invasion of **China** began in 1211 when the Mongols broke through the Great Wall. In 1215, Peking was captured and northern China was conquered.

The Mongols fought on horseback. Their horses were small and strong. They were bred to withstand the cold and heat and were trained to keep calm in battle.

The **Mongol Empire** was the largest land empire ever known. By 1279 it stretched from Hungary to Korea and included most of Asia.

Russia

Arabia

China

Pacific Ocean

India

Arabian Sea

The Mongol Empire

Crusaders

The Crusades were wars between Christians and Muslims. There were seven Crusades between the years 1095 and 1300.

The name 'Crusader' comes from the Latin word for cross. The Christian warriors were called Crusaders because they wore a cross as their badge.

Assassins were sent into Crusader camps by the Muslims to murder important leaders.

Richard the Lionheart was a King of England who led the Third Crusade in 1190. At the battle of Arsouf, in 1191, Richard defeated a large Muslim army and in the following year, he defeated another Muslim army at Jaffa. He led the Christian attack himself and acted with great bravery. Richard forced the Muslims to agree to a truce that allowed Christians to visit Jerusalem.

Warrior monks fought in the Crusades. These were special monks who made promises to God to fight against the Muslims. The Templar Order was the most famous group of warrior monks. The order was founded in 1118 to protect pilgrims going to Jerusalem. Other orders included the Hospitallers, the Trufac and the Teutonic.

Saladin was the great Muslim leader of the 1100s. In 1175, he became Sultan (ruler) of Damascus and went on to unite the Muslims. He defeated the Crusaders in many important battles and stopped them taking over Jerusalem.

El Cid was the nickname given to Rodrigo di Vivar. He was a great Spanish warrior who fought against the Muslims. El Cid means 'The Champion'. In 1094 he defeated the Muslims and captured the city of Valencia. He ruled it until his death in battle in 1099.

The Kingdom of Outremer

The Crusaders set up their own kingdom in Palestine called **Outremer**. The name means 'Beyond the Sea', because Palestine is across the Mediterranean Sea from Rome, the Christians' headquarters.

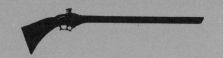

The Aztecs were a warlike people who lived in Mexico. By 1450, they had formed a large empire stretching from the Pacific Ocean to the Caribbean.

Aztec Empire

Inca Empire

The Incas came from Peru. Their empire covered an area four times as large as France. The Incas believed it was their holy duty to conquer other tribes and make them worship the Sun God.

The Aztecs and Incas used weapons made from wood with sharp polished pieces of a rock called **obsidian** set in them to make a cutting edge.

In 1423 Pachacuti, the Inca ruler, ordered work to start on the fortress of **Sacasahuaman**. The fortress had three massive towers and three walls made of stone. The walls were in a zigzag shape. The stones were specially shaped to fit into each other like pieces in a jigsaw.

Every Aztec man joined the **army** at the age of 17. If he had not performed a brave act by the age of 23, he had to leave the army to become a farmer or merchant. Very brave warriors were allowed to wear special animal skins.

Spanish troops, known as **Conquistadors** (meaning conquerors), attacked the Aztecs in 1519, and the Incas in 1532. The Conquistadors rode horses into battle and were armed with steel swords and guns. These modern weapons were too powerful for the Aztecs and Incas, and both their empires were conquered.

Prisoners captured by the Aztecs were taken to the temples in Tenochtitlán, the capital city. Priests killed the prisoners as a sacrifice to the gods. At least one person was killed each day. On special holy days, over a thousand people might be sacrificed at a time. Sometimes, wars were fought simply to capture prisoners.

Sitting Bull was the greatest leader of the Sioux people. He united the Sioux tribes.

With the help of the Blackfeet, Cheyenne and Arapahoe tribes, he led a war against the American settlers.

Warriors like the Sioux fought on horseback. They were armed with spears, bows and arrows, or guns bought from the white settlers.

The **first Indian War** began in 1608 when English settlers fought the Powhatan tribe in Virginia. The war ended in 1613 when the Indian princess Pocahontas married an Englishman.

Red Cloud was chief of one of the Sioux tribes. He fought against the American army to stop them from building forts and a road across land belonging to the Sioux and Cheyenne tribes. The war lasted for two years, from 1865 until 1867, when the government was forced to leave the tribes' land. Red Cloud made peace with the settlers, but continued to defend the rights of his people with many visits to the government in Washington.

When **gold** was found on Sioux land, the American government ordered Sitting Bull to move his people to a new reservation 380 km away. Sitting Bull refused to move and war broke out between the government and the Sioux.

In 1876, General Custer was sent with the 7th Cavalry to attack the Indian camp at **Little Big Horn**. Custer sent part of his troops to attack the Indian rear, and charged forwards with the remaining troops. He rode straight into a trap set by Sitting Bull and another chief, called Crazy Horse. Custer and all his men were killed.

Geronimo was the leader of the Apache, who lived in the deserts of the USA-Mexico border. In 1859, the Apache were attacked by Mexicans. After this the Apache fought a war against all whites. For many years Geronimo led his warriors in a brutal conflict until he surrendered in 1886.

Warriors of the Orient

The Orient is the name given to the lands to the east of the Mediterranean Sea, especially those in eastern Asia, such as China or Japan.

Many ruthless warriors have fought each other across this vast area of land.

Samurai warriors came from Japan. They were highly-trained fighters who were loyal to their local lord. All Samurai followed a strict set of rules, known as Bushido. These rules encouraged the Samurai to be brave, honest and live a simple life. If a Samurai broke the rules of Bushido or lost a battle, he had to kill himself. This was known as seppuku.

The **Great Wall of China** was built by the Emperor Shih Huang-ti around 220 BC. It was designed to protect China from invasions from the north. It is over 6,000 km long and wide enough to drive a chariot along the top. Today it is a major tourist attraction.

Early Chinese armies were made up of large numbers of peasants. They fought on foot as only the nobles could afford chariots or proper weapons. By 200 BC the Han Emperors had introduced cavalry. An example of what warriors looked like at this time can now be seen at Xian in China after the discovery of 6,000 life-size terracotta models of the Emperor Shih Huang-ti's army.

Timur the Lame, or Tamerlane as he was known in Europe, was the ruthless leader of the Tartar warriors from southern Asia. He was born in 1336 in Samarkand, which is in modern-day Tajikistan. By 1399, he had conquered or made treaties with all of central Asia, and invaded Russia and India. Timur was a cruel person who slaughtered thousands of people. He would build great pyramids of skulls from the people he killed before taking their treasure back to Samarkand.

An Lu-Shan was a Turkish warrior who became ruler of China. As a young man, he was a cavalry commander in the Chinese army. He won many victories against the enemies of China and was soon commander of the entire northern army. In 756, thinking the Emperor had ordered his death, An Lu-Shan attacked China. He overthrew the Emperor and became ruler of China. He was murdered one year later by a servant.

Freedom fighters are warriors who try to free their country from the rule of a foreign nation.

Most freedom fighters work in small groups rather than with a large army. Sometimes they win and their country is freed. Other freedom fighters fail but they become heroes and inspire others to follow their ideas.

Joan of Arc led the French in a war against the English. In 1429 England ruled most of France. Joan, a young farmer's daughter, persuaded the Dauphin (the French heir to the throne) to let her fight with a small army. Joan amazed the troops with her bravery and leadership. She was captured and executed by the English in 1431. Thousands of French people were inspired by Joan and within a few years France was free.

Simon Bolívar fought to free South Americans from the Spanish Empire. In 1810 Venezuela threw out the Spanish Governor. Bolívar took command of the rebel army and won many victories. In 1821 Spain accepted defeat. Bolívar then went on to lead rebels in Colombia, Peru, Ecuador and Bolivia.

Francois Toussaint L'Ouverture was a black slave who led the slaves of Haiti to freedom. In 1791 he led a slave revolt against the foreign rulers of the island and by 1797 he was ruler of Haiti. Toussant outlawed slavery and brought in many humane laws.

Giuseppe Garibaldi led a small group of followers to try and unite Italy. In 1860 Italy was made up of a large number of small kingdoms and much of the country was controlled by Austria. Garibaldi led just 1,000 men (called the 'Redshirts' due to the colour of their clothes) to Sicily. He began a revolution and swept northwards overthrowing many rulers. After only six months most of Italy joined together under the rule of the King of Piedmont.

Robert the Bruce led the Scots against the English. In 1296 Edward I of England was crowned King of Scotland. Robert the Bruce, a great grandson of an earlier Scottish king, claimed that he should be King. For years he was unsuccessful, until the Battle of Bannockburn in 1314, where the English army was smashed by Robert's Scottish troops. Scotland was a free nation again.

Mythical warriors appear in legends from many countries.

Although fantastic stories are told about these warriors, the legends are often based upon the lives of real people.

Horus was an Ancient Egyptian god. It is thought that the many stories told about his conflict with the god Seth refer to ancient tribal conflicts before the first pharaoh united Egypt in about 2800 BC.

Gilgamesh was a legendary hero of Ancient Persia in about 2000 BC. In the legend, Gilgamesh is a king who goes on a long journey to try to discover the meaning of life. It is thought that Gilgamesh was a famous warrior-king of Uruk in about 2500 BC.

The Ancient Greeks and Persians told stories of female warriors called **Amazons**. The Amazons were a race of war-like women who raided other countries to capture gold and men. In fact, the Amazon legend was probably based on a real-life tribe called Sarmatians, who lived near the Black Sea between 800 BC and 300 BC. Sarmatian women had equal rights with men and fought in battles. This seemed very strange to the Greeks and Persians of the time and led to the stories about the Amazons.

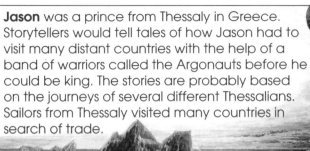

Jason was a prince from Thessaly in Greece. Storytellers would tell tales of how Jason had to visit many distant countries with the help of a band of warriors called the Argonauts before he could be king. The stories are probably based on the journeys of several different Thessalians. Sailors from Thessaly visited many countries in search of trade.

King Arthur is a legendary warrior of Britain. According to legend, Arthur was a great king who led a band of noble and gentle knights. The knights sat around a round table so that no one would appear to be more important than any of the others by sitting at the head of the table. In fact, Arthur was probably a Celtic warrior who fought against the Anglo-Saxons (who invaded Britain after the Romans left). He is thought to have been killed at the Battle of Camlann in about 515.

Sigurd was a great hero warrior of the Vikings. He was the last of the Volsung tribe and had many adventures, like fighting a dragon and finding treasure. Nobody has been able to discover who the character of Sigurd was based upon.

Before engines were invented nature was the only source of power available. Animals pulled carts, and the wind and running water moved windmills and water wheels. Water, wind and animal power are still important today.

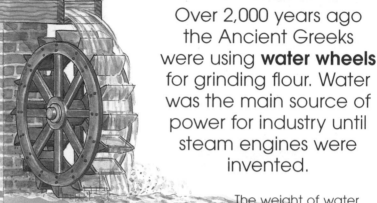

Over 2,000 years ago the Ancient Greeks were using **water wheels** for grinding flour. Water was the main source of power for industry until steam engines were invented.

The weight of water falling into the buckets turned the wheel.

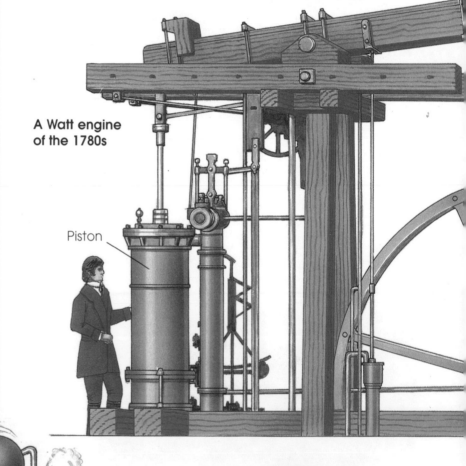

A Watt engine of the 1780s

Piston

However, engines are an important source of power. Cars, trucks, trains, aircraft and ships all have their own special engines to power them along.

The first **steam machine** was made before AD 100 by a Greek engineer, called Hero. It spun round as steam shot out of the pipes.

A **turbine** spins very fast when water flows through it. The turbine was invented in 1827. It soon replaced the water wheel.

Water in

Vanes

Water pours into the turbine through a narrow pipe. It pushes the vanes round.

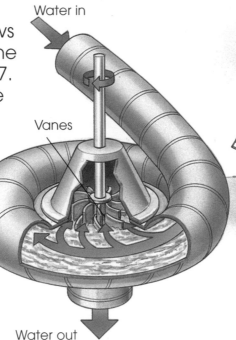

Water out

Windmills were first used around AD 650. They turned huge millstones which ground grain to make flour. They also pumped water and worked machinery.

In 1776 James Watt built a **steam engine** for pumping water out of coal and tin mines. Steam from boiling water moved a piston in and out. The moving piston worked the water pump.

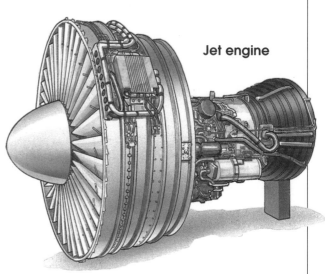

Jet engine

The sort of engine used in most modern cars is called an **internal combustion engine**. The first of these engines was built in 1860.

An internal combustion engine has cylinders and pistons like a steam engine. The first one used gas for fuel.

In 1939 the first aircraft with a **jet engine** took off. It was called the Heinkel He 178. Jet engines meant that aircraft could fly much faster than before.

The wheel was one of the most important inventions in history. Think how difficult it would be to get about without it. Cars, bicycles, trains and carts use wheels.

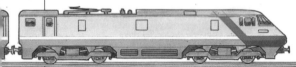

For thousands of years carriages and carts were pulled by horses. But as soon as engines were invented people began making powered vehicles.

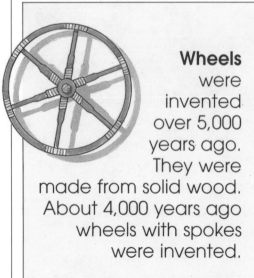

Wheels were invented over 5,000 years ago. They were made from solid wood. About 4,000 years ago wheels with spokes were invented.

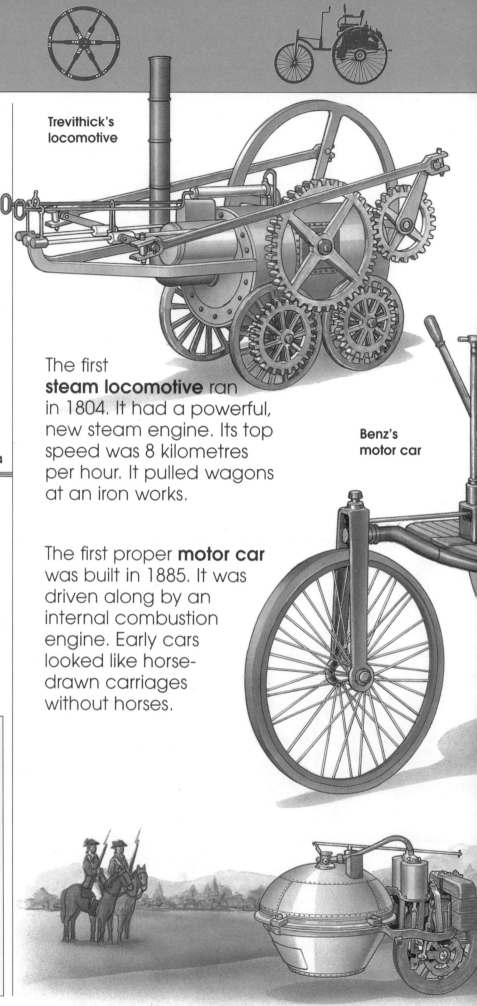

Trevithick's locomotive

The first **steam locomotive** ran in 1804. It had a powerful, new steam engine. Its top speed was 8 kilometres per hour. It pulled wagons at an iron works.

Benz's motor car

The first proper **motor car** was built in 1885. It was driven along by an internal combustion engine. Early cars looked like horse-drawn carriages without horses.

The first **electric locomotive** was demonstrated in 1879 in Berlin.

The pedal **bicycle** was invented in 1839 by a Scottish blacksmith, called Kirkpatrick Macmillan. He only built one machine, which he rode himself.

To make the bicycle go, the rider pushed the pedals backwards and forwards.

The first **motorcycle** was simply a bicycle fitted with a steam engine. It was built in 1868. The engine was under the saddle.

Steam engines powered tractors, trucks and buses. The first **steam vehicle** was designed to pull military cannons.

Cugnot built his steam tractor in 1769 or 1770. It was slow and quickly ran out of steam.

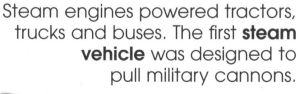

Ships and boats are very old inventions. Archaeologists think that people first made journeys in small boats 50,000 years ago. The boats were very simple canoes carved from tree trunks.

A triangular sail, called a **lateen sail,** was invented around 300 BC. Boats with lateen sails could sail where their crews wanted them to.

A type of boat called a dhow has a lateen sail.

In the 1400s **full rigging** was developed. Full-rigged ships had two or three masts with square and triangular sails.

In the 1400s and 1500s European explorers, such as Christopher Columbus, sailed small full-rigged ships across the oceans.

Ships and boats are not only used for transporting people, but for trade, too. Today, most of the goods traded between different countries are sent by ship.

Archaeologists don't really know when **sailing boats** were invented. However, the Ancient Egyptians sailed boats made of reeds along the River Nile over 5,000 years ago.

These reed boats had square sails.

Soon after small portable steam engines were invented engineers built **steam-powered boats**. The *Charlotte Dundas* was built in 1801.

For thousands of years sailors steered using large oars attached to the side of their ship. The **rudder** was invented in China around AD 700.

The engine turned large paddle wheels which pushed the boat through the water.

Most modern ships are pushed along by a **propeller**. It was patented in 1836 and soon replaced paddle wheels.

A hydrofoil has wings which lift it out of the water. This means it can go much faster than ordinary boats.

Forlanini hydrofoil

The idea for the **hydrofoil** was thought of in 1881. However, the first hydrofoil was not tested until 1905.

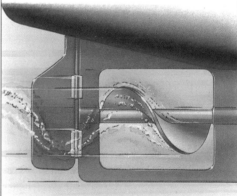

A **hovercraft** is half boat, half aeroplane. It skims across sea or land on a cushion of air. The first practical hovercraft was launched in 1959.

Flying machines

People dreamed of flying like birds for thousands of years before flying machines were made. Many people tried to copy the way birds flew. They tied wings to their arms, but with little success.

Today, there are many different types of aircraft. Every day, millions of people travel around the world in airliners and private aircraft. War planes include small fighters, bombers and huge transport planes.

The first aircraft with wings were **gliders**. Otto Lilienthal made many short glider flights in the 1890s.

The first machine to carry a person into the air was a **hot-air balloon**. It was built by the French Montgolfier brothers in 1783.

The balloon flew 8 kilometres on its first flight.

The first successful **airship** was built in 1852. In the early twentieth century, airships were popular for transport.

Airships were pushed along by propellers and steered by a rudder.

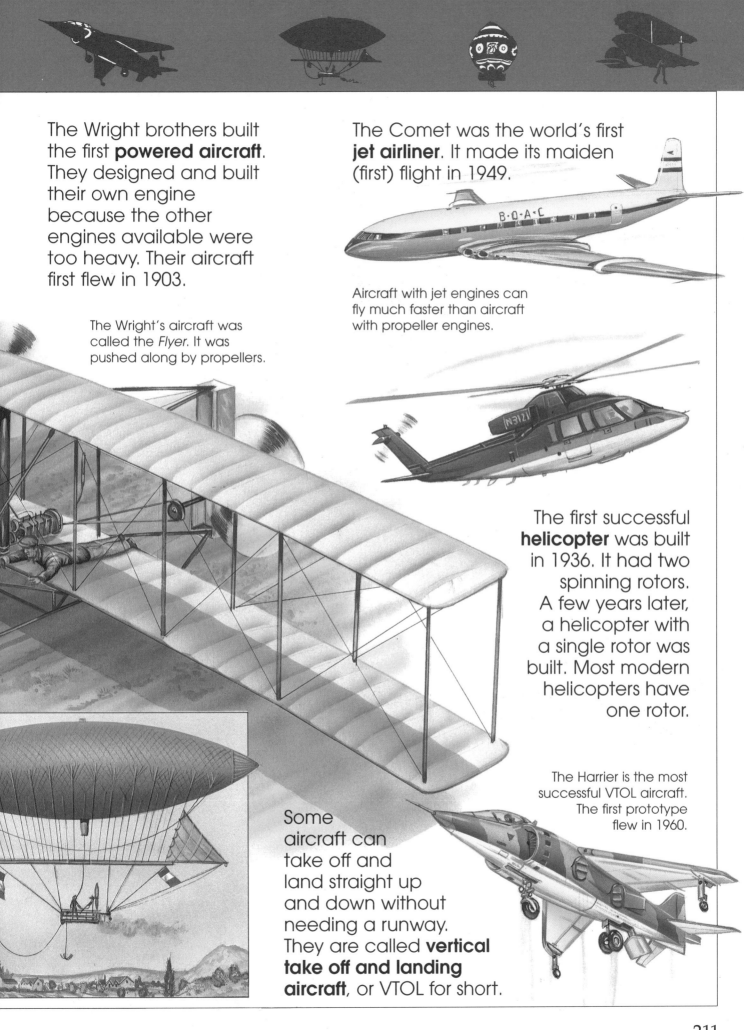

The Wright brothers built the first **powered aircraft**. They designed and built their own engine because the other engines available were too heavy. Their aircraft first flew in 1903.

The Wright's aircraft was called the *Flyer*. It was pushed along by propellers.

The Comet was the world's first **jet airliner**. It made its maiden (first) flight in 1949.

Aircraft with jet engines can fly much faster than aircraft with propeller engines.

The first successful **helicopter** was built in 1936. It had two spinning rotors. A few years later, a helicopter with a single rotor was built. Most modern helicopters have one rotor.

The Harrier is the most successful VTOL aircraft. The first prototype flew in 1960.

Some aircraft can take off and land straight up and down without needing a runway. They are called **vertical take off and landing aircraft**, or VTOL for short.

Five hundred years ago people could see only what was visible with their own eyes. Nobody knew how their bodies worked or what was out in space.

When the microscope and the telescope were invented, scientists and astronomers began to discover microscopic cells and millions of new stars.

In 1931, the first **electron microscope** was built. The picture of the object being studied appears on a screen.

An ordinary microscope can only make things look about 2,000 times bigger. An electron microscope can make things look millions of times bigger.

The first **microscope** was probably made in about 1590. In the 1650s, Robert Hooke used his microscopes to study plants. He drew sketches of what he saw.

Hooke's microscope was made from three lenses inside a cardboard tube.

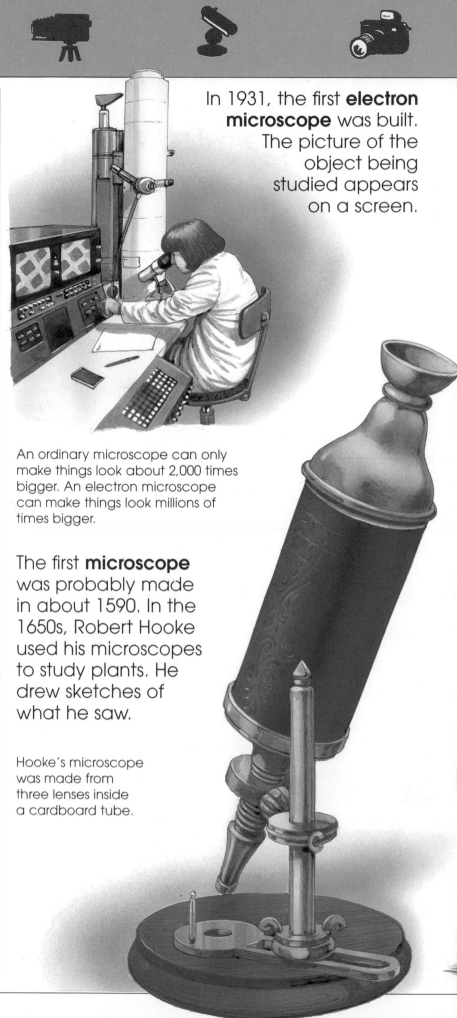

The first **telescope** was probably made in 1608. The next year Galileo Galilei built his own telescope and used it to study the stars.

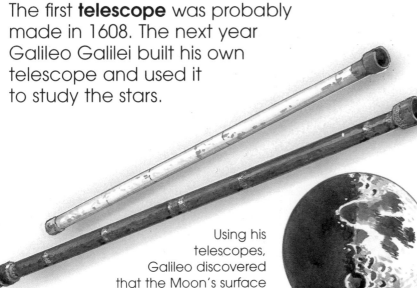

Using his telescopes, Galileo discovered that the Moon's surface is covered in craters.

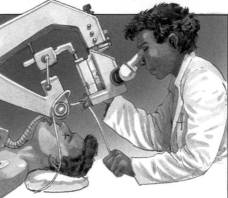

An **endoscope** is a long tube for seeing inside the human body. The first flexible one was built in 1956.

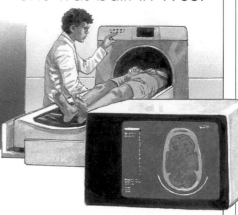

A **reflecting telescope** uses mirrors instead of lenses. It was first made in 1668. Most telescopes used by astronomers are reflecting telescopes.

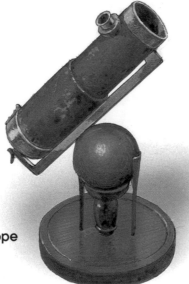

Isaac Newton's reflecting telescope

The first **medical scanner** was built in 1971 for looking inside the brain. Scanners for looking at the whole body soon followed.

Radio telescopes collect radio waves coming from outer space.

Radio waves from space were first detected in 1931.

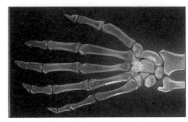

X-rays were discovered in 1895 by Wilhelm Röntgen. They were soon being used to take pictures of human bones.

Weaving a fabric

The first clothes worn by human beings were made from animal skins and fur. Later, people learned to make cloth from other natural materials, such as plants, and still later, from artificial fibres.

Most types of cloth are made on a loom. The loom weaves threads together. Modern looms work automatically. Some weaving is still done on traditional hand looms.

Some materials, such as cotton and wool, have to be spun before they are woven. Spinning makes short fibres into long thread.

People started to spin wool and cotton fibres into thread many thousands of years ago. The first **spinning machine** was like a long spinning top.

The **spinning wheel** was probably invented in India. People started using it in Europe about the year 1300.

A spinning wheel spins and collects thread at the same time.

Around 1767 James Hargreaves invented a machine that he called the **spinning jenny**. It spun thread automatically and made spinning much quicker.

The **loom** appeared around 5000 BC. The first looms were very simple.

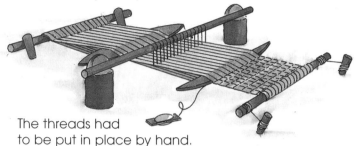

The threads had to be put in place by hand.

Weaving by hand was very slow. The **flying shuttle** was invented in 1733. It carried the thread from side to side automatically. Before this, it was passed through by hand.

The **Jacquard loom** was invented in 1801. It could weave complicated patterns into the cloth.

The loom was controlled by rows of holes in a long strip of card. Early computers used the same idea.

Rayon fibres, as seen under a powerful microscope.

The first **artificial fibre** was patented in 1892. It was an artificial silk, called rayon.

Thousands of years ago, people did not need to tell the time. They got up when the Sun rose and went to bed when it set. Gradually, as life became more complicated, clocks began to play a larger part in people's lives.

The first clocks were used for waking priests and monks in time for their nightly prayers. Today, clocks seem to rule our lives.

The first clocks were **shadow clocks**. The shadow moved as the Sun moved across the sky. They were invented around 3,500 years ago.

Mechanical clocks were probably developed in Europe during the 1200s. They did not have a face or hands, but rang bells.

The speed of the clock was controlled by a mechanism called an escapement, but it was not very accurate.

In a **water clock**, water drips out of a container so that the level of water inside gradually falls. The Ancient Egyptians were using water clocks about 1500 BC.

The **pendulum clock** was invented in 1657. It was much more accurate than the clocks before it.

Each swing of the pendulum takes the same amount of time. This keeps the clock running at the same speed all the time.

To know exactly where they were, sailors needed instruments for navigating. These included an accurate clock, called a **marine chronometer**. The first successful one was made in 1762.

JOHN HARRISON

It took 40 years for John Harrison to design his marine chronometer.

Inside a **quartz watch** there is a tiny crystal of quartz which controls the speed of the watch. The quartz clock was invented in 1929.

Atomic clocks are the most accurate clocks in the world. The first atomic clock was built in 1948.

An atomic clock will only gain or lose one second every million years.

For thousands of years, people did not write anything down. Instead, they passed on information and stories by word of mouth. Shapes and pictures were the first sort of writing.

The books that we know today were not made until printing was invented. Until then, every book was copied by hand by people called scribes. Long books took months to copy.

The Ancient Egyptians used **picture writing**. Each small picture stood for a word or sound. These pictures, or symbols, are called hieroglyphics.

The first simple **pens** were brushes, or hollow reeds, dipped in ink. The Ancient Greeks used a metal, or bone, stylus to write on soft wax tablets. Later, people used quill pens made from goose feathers.

The end of a goose feather was sharpened and then cut to make a nib shape. To write with a quill, you have to keep dipping the nib in ink.

The first **ballpoint pens** were made in 1938 by Lazlo Biro. When a cheap ballpoint pen runs out, you throw it away. For other pens, you can buy an ink refill with a new ball.

Inside the tip of a ballpoint pen is a tiny steel ball. It rolls around as you write, spreading ink on to the paper.

The first **printed book** that still exists was made in China in AD 868. It is a long roll of paper, and is called the *Diamond Sutra*.

The *Diamond Sutra* was printed by pressing carved, wooden blocks covered with ink on to the paper.

Around 1450, Johannes Gutenberg built the first **printing press**. It could print about 16 pages of a book every hour.

In 1939, **phototypesetting** was invented. It has now replaced metal type. The words are now typed on to a computer and printed out on photographic paper.

Gutenburg made up words by putting metal letters, called type, together.

Newspapers were first printed in Europe at the beginning of the 1600s. Before then, newspapers were only printed when there was a lot of news.

Listening to recorded music is something most people do every day. However, when sound recording was first invented it was a novelty, and nobody took it seriously.

Every so often, a new way of recording sound is invented. Recordings of speech and sounds are also important historical records.

The first machine to record sound and play it back was the **phonograph**. It was invented in 1877 by the American inventor Thomas Edison.

Speaking into the phonograph made a needle move up and down. As the drum went round, the needle made a groove in the tin foil.

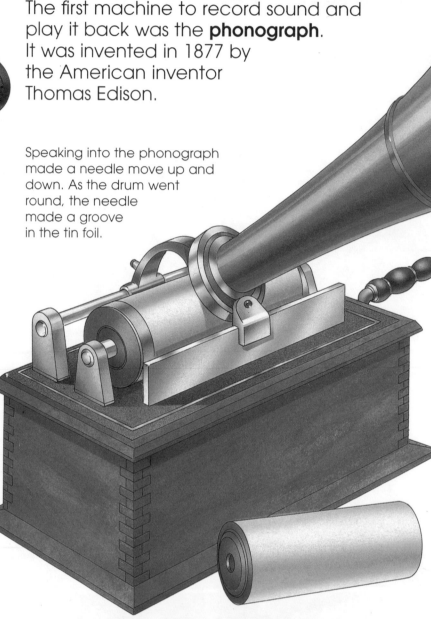

A **tape recorder** records sound as a magnetic pattern on a long strand of tape. The first tape recorder used iron wire. Plastic tape coated with magnetic material appeared in 1935.

Cassette tapes appeared on the market in the 1960s. Smaller tapes meant that smaller tape recorders were made.

The **gramophone** was invented in 1888. It played sounds recorded on metal discs. The discs worked like today's records.

Personal stereos were first sold in the late 1970s.

Compact discs were first made in the 1980s by the electronic companies Philips and Sony. The sound is recorded on the disc as a pattern of tiny pits in the disc's surface.

A compact disc player uses a laser beam to look at the disc and play the sound.

Until about 200 years ago the only way to send a message was by messenger or by post. Sometimes, hill-top bonfires were used to send emergency signals.

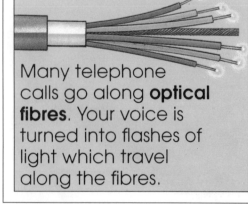

Today, you can talk on the telephone to friends and relations in almost any part of the world. It takes just a few seconds to dial. Your call might even travel via a satellite in space on the way.

Many telephone calls go along **optical fibres**. Your voice is turned into flashes of light which travel along the fibres.

The **semaphore** system was the first way of communicating over long distances. Semaphore stations were positioned on hill-tops, and the message was passed from one station to the next. The system was first used in France in 1794.

The message was shown by moving the arms on top of the semaphore station to different positions.

Messages were tapped with the key as dots and dashes.

The first simple electric **telegraph** was built in 1804. In 1837, Samuel Morse invented **Morse code**. It was used to send messages by telegraph.

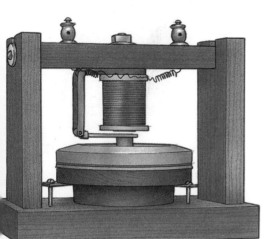

In 1876, Alexander Graham Bell patented the **telephone**. It converted sound into electrical signals. The signals were sent down a wire to another phone and turned back into sound.

Radio was first used in the 1890s. Sailors used it to send signals to the shore by Morse code. The first radio programme was broadcast in 1906.

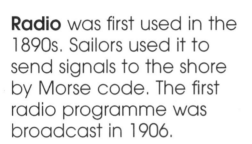

An automatic telephone exchange was in operation in 1897. **Electronic telephone exchanges** were built In the 1960s.

The first **telephone exchange** was built in 1878. Only a few people could use it, and it needed a person to operate it.

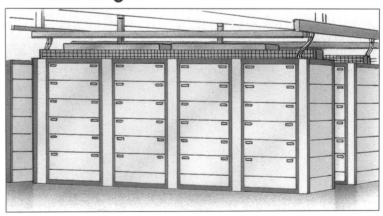

Facsimile machines (fax machines for short) send words and pictures along telephone lines. The idea for fax was first thought of in 1843, but it took until the 1980s for faxes to become common.

Until the 1820s there were no photographs or films. To make pictures of anything, people had to draw or paint them. Taking photographs is a much easier process.

When moving pictures first appeared nobody took them seriously. The machines that made the pictures move were thought of as toys.

Television is part of our everyday lives. We can watch soap operas, films, the news and sport. Thanks to satellites, we can even watch events happening live around the world.

The first **camera** of the type we use today was made by the Eastman company in 1888. It had film that you could send away for processing.

The **kinetoscope** was invented in 1891 by Thomas Edison. You had to look through the top and wind a handle. The film inside lasted only about 15 seconds.

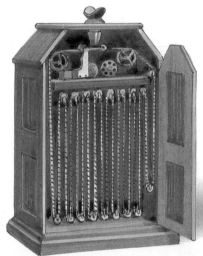

Inside the kinetoscope was a long strip of film with hundreds of pictures on it. Each picture was slightly different from the one before to make an action sequence.

The first **cinema** opened in Paris in 1895. The film was projected on to a screen. The projector worked like the kinetoscope.

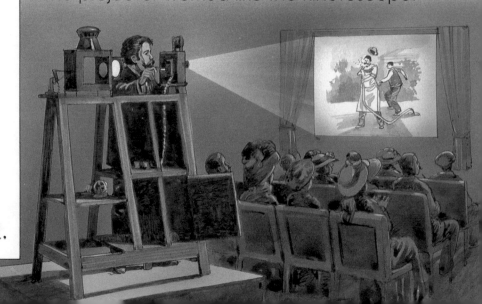

The first time **television** pictures were transmitted by electricity was in 1926. The pictures weren't very good - they were in black and white, wobbly and blurred.

The pattern of light and dark on the picture was made by a spinning disc with holes in it.

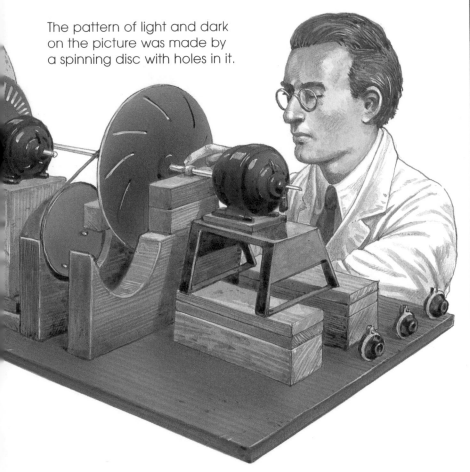

Satellite television receivers that could be installed in homes became popular in the 1980s. The pictures are beamed down from satellites orbiting in space.

In 1928, the first television programme was broadcast In America. It was used to test a new **television transmitter**. The pictures were of Felix the Cat™

Colour television pictures were first broadcast in 1953.

Video tape and **video recorders** were invented in 1956. Pictures are recorded on videotape just as sounds are recorded on audio tape.

225

Electronic circuits are often used to control and work machines. Computers, televisions and telephones all use electronics. So do some simpler machines, such as washing machines and alarm clocks.

Electronic circuits are made up of electronic components. There are many different sorts of components. One of the most important is the transistor. Its invention meant that electronic circuits could be made much smaller than before.

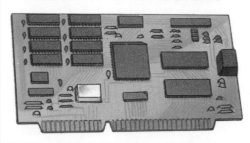

In the 1830s, years before electronics were possible, British scientist Charles Babbage designed a mechanical computer. He called it an **analytical engine**. It was never finished.

The first electronic device was called the **thermionic valve**. It was first made in 1904.

Thermionic valves were used in early radios and televisions.

The first general-purpose electronic **computer** was called ENIAC, which stands for Electronic Numerical Integrator and Calculator. It was built in 1946.

ENIAC used over 18,000 valves and filled a whole room.

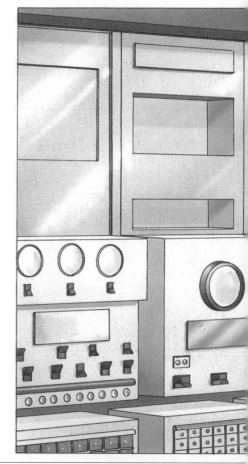

The **transistor** was invented in 1948 by a team of scientists in America. Transistors took over from valves, but were much smaller and cheaper.

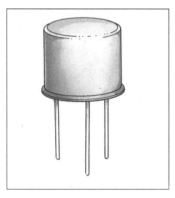

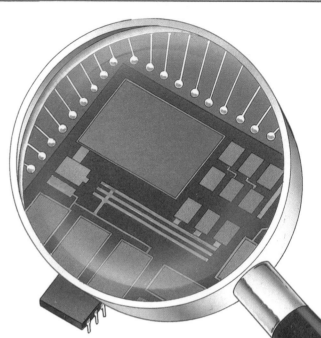

A **silicon chip**, or microchip, as small as a fingernail can contain many thousands of transistors and other electronic components. The first silicon chip was made in 1959.

A silicon chip in a plastic casing

Engineers began to fit more and more components on to a silicon chip. Eventually engineers at Intel built a complete computer on a single chip. This is called a **microprocessor**.

Every personal computer has a microprocessor 'brain'.

227

Until the eighteenth century people did all their household chores by hand. There were no washing machines or vacuum cleaners. No one had running water or a flushing toilet either.

The first domestic appliances were mechanical. It was still hard work to operate them. Things really changed when electric motors became cheap to make. Imagine what life today would be like without electricity!

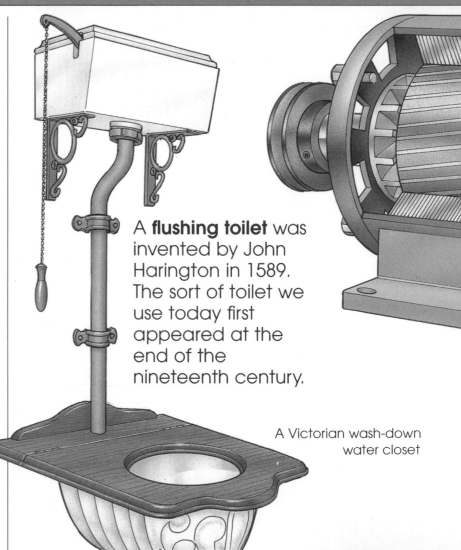

A **flushing toilet** was invented by John Harington in 1589. The sort of toilet we use today first appeared at the end of the nineteenth century.

A Victorian wash-down water closet

Englishman Joseph Swan made a long-lasting **light bulb** in 1878. The next year, Thomas Edison made a similar bulb.

In Edison's light bulb, the electricity flowed through a piece of carbonised bamboo, making it glow.

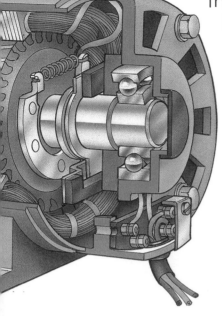

The first **electric motor** was made in 1835. Its power came from a battery because there was no mains electricity at the time.

Operating Booth's Patents

BRITISH VACUUM CLEANER Nº 11512

Before refrigerators, food was kept fresh in a cool place or boxes lined with ice. The ice had to be replaced as it melted.

The **vacuum cleaner** was patented by Englishman Hubert Booth in 1901. Booth's first machine had to be hired, together with people to operate it.

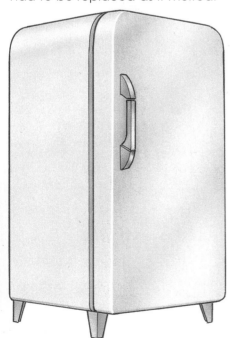

Microwave ovens appeared in the 1950s. They were used by catering companies.

Refrigerating machines were developed at the end of the nineteenth century. It was not until the 1950s, however, that domestic refrigerators became popular.

Microwave ovens cook most foods many times faster than electric or gas ovens.

For every invention that has been a success, there are many more that have been failures. The great age of crazy inventions was the nineteenth century when inventing things became many people's favourite hobby.

Some inventions have no chance of success because their inventor has not understood the scientific principles behind them. Others are simply flights of fancy, designed for fun.

In the fifteenth century, the artist **Leonardo da Vinci** made drawings of many machines, including tanks and flying machines, long before they were actually invented.

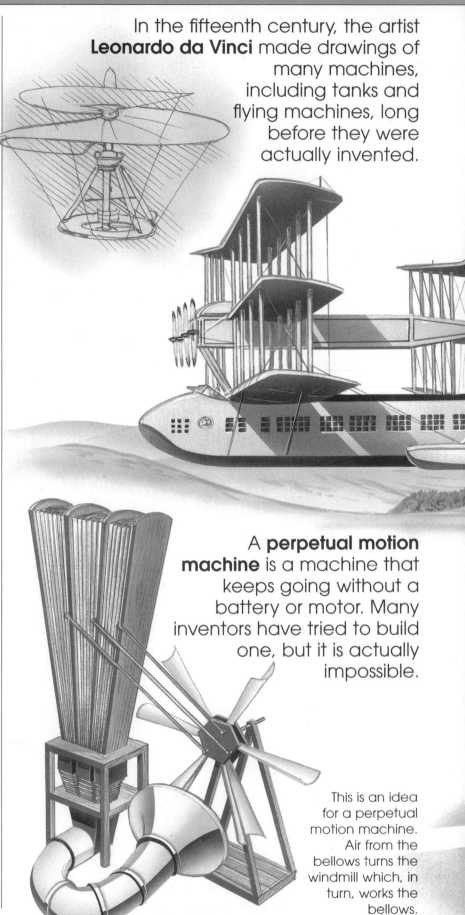

A **perpetual motion machine** is a machine that keeps going without a battery or motor. Many inventors have tried to build one, but it is actually impossible.

This is an idea for a perpetual motion machine. Air from the bellows turns the windmill which, in turn, works the bellows.

The Italian Count Caproni built several huge aeroplanes. The largest was the **Ca 60**, which had nine wings and eight engines.

The Ca 60 crashed just after take-off on its first flight in 1921.

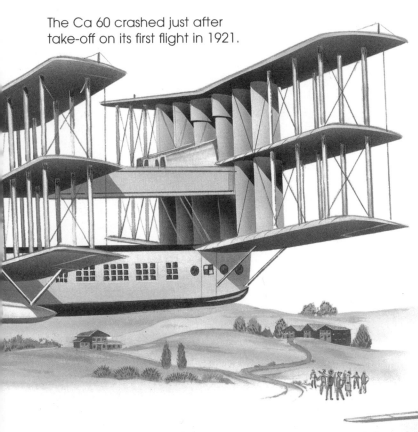

William Heath Robinson was a cartoonist who drew very complicated machines that were completely useless.

The airstrip was never built because it was too expensive.

The **Sinclair C5** was a tiny electric car. It was designed in the 1980s for cheap travel around town. However, most people thought it was too dangerous to drive.

Sir Clive Sinclair

In 1942, English inventor Geoffrey Pyke designed an **iceberg airstrip** on which aircraft could refuel in the Atlantic Ocean.

The existence of ghosts has never been proved scientifically. However, throughout history many people have reported sightings of ghosts.

Ghosts are believed to be the spirits of people who have died, but sometimes they seem to resemble living people. There are animal ghosts and even ghostly ships, cars, planes and trains.

It is said that there have been many appearances of **royal ghosts.** King Henry VIII's beheaded wife, Anne Boleyn, is said to haunt the Tower of London, England. Two of his other wives roam the corridors at Hampton Court Palace.

In 1962, English brothers, Derek and Norman Ferguson claimed to have seen lots of **ghostly animals** whilst driving their car along a motorway in Scotland.

A **bizarre bat** with a human head is a ghostly legend of Native Americans.

Haunted computers have been reported in many parts of the world.

Glamis Castle, the birthplace of Princess Margaret, is believed to be the most haunted royal building in Scotland. This 14th-century castle is said to be the home of a monster, a vampire and a whole host of ghosts.

Some people believe that ghosts like to haunt houses as well as ancient castles. In 1966, a British family had to be rehoused by their local council because they thought their house had been haunted for two years.

FOR SALE

Ghosts around the world

There have been hundreds of ghostly sightings. Such stories have been reported from many countries around the globe.

Often these stories reflect the legends and traditions of the country in which the hauntings occur.

Over 150 years ago, a **Danish** man was wrongfully hanged for stealing. It is claimed that a shadowy outline of a body, hanging from a gallows, still appears today, just before the death of a family member.

One of the best known English ghosts is that of **Dick Turpin** who was famous for robbing travellers. He was a hero of the poor people because he stole from the wealthy. Turpin was hanged in 1739. It is widely believed that his ghost still appears on Hounslow Heath – now known as **Heathrow Airport**!

Abraham Lincoln was one of the most influential presidents of the United States of America. He was assassinated in April 1865. It is said that every year during the month of April, the President's funeral train appears. It can be seen travelling along a stretch of track in New York State.

It is said that whenever the President's ghostly train appears, a complete military band can be heard blasting away.

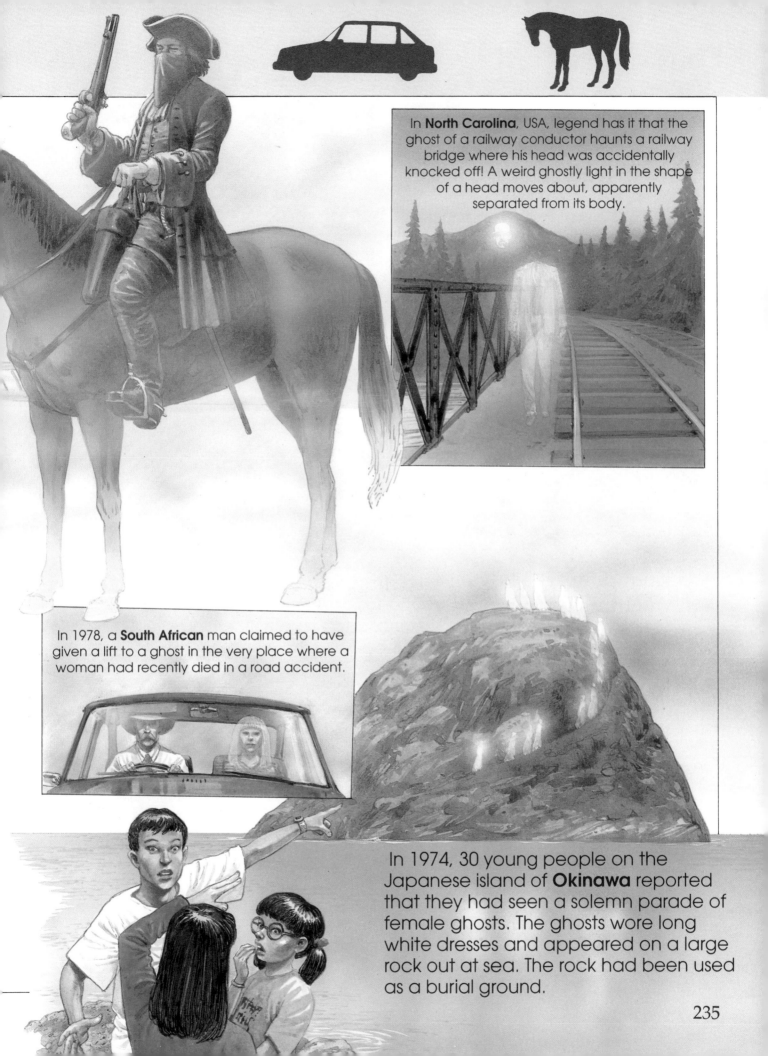

In **North Carolina**, USA, legend has it that the ghost of a railway conductor haunts a railway bridge where his head was accidentally knocked off! A weird ghostly light in the shape of a head moves about, apparently separated from its body.

In 1978, a **South African** man claimed to have given a lift to a ghost in the very place where a woman had recently died in a road accident.

In 1974, 30 young people on the Japanese island of **Okinawa** reported that they had seen a solemn parade of female ghosts. The ghosts wore long white dresses and appeared on a large rock out at sea. The rock had been used as a burial ground.

Poltergeists

A poltergeist is described as an invisible and noisy ghost. It is said that when a poltergeist is present people hear scratching, banging and mysterious voices. Sometimes fires start and strange smells fill the air.

Often poltergeists throw things around, smash ornaments and move heavy furniture. They are said to be invisible vandals!

In 1661, a magistrate confiscated a drum from a local beggar in **Tedworth**, England. Legend has it that a phantom drum could be heard frequently and lighted candles floated up the chimney. The magistrate's horse was even found with its hind leg stuck in its mouth!

A family in **Barbados** buried deceased relatives in a big tomb. Each time the tomb was opened the coffins were found scattered around.

In 1960, an 11 year old Scottish girl, **Virginia Campbell**, claimed she was being aggravated by a poltergeist for two months. It followed her wherever she went. One night her bed started shaking as if there was an earthquake. The haunting stopped once her parents held prayer meetings in their house.

Objects were said to fly around when a poltergeist made its home on a farm in **Lancashire**, England. A cow was even lifted to a hay loft. How it got there nobody knows – it certainly could not have climbed up the rickety ladder.

In 1951, a family reported strange happenings in their **London** home. A policeman found furniture being thrown across a room. Strangely, the violent activity stopped instantly once a light was turned on.

During 1967, a poltergeist started creating a disruption around 11 year old **Matthew Manning** from Cambridge, England. Furniture began to move all over the family home and strange scratching noises could be heard. The haunting ended when Matthew began to create strange and beautiful drawings.

Funny ghosts

It is said that ghosts like playing tricks. But ghosts and people seem to have a very different sense of humour. Often people do not find what ghosts do very funny. Ghosts are more likely to terrify people than make them laugh.

Over 25 years ago, a derelict hotel in Wales was being demolished. Even though the electricity to the building had been cut off, the **electric lift** kept on working.

Over 60 years ago, on the Isle of Man in the Irish Sea, a ghostly **mongoose** was said to haunt an old farmhouse by the sea. It told jokes, sang songs and even swore. It told everyone its name was Gef. When the farmhouse was sold the new owner shot an unusual little furry animal. Gef has never been seen since.

Twelve year old English boy, **Michael Collingridge**, was recovering from tonsillitis when a walking stick in his bedroom appeared to dance. It jumped all around the room and began to tap out well-known tunes!

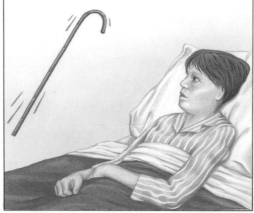

When the Pritchard family from **Pontefract** in Wales was plagued by a ghost, a woman from a Christian charity tried to drive the ghost away by singing *Onward Christian Soldiers*. The ghost responded by picking up her gloves and conducting her as she sang!

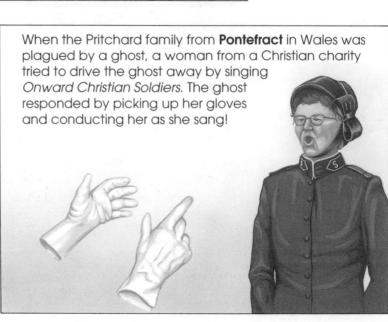

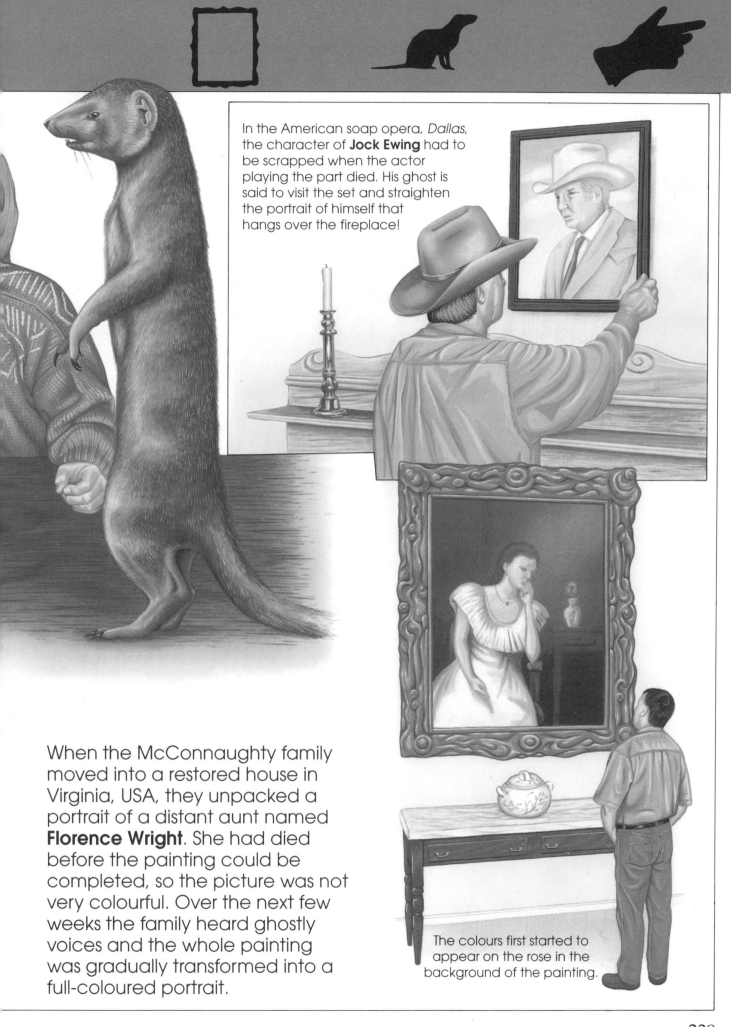

In the American soap opera, *Dallas*, the character of **Jock Ewing** had to be scrapped when the actor playing the part died. His ghost is said to visit the set and straighten the portrait of himself that hangs over the fireplace!

When the McConnaughty family moved into a restored house in Virginia, USA, they unpacked a portrait of a distant aunt named **Florence Wright**. She had died before the painting could be completed, so the picture was not very colourful. Over the next few weeks the family heard ghostly voices and the whole painting was gradually transformed into a full-coloured portrait.

The colours first started to appear on the rose in the background of the painting.

Haunted houses

It is said that haunted houses creak and ghosts glide through the walls.

It is believed that ghosts haunt places where they once lived, but no one knows if hauntings really happen!

Legend has it that **Ballechin House** in Scotland is haunted by invisible dogs who hit guests with their tails. It is also said to be home to ghostly nuns and a disembodied hand!

Raynham Hall in Norfolk, England, is thought to be haunted by the ghost of Dorothy Walpole who died there. In 1936, a photograph of a ghostly woman in a veil was snapped by a professional photographer visiting the hall.

After studying the picture, some experts believe that it is genuine.

The most haunted house in Britain was said to be **Borley Rectory**. Even though it burnt down in 1939, poltergeists are said to haunt the ruins. Two headless ghosts and a phantom nun are also believed to have appeared.

The home of the British Prime Minister, **Number 10 Downing Street**, London, is said to be haunted by a politician from regency times.

Between 1883 and 1934, number **16 Montpelier Road** in London was the scene of 20 suicides and one murder. The victims had fallen from the top of the tower. In 1944, an investigator visited the house and was almost thrown from the tower himself. A photograph taken shows a ghost in Victorian clothing in an upstairs window!

People have invented all kinds of weird ways to ward off ghosts. Good luck charms and complicated rituals are used to scare ghosts away.

Inuits never remove someone who has died in an **igloo** through the front door. It is thought the spirit of the dead person would return if it knew where the front door was!

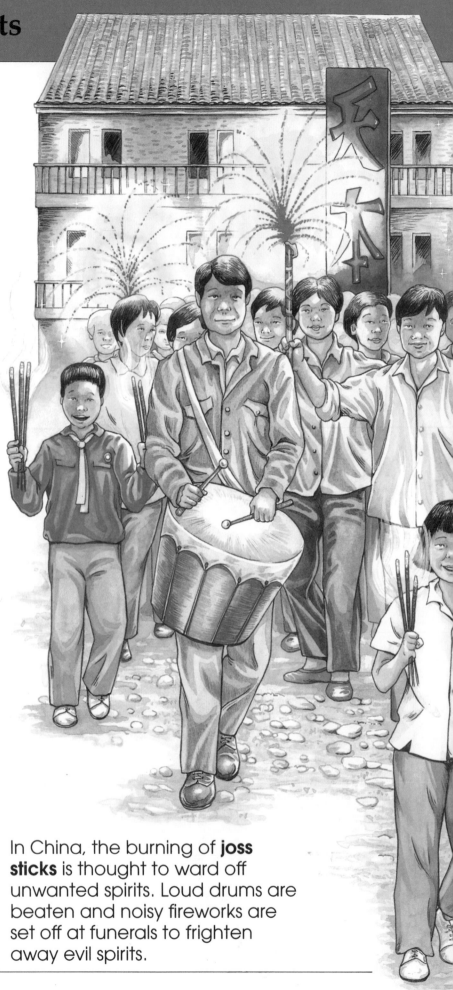

In China, the burning of **joss sticks** is thought to ward off unwanted spirits. Loud drums are beaten and noisy fireworks are set off at funerals to frighten away evil spirits.

Some people wear **amulets** and **talismans** (good luck charms) around their necks to scare off evil spirits and bring good fortune.

Some Asian communities will demolish the house someone has died in and then build a new home. It is believed that this gives the dead a resting place before finding **eternal peace**.

Many societies believe everyone has a **guardian spirit**. Mohammedans believe that we have four – two for the day and two for the night!

In many parts of the world it is still the custom to cover all the **mirrors** in a house until after a funeral. This protects against a spirit stealing the reflection of a living person and taking them off to the spirit world.

Mysteries in the sky

Thousands of people have reported strange sights in the sky, from frogs to unidentified flying objects (UFOs).

There have even been stories of close encounters with aliens. As a result, many people are convinced that there is life beyond planet Earth.

The first reported sighting of a **UFO** was during the 1200s, long before the invention of the aeroplane!

In 1975, a farmer in Switzerland sighted a **flying saucer**. Over the years he said he was visited by its three passengers called Somjasc, Ptaah and Asket. They told him that they were from the planet Erra, about 400 light years away.

In 1985, writer Whitley Strieber claimed that he had been abducted by **aliens** who gave him a thorough scientific examination. So disturbed was he by the experience that he sought the help of a hypnotist. Hypnosis revealed that he believed that aliens had been visiting him since childhood!

Numerous sightings of aliens have been reported in the **Broadhaven Triangle** in Wales. A luminous ball chased one car for miles. The occupants reached home to find a burnt-out television in their living room and a glowing figure in a silver suit in their garden.

In 1954, shoppers in Birmingham, England, were rained on by hundreds of tiny **frogs**! Many similar instances have been reported. Sometimes these are believed to be caused by supernatural forces.

In 1948, a **spacecraft** was reported to have crash-landed in New Mexico, USA. Eye-witnesses claimed that fourteen aliens were discovered on board the spacecraft. It has been said that the aliens were one metre tall and looked like humans with green, webbed feet.

Throughout history there have been reports of people vanishing without trace. Ships and aeroplanes seem to have disappeared into thin air! Some of these cases are still shrouded in mystery.

Sometimes stories have been made up to explain disappearances. When famous band leader, **Glenn Miller**, vanished in 1944, some people believed that his face had been so disfigured in a plane crash that he had decided to hide away for the rest of his life.

The crew's meal was found half-eaten on the table.

In 1872, the entire crew of the merchant ship, the **Marie Celeste**, vanished. The ship was completely undamaged but no one on board was ever seen again.

Often disappearances are hoaxes. In 1880, the story of a farmer who had apparently vanished hit the headlines in **Tennessee**, USA. It turned out that a hardware salesman, who had been snowed into his house, had invented the whole story out of boredom!

In 1937, **Amelia Earhart**, a record-breaking pilot, disappeared en route to an island in the Pacific Ocean. No one has ever been able to explain this mysterious disappearance.

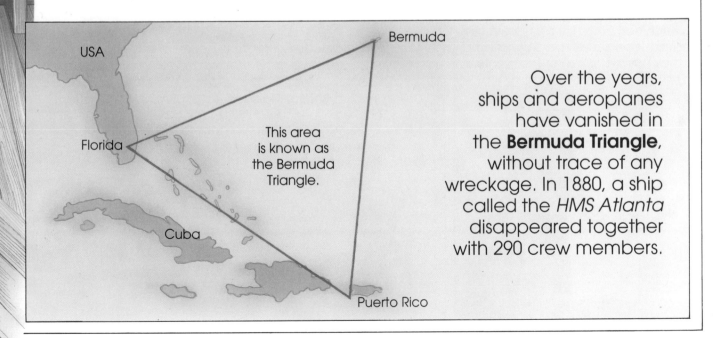

USA

Bermuda

Florida

This area is known as the Bermuda Triangle.

Cuba

Puerto Rico

Over the years, ships and aeroplanes have vanished in the **Bermuda Triangle**, without trace of any wreckage. In 1880, a ship called the *HMS Atlanta* disappeared together with 290 crew members.

Witchcraft

Witchcraft comes from two old English words, *wita* and *craeft* which means craft of the wise. Some witches are thought to have special knowledge of the plants and herbs used to cure sickness.

In the past witches were thought to use their powers in an evil way.

In the past, anybody accused of **witchcraft** could be brought to trial. They were sometimes tortured until they had no option but to 'confess'.

Witchcraft was outlawed in the United Kingdom until 1951, when the old law was overturned. Today, it is quite legal to be a witch and join a **coven** or group of witches.

During 1692, in **Salem**, Massachusetts, USA, a group of children accused 200 residents of being witches. The 'witches' were brought to trial and 20 were executed. It was later agreed that it had all been a terrible mistake.

At the time of the **winter solstice,** in December, witches perform 'The Dance of the Wheel', a special ceremony to coax back the sun. They dance and leap around a boiling cauldron to represent the spring.

Traditional doctors in Africa used to be referred to as **witch doctors.** These doctors are expert herbalists and they sometimes call upon spirit powers to help cure their patients.

During the 1300s, the **Christian Church** formed a group called the **Inquisition** to find people who disagreed with the church, including witches. They falsely believed that 'witches' made pacts with the devil, flew on broomsticks and even ate babies!

Many people believe that fortune tellers can look into the future. Some of them look at cards or tea-leaves. Others look to the stars to see what lies ahead.

Rune stones are a set of 25 small tablets or stones which are believed to have special meaning. A rune reader can recognise what the stones represent according to the way they are laid out.

Most fortune telling methods originated in China. **I Ching** is an ancient Chinese book of knowledge which is believed to have the answer to everything!

No two hands are the same. **Palmists** read people's hands to predict how long they will live and even how many children they will have.

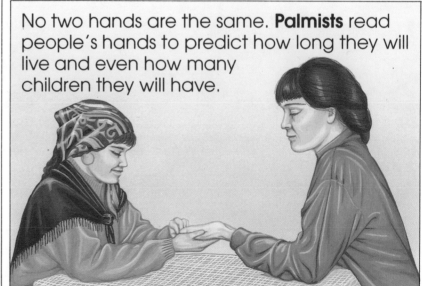

Astrology places people into twelve different groups which correspond with their birth dates. Maps of the stars and planets are consulted to forecast what the future holds.

Phrenology is the art of telling a fortune by feeling the bumps on a person's head.

Some people read their **horoscope** to predict what will happen during a day, week or month.

The Chinese invented **dominoes** as a method of predicting the future. The dominoes are put in a pouch, shaken and removed. Fortunes are read according to the position in which the dominoes are laid out.

Second sight

Some people claim to have second sight. They believe that they see or sense things which are invisible to other people. Sometimes they even say that they can tell when a terrible event is about to happen.

In 1898, **Morgan Robertson**, wrote *Futility*. It told the story of a massive luxury liner, called the *Titan*, which hit an iceberg and sank. The *Titanic* did exactly that 14 years later and hundreds of the passengers were drowned.

In 1925, a famous palmist predicted that **Edward, Prince of Wales** would be forced to abdicate soon after he became King. Amazingly, 11 years later this premonition became fact!

In May 1979, an American called **David Booth** dreamt of a terrible air crash. He informed the airline but they took no notice of him. The next day an aeroplane crashed at Chicago airport killing 273 people.

Jeane Dixon, an American who claimed to have powers of second sight, warned that the President would be assassinated. Eventually, on 23 November 1963, she told friends that the day had come.
John F. Kennedy was shot dead that afternoon.

The police have often been helped by people with second sight. **Gerald Croiset** spent his life helping Danish police to find murderers and to locate missing people and buried bodies.

253

It is said that some people are gifted with bizarre powers. They claim to be able to make things rise above the ground and to make objects change shape.

Astral projection is when a person feels that their spirit is rising out of their actual body. Such people claim that while sleeping they can sit on the end of their bed and watch themselves.

Many people believe that **dowsers** can sense where gold and oil are hidden in the ground. They use instruments, such as bent metal rods or forked twigs, which tremble or rotate when they have found the hidden treasure.

Levitation is said to defy the law of gravity by making bodies or objects rise and float in the air. Some eastern holy men are supposed to be able to levitate themselves at will.

Experts are unable to explain the strange pictures created by psychic photography.

It is claimed that **psychic photography** is the ability to take photographs of thoughts. Ted Serios from Chicago believed that when he took a photograph of his face an image in his thoughts would appear on the film!

Psychokinesis is the ability to affect objects by mental means alone. **Uri Geller** from Israel, for example, is famous for bending keys. He has even claimed to be able to stop a cable car in mid-air. Many magicians believe he is a fraud.

For hundreds of years sightings of strange creatures, mysterious monsters and bizarre landmarks have been reported all over the world. Even today experts are unable to find scientific explanations for many of these mysteries.

Bigfoot-Sasquatches are described as tall, hairy monsters that live in Washington State, USA. A Bigfoot sighting is reported regularly so there must be lots of these monsters!

Yeti, or the **Abominable Snowman** is thought to be a tall, white, furry monster. The first sighting was reported in Tibet in 1921 and there have been numerous reports of appearances ever since.

Enormous, elaborate shapes known as **crop circles** have appeared in the crop fields of Hampshire and Wiltshire, England. No one is sure how they are formed or where they came from although many explanations have been suggested.

It is said that the **pyramids** in Egypt are surrounded by strange powers. Plants apparently grow faster and it is even claimed that people are filled with amazing energy around the pyramids!

Nowadays modern technology, from radar to the latest computers, is used to investigate sightings of unknown creatures.

The **Loch Ness Monster** is believed to be a gigantic prehistoric reptile which still survives in Loch Ness, Scotland. Sightings of it have been reported as long ago as 565 BC. Although there are numerous photographs, the existence of this 'monster' has never really been proved.

More spooky cases

Tradition has it that when a dramatic event has occurred, ghostly phantoms will return to haunt the place where the disturbing incident happened.

Here are two especially chilling phantom stories.

During the 1600s, the owner of **Bettiscombe Manor** in Dorset cruelly enslaved an African man and brought him back to England. The slave said that if he was not buried in his homeland he would return to haunt the manor. The slave's request was ignored and he was buried in the local churchyard.

It is said that such terrible screaming could be heard in the churchyard that the owner was forced to dig up the coffin and put it in the loft of Bettiscombe Manor.

The skull remains at Bettiscombe Manor and seems to guard it. If the skull is taken outside, it is said that screams shake the house.

The Flying Dutchman was a ship which sank in the 1600s. Its ghost is said to haunt the oceans. In 1881, the crew of *HMS Inconstant* thought they saw the ship.

In 1939, over 100 people claimed to have seen the ship as they sunbathed on a beach near Cape Town, South Africa.

During World War II, a German admiral reported that the crew of his U-Boat submarine had seen the phantom ship.

In 1911, the crew of the steamer, *Orkney Belle*, encountered **The Flying Dutchman**. It was totally deserted. It is said that three bells were heard and the ghost ship vanished into the fog.

When your eyes are open light travels into them from the world outside. The source of the light could be the Sun, or a light bulb.

Before it enters your eyes, light reflects off objects that are in your **field of vision** – the things you can see.

Sometimes there is not much information for the brain to work with. It must use other information to understand what it is seeing. If you cover up the second of the two words below it is not so easy to see that the first word is FISH. Your brain fills in the gaps by using any other available information.

FISH FINGERS

There is a **blind spot** at the back of your eye where the optic nerve connects to the brain. It is an area which is insensitive to light.

The image on the **retina** is actually upside-down but your brain flips the image allowing you to see it the right way up.

The eye

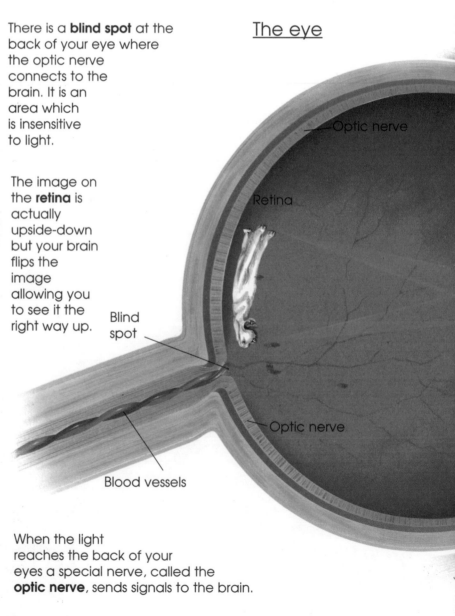

Optic nerve

Retina

Blind spot

Optic nerve

Blood vessels

When the light reaches the back of your eyes a special nerve, called the **optic nerve**, sends signals to the brain.

Even when your eyes are shut your brain still thinks it sees. When your eyes have been looking at a bright light or you have been staring hard at something, an **after-image** can stay on the back of your eye for some time. Try staring for a minute or two at the black cat, then close your eyes. You should see an image of the cat even though your eyes are closed.

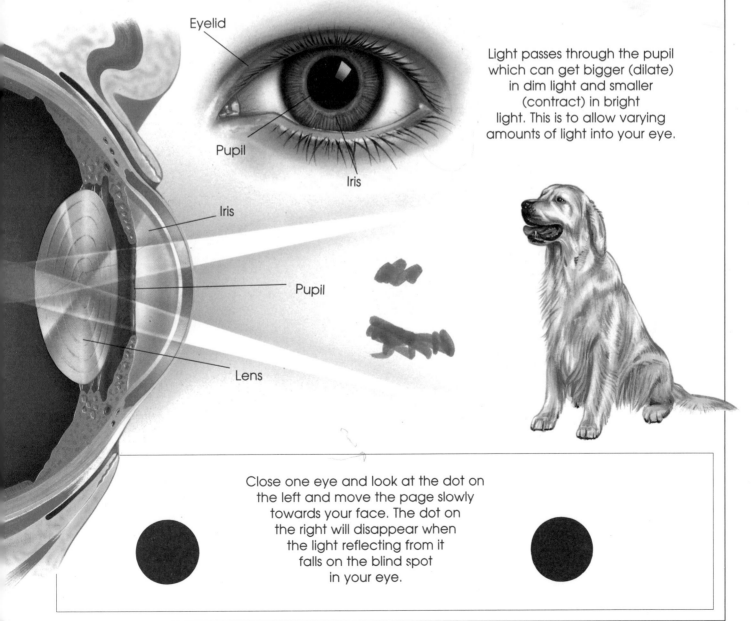

Eyelid

Pupil

Iris

Iris

Pupil

Lens

Light passes through the pupil which can get bigger (dilate) in dim light and smaller (contract) in bright light. This is to allow varying amounts of light into your eye.

Close one eye and look at the dot on the left and move the page slowly towards your face. The dot on the right will disappear when the light reflecting from it falls on the blind spot in your eye.

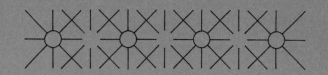

Simple lines and shapes can fool your brain. Phantom blobs can appear from nowhere and straight lines can seem to bend.

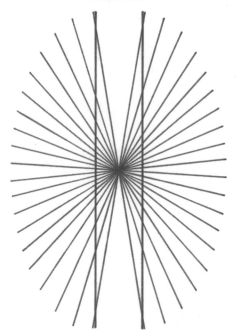

Here are some diagrams that will trick your eyes.

Try staring at the circle. You will find it hard to see a steady picture. Your eyes are being drawn to the centre of the circle where the black stripes get closer and closer together. The lines appear to 'interfere' with each other, producing a shadow effect around the circle. This is known as the **Mackay Effect**.

The unenclosed circles at the centres of the crossed lines seem to be brighter than the enclosed outlined circles.

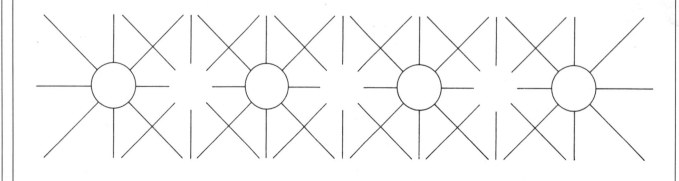

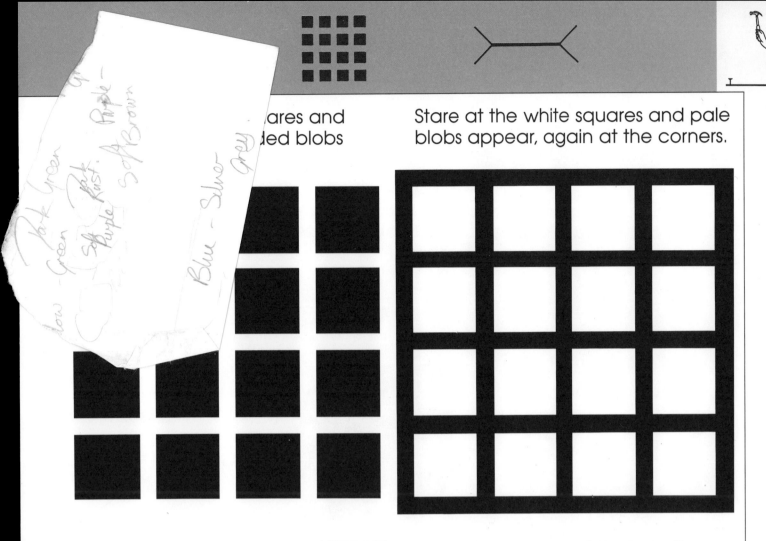

...ares and ...led blobs

Stare at the white squares and pale blobs appear, again at the corners.

Which of these lines do you think is longest? A or B? In fact they are both the same length. Your eyes follow the direction of the arrows which makes your brain think one line is shorter than the other.

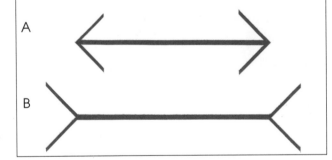

A

B

Parallel lines are lines that are the same distance apart, however long they are. Here, the parallel lines seem to curve away from each other.

The diagonal lines draw your eyes away from the horizontal lines, making them appear to bend.

Do the bricks in this wall seem as if they are being partly squashed? Although they are, in fact, all rectangles, they appear to be wedge-shaped. This interesting optical illusion only works when the lines between the bricks are brighter than the dark bricks and darker than the light bricks.

We live in three-dimensional space. This means we can move from side to side (one dimension), forwards and backwards (the second dimension) and we can jump up and down (the third dimension).

A flat sheet of paper has only two dimensions, but an object can be drawn so it looks three-dimensional.

This drawing of a cube appears to be a three-dimensional (3-D) shape, even though the paper it is printed on is only two-dimensional (2-D). The brain is being tricked into believing the lines form a 3-D figure.

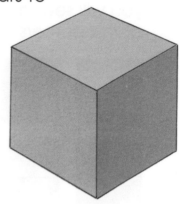

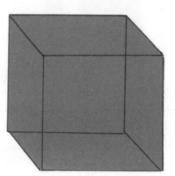

There is no way of knowing which is the front or back of the cube.

This type of cube is known as the **Necker cube**, named after the man who first drew it.

This 3-D triangle, sometimes called a **tribar**, appears to be a picture of a simple 3-D shape. However, on closer inspection it is clear that it could not exist in a real three-dimensional space!

Railway lines are parallel lines. However, a picture of a railway track disappearing into the distance shows the lines getting closer and closer together. This is called perspective. **Perspective** is used to show 3-D pictures in 2-D.

To learn the rules of perspective, artists sometimes paint what they see through a window on to the glass itself!

The Dutch artist **Maurits C Escher** produced amazing geometric drawings. Some are of buildings that at first glance appear quite normal, but would be quite impossible to build in real life.

265

A mouse looks tiny when compared to a human, but compared to a flea it looks huge.

The brain always compares one thing with another to decide their size or position. However, these comparisons can often confuse the brain!

Clouds are a **scaled** phenomenon. This means it is impossible to tell how near or far away they are, as there is nothing to compare the clouds to in order to guess their size.

At a reading distance of 30 cm, the mouse and the elephant appear to be the same size. In real life, if the mouse (40 mm high) were in the foreground the elephant (three metres high) would have to be 32 metres behind the mouse to appear to be the same size.

A constellation is a group, or pattern, of stars. The Plough, part of the Ursa Major constellation, is made up of seven bright stars. When viewed from Earth they all appear to be the same distance away, but in fact some are much closer than others.

A light year is the distance light travels in a year. Light travels at 300,000 km per second, so a light year is around 9,460,000,000,000 km!

The closest star in the Plough to Earth is 60 light years away, the furthest is an amazing 110 light years away!

As the light from the furthest star in the Plough takes 110 years to reach us, it may not even be there any more and we would not realise. If the star had burnt out five years ago we would not be able to tell for another 105 years!

Which is the largest of the centre circles? They are both the same size! Your brain compared them with the circles that are surrounding them and decided that one was 'small' in comparison with other circles and the other was 'big'.

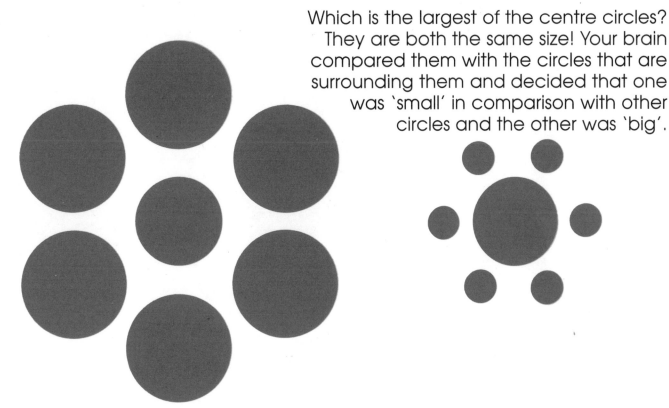
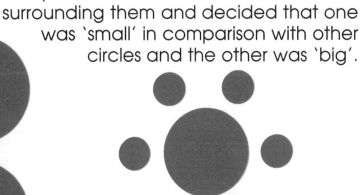

267

Light can be split into different colours. These colours are red, orange, yellow, green, blue and violet, and are called the spectrum.

Rainbows are a natural example of how sunlight can be split into the colours of the spectrum (see page 28).

You can try a simple experiment to see how the colours of the spectrum combine to make white light. Divide a card circle into six sections and colour the segments the colours of the spectrum. Push a pencil through the centre of the card. When you spin the pencil fast, the colours will blend together until they look white.

There are two sorts of cell in the human eye which are sensitive to light. They are shaped like **cones** and **rods**. The cones are sensitive to bright light and the colours red, blue and green. The rods are sensitive to dim light, but not colour.

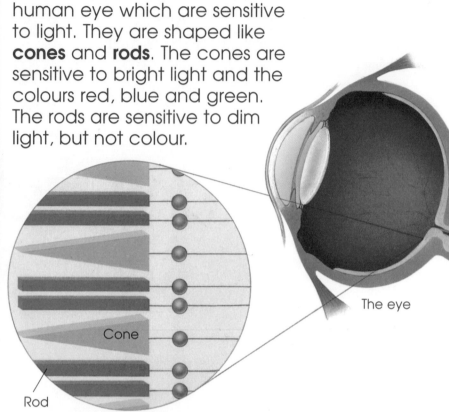

The eye

Cone

Rod

Sometimes photographers use coloured **filters** on the camera lens. The filter blocks some of the colours in the spectrum and can make photographs look very dramatic.

Using a yellow filter makes blue sky look darker and makes white clouds stand out more.

 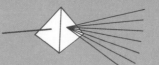

Stare at the red square in the centre of the red and white checkered pattern for about a minute. Now stare at the white square to its right. The white square will seem to change to a faint cyan (a shade of blue).

When two colours can combine to produce white light, they are said to be **complementary** colours.

The cones in your retinas have become tired of taking in the red light. So, for a while, your eyes will ignore it. The colour produced by the rest of the light is cyan. Cyan is the complementary colour to red.

If a person cannot see some colours, they are called **colour blind**. Colour blindness is 20 times more common in men than in women.

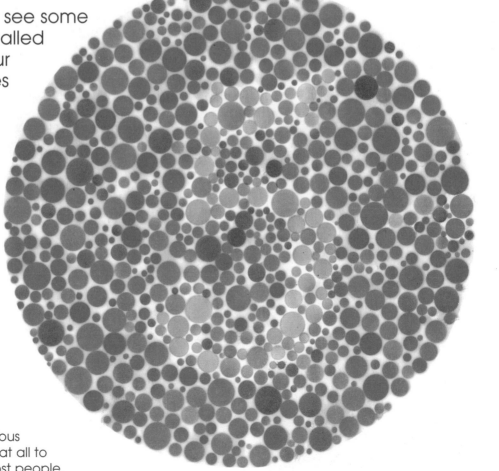

Tests like this are used to see if people are red-green colour blind.

Colour blindness is not serious and makes no difference at all to the day-to-day lives of most people.

Cinema films are often called 'movies'. However, when you watch a 'movie' you simply see a series of still pictures shown quickly one after another. Each picture or **frame,** is slightly different from the previous one so an illusion of movement is created.

Sometimes when watching a film or the television you might see a car wheel apparently spinning the wrong way. This happens when the position of the wheel's spokes in each frame makes it easier for the brain to think that the wheel is moving slowly backwards than very fast forwards.

A technique often used in nature films is **time-lapse photography**.

Individual pictures are taken of an object every day, and are then joined in sequence to make a film. In this way, a week in the life of a plant can be seen in a matter of seconds. This is an extreme form of fast-motion.

In the 19th century, before moving film was invented, you could have seen simple animation with a toy called a **zoetrope**.

The spinning drum had evenly spaced slits cut into it. Through each slit you could see a small image that was drawn slightly differently to the one next to it. Spinning the drum let you see one image after another, creating the illusion of movement.

Television pictures are made up of many tiny luminescent dots that form several lines across the screen. The dots are constantly changed from top to bottom, producing 25 frames every second. As the images change so quickly they appear to be moving.

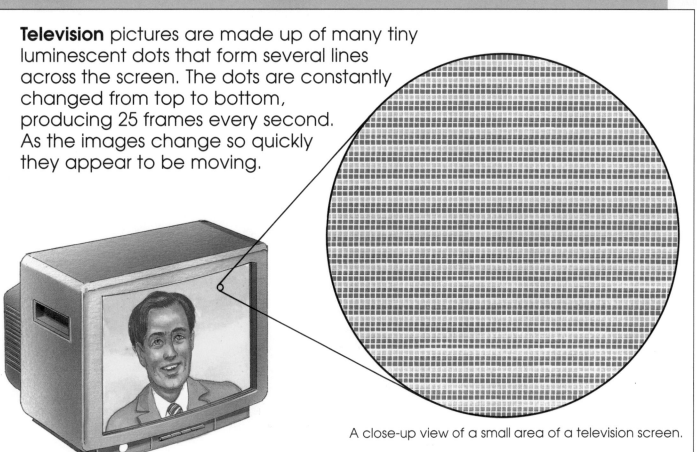

A close-up view of a small area of a television screen.

Animated films or **cartoons** work like normal films, except that between each frame the picture, or model, is changed slightly, either by hand or on a computer.

Some animated films use models made from modelling clay. The models must be changed slightly between each frame. It can take up to two years to make a 30-minute film using animated models.

271

As your eyes are about six centimetres apart you see things from two slightly different angles. This is called **binocular vision**.

Your brain has two views of the same thing to deal with, but it cleverly combines the two views so that your mind sees in 3-D. This is **stereo vision**.

The field of vision is the area in which you can see things without moving your eyes. A fly has hundreds of eyes, giving it a very wide field of vision. This makes it very difficult for a predator to sneak up on it, or a human to swat it!

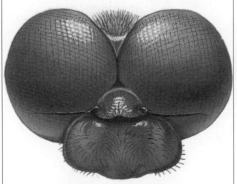

A close-up of a fly's head.

Stereo vision allows people to judge how far away an object is. This is called **spatial awareness**. It is much harder for your brain to judge the position of an object when it only sees the object through one eye (from one angle). You can try this yourself by throwing and catching a ball, or picking a ball up off the floor, when you have one eye closed.

Put the tips of your index fingers together and hold them about 20 cm away from your eyes. Relax your eyes or look at something a few feet in front of you. You will see that the ends of your fingers appear to overlap. A sausage-like object appears between your fingers.

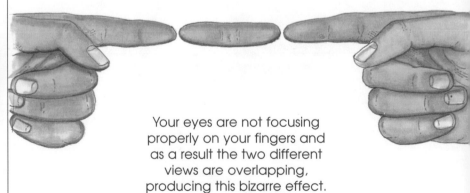

Your eyes are not focusing properly on your fingers and as a result the two different views are overlapping, producing this bizarre effect.

Each eye has a different view of the same object. If you close your left eye and point at a small object in the distance, and then close your right eye and look with the left, you will no longer be pointing at the object.

You can see 3-D pictures and 3-D films by wearing special glasses with one red and one green lens.

Two slightly different views of the picture are drawn on top of each other. Each view can only be seen through one lens of the coloured glasses. As each eye has a different picture, your brain then combines them to produce a 3-dimensional picture.

Holograms and stereograms are two ways of representing a 3-D image.

When lit correctly, a hologram can make a 2-D image appear to be in 3-D.

They are both created using technology developed in the last few decades.

The first laser beam was generated by **Theodore Maiman** in 1960 using a flash tube and a ruby crystal.

A hologram is created using **laser light**. The laser beam is split in two. One half of it is reflected from the object on to the film material. The other half is directed straight on to the film without reflecting from the object. When the hologram film is lit in a certain way, a 3-dimensional picture can be seen.

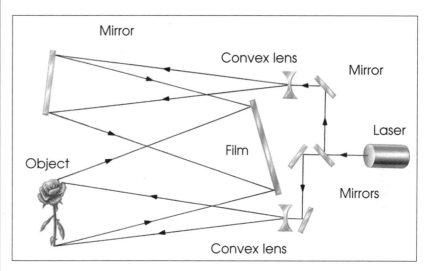

Laser light waves are coherent – they are the same length and go up and down together. Holograms can only be made using laser light as the process requires regular light waves. Unlike laser light, ordinary light waves are highly irregular, and therefore useless for the job.

A **stereogram** is a computer-generated picture that seems, at first, to be a random pattern of coloured dots and squiggles. But if you look at a stereogram in a particular way, a seemingly 3-D image emerges from within the pattern.

To see the stereogram try focusing on a point beyond the stereogram. It is not as easy as it sounds. Focus and then relax your eyes.

A 3-D picture is hidden in the scattered dots of a stereogram (the answer is at the bottom of the page). A computer is used to work out where the dots should be positioned. The dots make up two images of the same shapes – one for each eye. When you stare at the stereogram in the right way, your brain mixes the two images and magically recognizes the shapes in the picture.

Answer: It is a picture of a dinosaur.

Stage and screen

These days most films are full of incredible special effects, which can be created using computers.

Film makers have always used visual illusions, even in the early days of cinema, over 100 years ago. Then illusions were based upon the successful techniques used on stage.

In the 1902 film, *A Trip to the Moon*, film makers used trick photography to show a rocket crashing into the moon.

Early comedy film makers like **Max Sennet** and **Charlie Chaplin** used simple filming techniques to produce hilarious results. Although their special effects do not seem very convincing compared with modern techniques, they were revolutionary at the time.

One of the earliest special effects used in the theatre was **Pepper's Ghost**. A large mirror, hidden beneath the stage, reflected the figure of an actor on to a large piece of glass at the front of the stage. As the glass was invisible on the darkened stage, the audience saw a transparent phantom appearing in front of them!

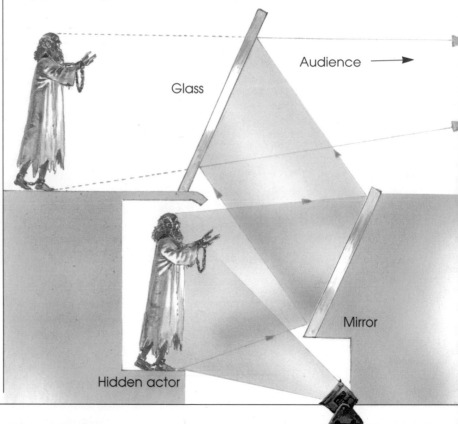

Glass

Audience →

Mirror

Hidden actor

A technique that is used a lot in film and television is **superimposition**. Two film sequences are shown at the same time. This gives the illusion that the actor is appearing twice in the same shot.

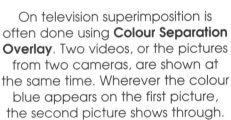

On television superimposition is often done using **Colour Separation Overlay**. Two videos, or the pictures from two cameras, are shown at the same time. Wherever the colour blue appears on the first picture, the second picture shows through.

With the help of computers it is possible to create almost any visual effect you could wish for on television or film. A picture can be stored **digitally** as trillions of binary numbers (ones and zeros). Computer software can perform complicated calculations with the stored numbers to produce spectacular effects.

Morphing is an effect where one object can appear to be smoothly transformed into another.

Most magic tricks are optical illusions that require years of practice. Magicians, or illusionists as they are sometimes known, are skilled at deceiving the eye.

To aid sleight of hand and palming, magicians try to distract the audience's attention, often by waving a 'magic' **wand.**

Magicians use **sleight of hand** to deceive their audience. This means they can cleverly move a small object, such as a coin, without anyone noticing.

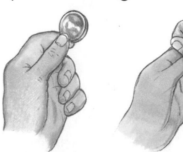
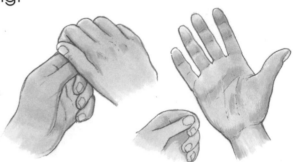

Palming is a method of holding playing cards or coins, without the audience seeing. It takes a lot of practice to make hand movements look natural whilst concealing an object.

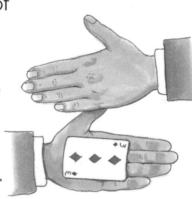

David Copperfield is one of the most famous magicians in the world today. One of his most successful illusions is when he appears to fly around the stage.

Drop a one pence coin into an empty drinking glass. Pour water into the glass and the coin will appear to become a two pence coin!

The water distorts the audience's view of the coin making it appear larger than it really is.

Make sure your audience only sees the coin through the side of the glass by holding your hand around the rim.

Hold two coins between your index fingers. Rub the two coins quickly together and it will appear that there are now three coins.

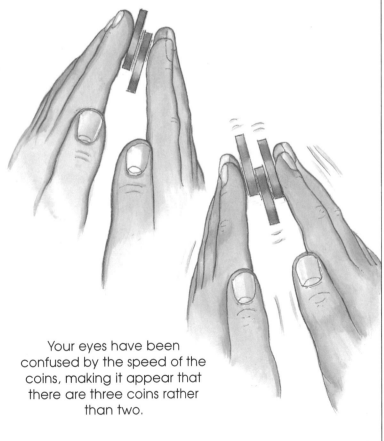

Your eyes have been confused by the speed of the coins, making it appear that there are three coins rather than two.

Light can bounce and bend. This is known as reflection (bouncing) and refraction (bending).

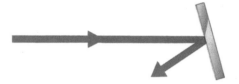

Light reflects from a mirror and refracts on entering and leaving water, sometimes producing amazing effects.

When light passes from air to water, it refracts. **Refracted light** distorts images. If you stand in the shallow end of a swimming pool and look down at your legs, they appear to be much shorter and stubbier than when you are out of the water. This is not because they have shrunk, it is because light is bent, or refracted.

A simple experiment to see how light refracts can be tried using a straw and a glass of water. Dip the straw in the glass of water and view it from different angles. The light bends on contact with the water, distorting the image of the straw.

The famous artist Leonardo da Vinci did not want other people to copy his ideas. So he sometimes used **mirror writing** when making his notes. Mirror writing can only be read if it is held up to a mirror.

A **concave** mirror curves inwards, like the bowl of a spoon. Light that reflects off it **converges** (comes together). The light focuses at a point in front of the mirror. After it has focused, the light **diverges** (separates).

The reflection in a concave mirror is upside down.

A **convex** mirror curves outwards, like the back of a spoon. It produces a small upright image, but also has a wide field of view. This means it shows things to the sides which a normal mirror would not reflect.

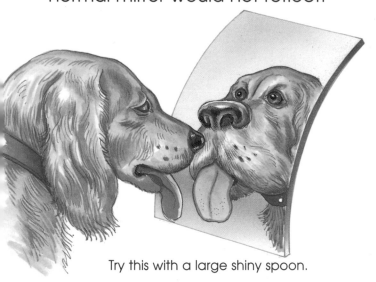

Try this with a large shiny spoon.

You may have seen weird images of yourself in a **Hall of Mirrors** at a fairground. The mirrors are curved so that some parts are concave and some are convex.

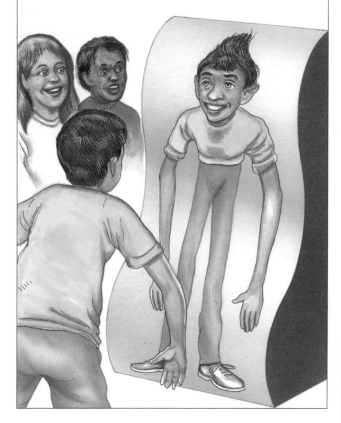

If the light meets your eye before it focuses, you see a magnified image of your face. If the light meets your eye after the focal point, you see an upside down image of your face.

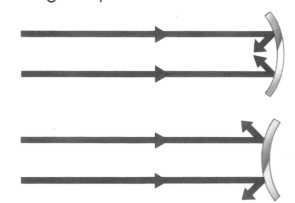

Useful illusions

Optical illusions are often entertaining, but they can also be very useful.

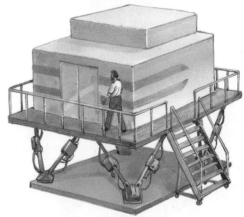

Deceiving our eyes can allow us to practise dangerous activities – but without the danger.

Pilots who fly large modern aeroplanes have to be very well trained in order to prevent accidents. Pilots can practise their skills using specially built machines called **flight simulators**.

Simulators are built to be exactly like the cockpit of the plane. Large computer screens display a realistic moving picture of what the pilots would see if they were really flying the plane. The computer-generated pictures respond to the controls as the pilot manipulates them.

Fashion designers use optical illusions when designing clothes.

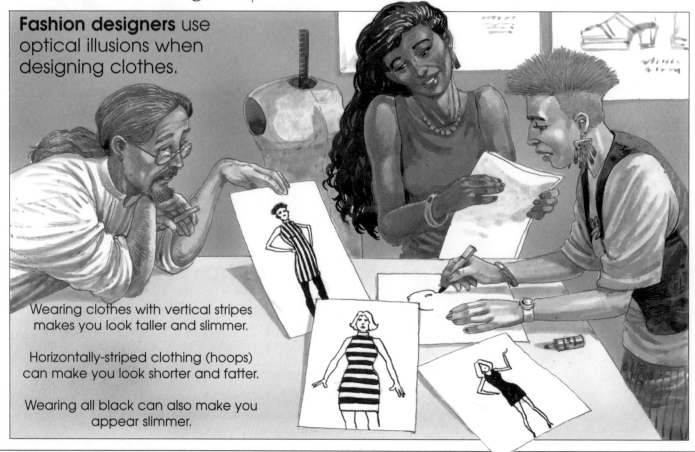

Wearing clothes with vertical stripes makes you look taller and slimmer.

Horizontally-striped clothing (hoops) can make you look shorter and fatter.

Wearing all black can also make you appear slimmer.

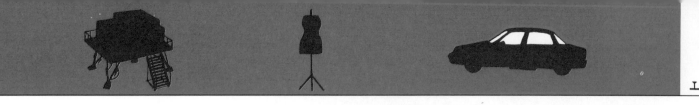

Using a design method called **Computer Aided Design**, architects can design a house, and see inside the rooms using the 3-D image on the computer screen. House buyers can be shown around the house as if it was already built.

Landscape architects can design a garden to make it look bigger than it really is. If a path gradually becomes narrower as it gets further away, the garden will look longer.

If you looked down the garden your brain would assume that the path was the same width from one end to the other and, therefore, that the end of the garden was further away.

In some countries, the stretch of road approaching a roundabout is striped with **yellow lines**, which get closer and closer together towards the roundabout. This creates the illusion that vehicles are travelling very quickly and encourages drivers to brake earlier to reach a safer speed.

Some optical illusions occur naturally. They are all around us.

Strange illusions appear in the sky, certain animals can blend into their surroundings, or look like something completely different.

On some clear days at sunset the sun will appear to turn bright green for a few seconds. This is called the **green flash**.

WARNING: NEVER LOOK DIRECTLY AT THE SUN!

A **rainbow** is a natural optical illusion that can appear when sunlight reflects off raindrops.

The light from the sun is bent as it travels through the drops. The different colours that make up white light do not bend at the same angle, so they are split into the six colours of the spectrum. Although it can appear as if there are seven colours in a rainbow, most experts agree there are only six.

On sunny days, pools of water seem to appear on the road. This is known as a **mirage**. The light has been refracted by the rising hot air close to the ground. The expanding hot air also makes the light shimmer, giving an overall effect of blue rippling water.

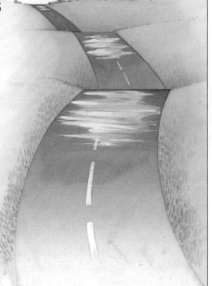

Peacock butterflies scare off predators with the vividly-coloured circles on each wing. These look like a pair of ferocious eyes.

Some animals have evolved ways of hiding themselves from other creatures. They use **camouflage.** A lion has sandy coloured fur to make it hard to see in the long dry grass.

Zebra, which might be a lion's prey, are marked with irregular black and white stripes. The stripes make it hard for the lions to tell one zebra from another in a large herd.

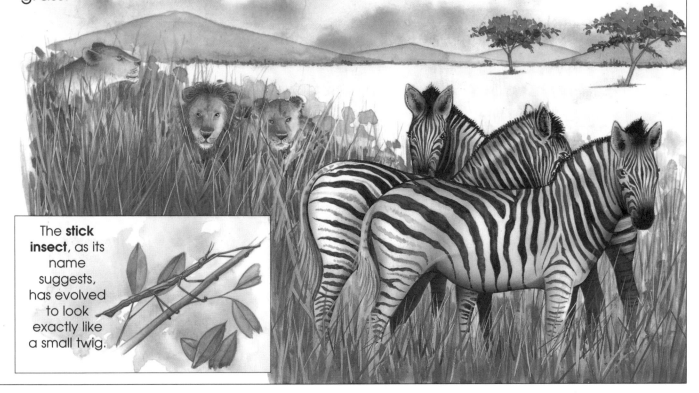

The **stick insect,** as its name suggests, has evolved to look exactly like a small twig.

Imagine wandering through a world that does not exist, or catching a ball that is not there. It is all possible with virtual reality.

Virtual Reality is anything that seems to exist but does not. A painting you might do of an imaginary house is virtual reality! The house only exists in the painting. With modern computers we can experience **Interactive Virtual Reality**. Interactive means it responds to things that you do.

Virtual Reality computer programs can create imaginary landscapes that seem as real as the view you might see from the window of a train. Computer programmers use mathematical formulae to generate very realistic landscapes that move with you through this virtual world.

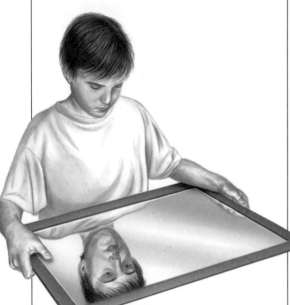

If you look into a **mirror**, you can see a virtual world behind your reflection. Try holding a mirror horizontally in front of you while you walk from room to room. It seems like you are walking on the ceiling.

> WARNING:
> BE VERY CAREFUL IF YOU DO THIS, AS IT COULD BE VERY DANGEROUS

There are various items of equipment that can be used for exploring virtual reality. The most well known is the **headset.** In front of the eyes are two tiny TV screens that give you a 3-D view of the computer generated landscape. Some more expensive headsets change the view as you move your head up and down or from side to side.

A **VR glove** contains sensors that can detect the movements of your fingers. Soon gloves will have sensors that make it seem as if you can actually feel virtual objects, objects that do not really exist.

The history of ballet

The tradition of dance dates back thousands of years. People danced to worship their gods, to bring good fortune and to celebrate festivals.

The true origins of ballet, however, date back to Italy, 500 years ago.

Today, ballet is full of variety because of its rich history. Film and television have made it more popular than ever.

During a period in history known as the **Renaissance**, wealthy Italian families entertained visitors at exciting parties with poetry, music, mime and dancing.

Catherine de Médici, an Italian courtier, became Queen of France in 1547. She introduced spectacular dance pageants. They were known as *ballet de cour* as they were danced by the courtiers themselves.

King Louis XIV of France was an enthusiastic dancer. In 1661, he set up a school for dance where the five basic ballet positions were first written down.

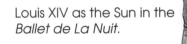

Louis XIV as the Sun in the *Ballet de La Nuit*.

In 1760, **Jean Georges Noverre** introduced story ballets or *ballet d'action*. An early story ballet was *La Fille Mal Gardée* which is still danced today.

A French dancer, called **Marius Petipa**, joined **The Imperial Ballet** in Russia in 1847. He created famous ballets, such as *The Sleeping Beauty*.

In 1909, **Serge Diaghilev** formed **Les Ballets Russes** with the most talented dancers he could find. Diaghilev brought audiences ballets such as *The Firebird* and *Rite of Spring*.

Modern dance began in America with **Isadora Duncan**. She danced barefoot in flowing tunics inspired by Ancient Greece.

In the 1930s, a new dance technique, with awkward, angular movements, was developed by **Martha Graham**.

Martha Graham in *Night Journey*.

Popular ballets

Ballets old and new entertain audiences with stories of love, magic and far away places.

Some ballets are long, with three or four acts, while others last for just one act.

Not all contemporary ballet and dance tells a story. Sometimes just music and movement alone are fun to watch.

Frederick Ashton's modern ballet brings the best-loved Beatrix Potter characters to life. Peter Rabbit, Jemima Puddle-Duck and Pigling Bland all star in the fun-packed **The Tales of Beatrix Potter**.

In the romantic ballet **La Sylphide**, James falls in love with a forest sprite (a *sylphide*) on the eve of his wedding. He is tricked by a witch and kills the sprite by accident.

The Nutcracker story is set at a Christmas Party. Little Clara dreams that she and her toys are attacked by a mouse king. She defeats him and her favourite toy, the Nutcracker, becomes a handsome prince.

Appalachian Spring is a famous ballet choreographed by Martha Graham. It tells the story of a newly married pioneering couple starting their life on the prairies of America.

Set in a crowded fairground, Fokine's **Petrushka** captures all the excitement of the fair. A magician makes three dolls dance and, when night falls, they secretly come to life on their own.

In **Coppélia**, Dr Coppelius, a toymaker, is tricked into believing that his beautiful doll has come to life!

Unforgettable dancers

Ballet moved to the theatre from the royal palaces over 200 years ago. Ballerinas and male dancers have been popular ever since.

While many dancers are famous for their incredible technique, others have brought something new and exciting to the world of dance.

Taglioni was perfect in the role of the forest sprite in *La Sylphide*.

In the 1830s, **Marie Taglioni** was the first great ballerina. Her lightness and poise brought beauty to every performance. People had never seen such graceful jumps and landings.

One of the most famous male dancers of all time was **Vaslav Nijinsky**. He brought dramatic skill and physical presence to ballet. His amazing leaps and expressive movement gave a special quality to every role he played.

Nijinsky caused a sensation in *L'Après-midi d'un Faune.*

Anna Pavlova was one of the world's greatest dancers. She devoted her whole life to dance. Every role she played seemed magical. She could transform herself into many graceful images.

Pavlova as *The Dying Swan*.

Isadora Duncan is famous for beginning the modern dance movement. She danced freely, wearing a simple tunic.

After defecting from Russia in 1961, **Rudolf Nureyev** danced with the Royal Ballet. He was an exciting, dynamic and strong performer. Male dancing became very popular because of him.

Isadora's movements were inspired by nature.

The choreographer Kenneth MacMillan created *The Prince of the Pagodas* specially for Darcey Bussell.

Margot Fonteyn was a leading ballerina of this century. Her partnership with Rudolph Nureyev was very famous.

Trained at the Royal Ballet School, **Darcey Bussell** is one of today's leading ballerinas.

Ballet around the world

Ballet is performed and enjoyed throughout the world.

Each country and culture brings something different and new to ballet.

From the English Classical style to Cunningham's technique, there is a rich variety of work that celebrates people's love of dance.

The **Royal Danish Ballet Company** is the world's oldest ballet company. Founded by **August Bournonville**, this company is famous for its powerful male roles and enchanting female stars.

The Australian Ballet is internationally renowned for performances of classical and modern ballets.

Edward Borovansky from the famous Ballet Russes started the Borovansky Ballet in 1939. When he died the company was renamed **The Australian Ballet**.

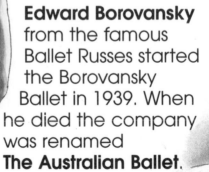

Arthur Mitchell formed the first black classical ballet company in the US, in 1971. It is called **The Dance Theatre of Harlem**.

The Royal Ballet was originally called the Vic-Wells Ballet. It is now one of the great British ballet companies.

The **Merce Cunningham Dance Company** from the US, is at the forefront of modern dance. Many of the dancers are classically trained.

Merce Cunningham mixes ballet steps with everyday movements.

One of the largest and best known companies is the **Bolshoi Ballet** from Russia. Its colourful and dramatic story ballets are seen all over the world.

You can start dancing from the age of three. In your first lesson you will learn basic steps and exercises.

Stepping, jumping, walking and running will all help to strengthen your muscles, give you better coordination and help you dance in time to the music.

Dance classes are held at local dance schools in the evenings and at weekends. If you want to be a professional dancer you can join a dance academy when you are about eleven years old, or later at sixteen or eighteen years old.

Clothes for dance classes must be light and simple to allow you to move easily.

Boys dance in leotards or T-shirts and tights.

Girls usually wear leotards and tights.

For other dance forms, bare feet, jazz shoes and tap shoes are used.

In a **dance studio** there are usually mirrors on the walls so that you can see that you are moving correctly. The floor is made of wood or vinyl and can be sprung to help you jump.

Ballet shoes are soft and flat, and made from satin, canvas or leather.

The **barre** is a wooden rail attached to the wall which is used to give the dancer support while exercising.

All dance classes are accompanied by **music**. As a dancer you learn to feel and express the music in the way you move.

To become a strong, expressive dancer you must **practise**. Even the most famous dancers go to class every day to stay strong and supple.

When you have learnt the basic ballet steps and can put them together, you are ready to start taking **ballet exams**. Exams test how much you know and show that you are ready to learn more.

The first ballet school was founded by King Louis XIV of France. It was here, in Paris, that the first ballet steps were set and written down. Ever since, the language of ballet has been French.

In a ballet class, you learn each position, or exercise, by its French name.

Before making any shape or position you must have the correct **posture**. This means standing tall with your hips directly over your feet. The back must be straight to give the body a slim line.

En seconde
Second position

En première
First position

En troisième
Third position

It is important to keep the neck relaxed, the head poised and the shoulders open and low.

The first exercise in any ballet class is the **plié**, which means 'to bend'. *Pliés* give the legs strength and suppleness.

Turn out is the amount you can turn your feet sideways in any position. Your legs must be turned outwards from the hip.

The way you carry your arms is called **ports de bras**. Arms should make a gentle curve and move gracefully.

Fingers should always be slightly curved and soft.

En quatrième
Fourth position

En cinquième
Fifth position

There are **five basic positions** for the feet and arms. They are used at the beginning and end of movements and in passing from one movement to another.

The order of exercises in a ballet class has been developed over hundreds of years. Each class starts at the **barre**.

After exercising at the *barre*, dancers move to the centre of the room for **centre practice**. Here the *barre* exercises are practised without support.

Pointing the toes correctly is an important part of ballet. Your foot should be pointed from the ankle with the leg turned out. This way your foot should make a straight line with your leg.

299

To become a professional dancer takes a great deal of dedication and hard work.

There are many complicated movements to learn and master.

Ballerinas and leading male dancers have studied, practised and performed for many years before gaining world fame.

Girls start to learn **pointework** at about age eleven. This means dancing on the tips of their toes, wearing special **pointe shoes**.

The toe of a **pointe shoe** is hardened with layers of satin, paper and coarse material called **burlap**.

A series of exercise positions and movements, performed together, is called an **enchaînement**.

Many dancers join a ballet company as a member of the **corps de ballet** or chorus. Performing as a group of dancers they learn to work together and to play a character on stage.

You can start training to become a professional ballet dancer aged sixteen. This takes at least two years, working and dancing for many hours a day.

The **arabesque** is one of the most beautiful ballet positions. It requires perfect balance while standing on one leg, with the other stretched out behind.

As dancers complete their training, they start to look for jobs. To become a member of a **dance company** they must **audition**. This means taking part in a class and performing a solo in front of a panel of experts.

A **pirouette** is an exciting and difficult step where the dancer spins on one leg. This needs balance and strength.

The **pas de deux** is a partnership between two dancers. The male dancer lifts and supports his partner.

Modern dance

Ballet is the oldest dance technique in the Western world, but many other dance forms are taught at schools throughout the world. These include contemporary dance, tap and jazz.

These techniques are very different from ballet, but a knowledge of ballet can help when learning them.

Contemporary dance is about a hundred years old. Its founders wanted to make movement more natural and expressive. **Graham**, **Cunningham** and **Humphrey** are names of techniques.

Contemporary dancers usually dance barefoot.

Contemporary dance has different sets of positions to ballet. There may be **floor movements** and dancers can use their breathing to help form the different positions.

Tap dancing was started by African slaves in America. Traditional African dances were mixed with those of white people. Over the years, tap steps have been made into the method which is taught in schools today.

Fred Astaire was one of the most famous tap dancers. He was both a talented dancer and choreographer.
Today, dancers such as **Savion Glover** continue to make tap dancing very popular.

Tap dancing is very fast and rhythmic. In **musicals** there are often as many as thirty dancers all tap dancing at the same time. The sound they make is very exciting.

Jazz dancing started in America. It developed from a mixture of African and European dances. Like tap dance, it is used in musicals and is also known as **show dancing**.

Tap shoes have metal toe and heel plates fitted to make a special sound on the floor.

Dancers who work in musicals are trained in many dance techniques. They are adaptable and perform ballet, tap and jazz.

303

Ballet does not use speech, so dancers must use all their expressive skills to convey their mood and character.

Early ballet dancers started to wear shorter and looser clothes as they began to perform more complicated steps.

Costumes, make-up and mime are all important for telling a ballet story and setting the scene.

Dancing tights were invented by Maillot at the Paris Opera in the early 1800s. They allowed dancers to wear shorter dresses without showing their bare legs!

Early ballet masters created **mime gestures** which have become part of today's choreography. Using movements of the eyes, arms and head, dancers can convey the emotions and intentions of the characters they play.

Some costumes look as if they are very hard to dance in but they are made of very light-weight materials.

Theatre lights are so bright, dancers wear make-up to stop their skin from looking pale and shiny.

A dancer's hair is usually tied back from her face so that her eyes and mouth can be clearly seen.

Costumes must be strong and easy to move in. They can be made from silk, velvet, chiffon or lycra and decorated with beads, braid and ribbons.

Hair is often decorated with a **head-dress** or flowers.

Tutus have short, stiff skirts which stick out from the waist.

The **classical tutu** was designed so that dancers could perform difficult turns, such as *fouèttés*, for which their legs needed to move freely.

Stage make-up is bright and heavy. It has to be applied boldly so that it can be seen from a distance.

Some dances look so natural and spontaneous it seems as though the dancers are making up the steps.

Every dance has been carefully worked out and set to music by the choreographer.

The **choreographer** chooses the story, selects the music and arranges the steps for a ballet. The ideas may come from a fairy tale, a painting or a poem.

Movements from *Square Dance* by Balanchine.

George Balanchine was a famous choreographer who created over a hundred ballets. He made dances which were both graceful and athletic.

Modern choreographers often create abstract dances with no story.

Twyla Tharp is a contemporary choreographer who uses movement of all kinds. Her work includes ballet and jazz dance.

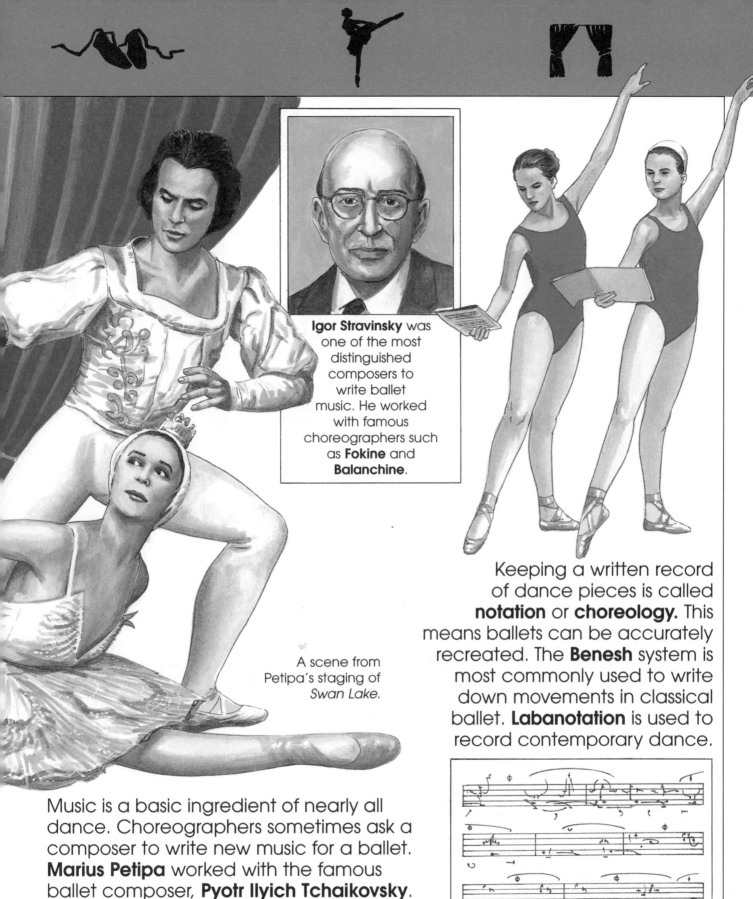

Igor Stravinsky was one of the most distinguished composers to write ballet music. He worked with famous choreographers such as **Fokine** and **Balanchine**.

A scene from Petipa's staging of *Swan Lake*.

Keeping a written record of dance pieces is called **notation** or **choreology.** This means ballets can be accurately recreated. The **Benesh** system is most commonly used to write down movements in classical ballet. **Labanotation** is used to record contemporary dance.

Music is a basic ingredient of nearly all dance. Choreographers sometimes ask a composer to write new music for a ballet. **Marius Petipa** worked with the famous ballet composer, **Pyotr Ilyich Tchaikovsky**. He wrote the magical music for *The Sleeping Beauty, The Nutcracker* and *Swan Lake.*

Benesh notation from *Les Sylphides.*

On with the show

Everyone in a ballet company has a part to play in putting on a successful show.

The dance is choreographed, or designed, to fit the theatre. The stage is carefully lit and the scenery painted.

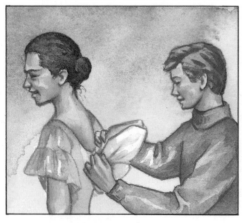

There must be rehearsals and time for costumes to be made or repaired.

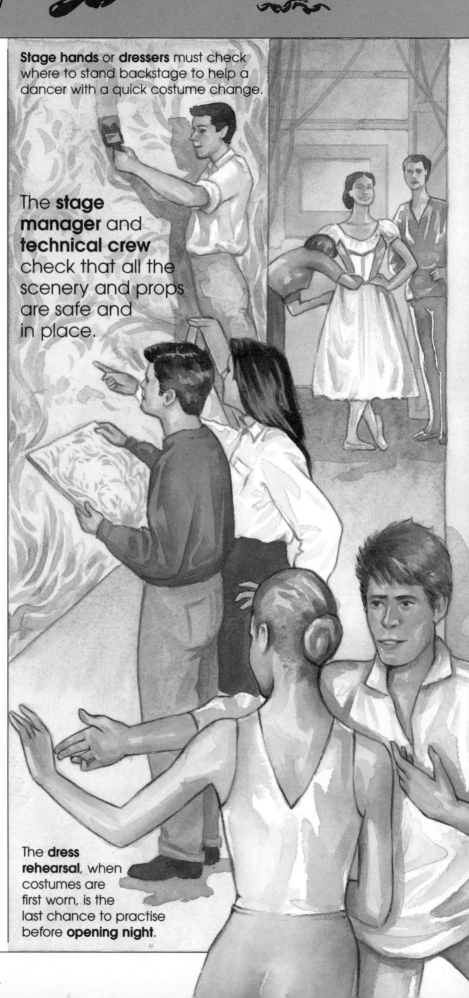

Stage hands or **dressers** must check where to stand backstage to help a dancer with a quick costume change.

The **stage manager** and **technical crew** check that all the scenery and props are safe and in place.

The **dress rehearsal**, when costumes are first worn, is the last chance to practise before **opening night**.

A good **lighting designer** can transform the stage and create a magical atmosphere by the way the lights are positioned.

The **designer** and choreographer plan the **scenery** and **costumes**. The designer makes a model to check everything will fit on stage.

A technician organises the **special effects**. A dry-ice machine might be used to blow mist across the stage.

The **publicity officer** lets the public know about the show. Programmes and posters are printed and the stars of the show may appear on television or radio.

Dancers practise with the **orchestra** for the last few rehearsals.

The stage has clear markings so that everyone knows where to stand.

Dancers spend many hours with the **choreographer**, rehearsing for the show. They start by learning the basic steps, then put them to music.

Dance for fun

People all over the world get together to dance for fun and to meet people.

Ceroc is a new and exciting form of modern jive based on French Rock 'n' Roll. There are steps to learn but you can dance to almost any kind of music.

Social dance is affected by fashion and is often inspired by films and music.

Rap, rave and **cult dance** all rely on the beat and sound of the loud music. The DJ plays the music the dancers want to hear!

The Waltz is perhaps one of the most famous social dances. It was first danced in Germany in 1780 when the swinging turns and the close contact between partners were considered shocking!

Johann Strauss wrote the music which made the waltz popular.

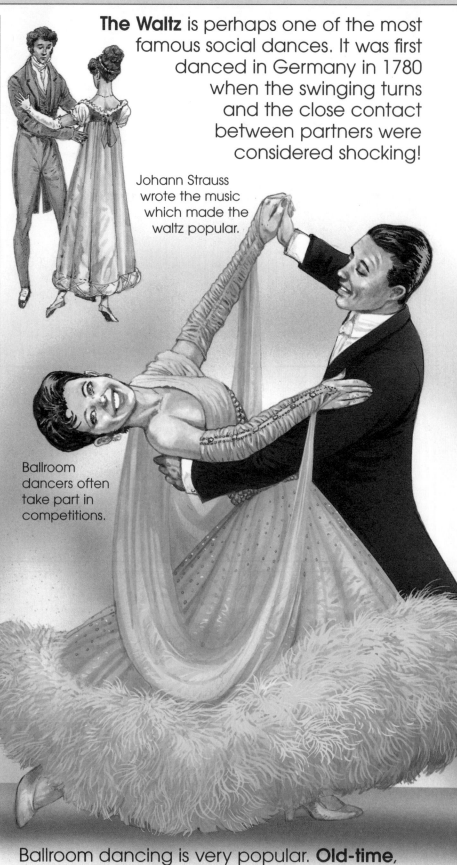

Ballroom dancers often take part in competitions.

Ballroom dancing is very popular. **Old-time, Modern** and **Latin American** are all types of ballroom dancing.

Latin dance came from South America, with lively dances such as the Rumba, Samba and Mambo.

Latin music is very rhythmic and noisy!

The **Jitterbug** and **Boogie-Woogie** were thrilling new dances in the 1940s. They were brought to Great Britain by American and Canadian soldiers during World War II. These dances are now known as **jive**.

Rock 'n' Roll became popular in the 1950s when records became cheap enough for young people to buy. Dancers jumped, turned and twisted to music by popular singers such as Bill Haley and Elvis Presley.

The **Alligator** and **The Monkey** were fashionable 1960s dances.

Dances like **The Twist** and **The Mashed Potato** were invented in the 1960s when people began to dance on their own.

Disco dancing began in the 1970s. You do not have to dance in pairs and there are no set steps. The way you look and move are more important.

311

National dance

Every country has its own dance form. National dances grow from religion, folk tales and even the weather.

Colourful costumes and decorations are part of each country's national dance.

India has a tremendous diversity of peoples, climates, languages and dances. One of the most popular is **Bharata Natyam** which started as part of religious worship, 2,000 years ago. A story is told using hand movements and facial expressions.

The dancer's bare feet tap out complex rhythmic patterns.

In England, **Morris dancing** is traditionally danced by men. They wear bells and ribbons and dance in lines facing each other. A man called the 'fool' carries a colourful stick and hits anyone who misses a step!

The Polish **Mazurka** is danced by eight or sixteen couples in a circle.

The main Spanish dancing styles are regional dances like the **fandango** and **flamenco**. Flamenco has developed from Asian, Arabic and gypsy dancing.

Flamenco is often danced to the music of guitars and castanets.

Settlers in the USA have created many country dances. At a **Square Dance** the 'caller' tells the dancers what to do. Dancers swing their partners as the banjo and fiddle play.

In **Irish dancing**, the upper body is kept straight and stiff while the legs and feet kick and step.

Irish dancers' costumes are embroidered with Celtic designs.

The **Maoris** of New Zealand use dance to communicate. As they dance they chant, quiver their hands and use facial expressions. The dancing is often accompanied by a sung poem.

The **Scottish Reel** is a gliding and springing dance performed by couples. Music is played on the bagpipes. The men wear a pleated, tartan kilt which is like a skirt.

Women wear a white dress with a tartan sash for dancing.

Ballet school life

Anyone who wants to become a professional ballet dancer will need to train hard for many years.

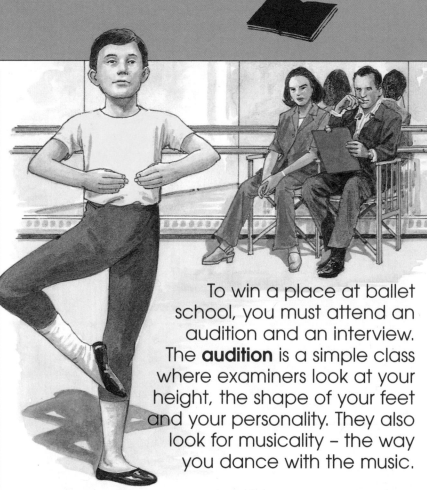

To win a place at ballet school, you must attend an audition and an interview. The **audition** is a simple class where examiners look at your height, the shape of your feet and your personality. They also look for musicality – the way you dance with the music.

Ballet schools give every student the chance to dance the best they can, to discover their talents and, perhaps, become a famous dancer.

Ballet schools are much like any other schools. Pupils study for exams and learn the usual subjects, such as English, Maths and Biology. They also have special lessons including Music, Drama, History of Dance, Singing and Contemporary Dance.

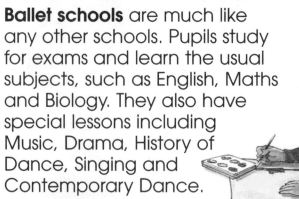

When pupils reach the age of sixteen, they begin to learn **ballet repertory** and **classical pas de deux**.

Once a year, pupils at **The Royal Ballet School** put on a performance at Covent Garden Opera House in London.

Being involved in a performance is excellent practice for the future. Not only do dancers learn about the art of performing but also the demands of **rehearsals** and the many jobs involved in producing a show.

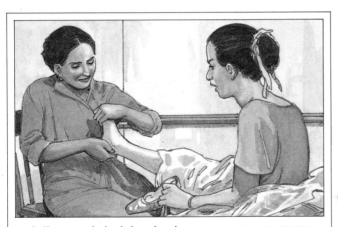

A thorough training in dance opens up many career opportunities. Dancers can become choreographers, stage managers, administrators, teachers and **physiotherapists**.

Days are long and demanding but dancers must have a good all-round education as not every student will take up a career as a dancer.

A career as a dancer is not easy or secure. Not everyone will grow to the right height and there is always the risk of injury. Dancing is not just a career - it is a way of life which can be very exciting and rewarding.

Fact*finder*
Index

A

A Trip to the Moon 276
Abominable Snowman 61, 256
Abu Simbel 128
Abuja 111
Acid rain 173
Aconcagua, Mount 105, 106
Acorn weevil 53
Active 150
Afghanistan 112
Africa 95, 101, 108-111, 161
African bee 57
African bush-cricket 26
African giant snail 24-25
African monarch butterfly 28
African wild dog 56-57
After-image 261
Airship 210
Alaska 100, 102
Albatross 41
Alexander the Great 178-179
Alexandria, Pharos of 120
Aliakmon River 98
Aliens 244-245
Alps 92, 94,133
Amazon River 104-107
Amazons 202
Americans 196-197
Amritsar, Golden Temple at 139
Amsterdam 97
Amulets 243
An Lu-Shan 199
Analytical engine 226
Andean condor 40-41
Andes Mountains 104-107, 125
Angel Falls 130
Angkor Wat 138
Angler fish 43
Anglo-Saxons 203
Animal pests 170-171

Animated film 271
Antarctic 82
Antarctica 164-166
Antibiotics 169
Antipater of Sidon 120
Antlion larva 13
Antony, Mark 183
Apache 197
Aphid 16
Appalachian Mountains 100
Appalachian Spring 291
Apple sucker 23
Aqueducts 144
Arab 188
Arabesque 301
Arabian Sea 115
Arapahoe 196
Arc, Joan of 200
Archelon turtle 88
Arctic 82
Arctic Circle 92, 96, 100, 102
Arctic giant jellyfish 38
Arctic Ocean 100
Argentina 105, 106
Argonauts 203
Arizona 174
Arminius 185
Army ant 56
Arsouf, Battle of 192
Artemis, Temple of 120
Arthur, King 203
Artificial fibre 215
Ashanti 177
Asia 92, 99, 108, 112-118
Asian Russia 116
Asir Range 114
Assassin bug larva 26
Assassins 192
Assyrians 177
Astaire, Fred 303
Astral projection 254

Astrology 251
Atacama Desert 105
Athens 98
Atlantic 166
Atlantic Ocean 102, 105, 106
Atlas moth 41
Atmosphere 173, 174
Atomic clocks 217
Attila the Hun 180
Auditions 301, 314
Australasia 116, 117, 119
Australia 64, 84, 116, 117, 119, 162, 171
Australian Ballet, The 294
Avalanche 158, 159
Ayers Rock 124
Aztecs 194-195

B

Babbage, Charles 26
Babylon, Hanging Gardens of 121
Balanchine, George 306, 307
Baleen 74
Ballechin House 240
Ballet de cour 288
Ballet steps 298-299
Ballets Russes, Les 289, 294
Ballpoint pens 218
Ballroom dancing 310-311
Baltic Sea 99
Banded sea-snake 85
Banded snail 27
Bangladesh 112, 155, 157
Bannockburn, Battle of 201
Barbados 236
Barnacles 73
Barracuda 49
Barre 297, 299
Basiliosaurus 74
Basilisk 61
Bay of Bengal 112, 115

Bayeux Tapestry 140
Beetle 18
Beijing 118
Ben Nevis 94
Benesh 307
Berlin 95
Bermuda 100
Bermuda Triangle 247
Bettiscombe Manor 258-259
Bharata Natyam 312
Bhutan 112
Bicycle 207
Bigfoot-Sasquatch 256
Biggest wave 167
Binocular vision 272
Biosphere 123
Bishop Rock Lighthouse 127
Black Death 168
Black fly larva 11
Black Forest 95
Black widow spider 54

Blackfeet 196
Blind-spot 261
Bloemfontein 110
Bloodaxe, Eric 189
Blue Mountain Peak 103
Blue shark 65, 81
Blue whale 39, 75
Blue-black spider wasp 13
Boeing 707 153
Boleyn, Anne 232
Bolívar, Mount 107
Bolívar, Simon 200
Bolshoi Ballet 295
Boogie-Woogie 311
Booth, David 252
Booth, Hubert 229
Borglum, Gutzon 129
Borley Rectory 241
Borobudur, Temple of 138
Borovansky, Edward 294
Boru, Brian 186
Bottle-nosed dolphin 79
Boudicca 185
Bournonville, August 294
Bouto dolphin 78
Brahmaputra River 115
Brasilia 106
Brazil 105, 106
Brimstone butterfly 27
British warriors 176
Broadhaven Triangle 245
Bruce, Robert the 201
Bubonic plague 168
Buddha, statue of 129
Buenos Aires 106
Bumblebee 35
Burlap 300
Bush fire 162
Bussell, Darcey 293
Butterfly 10, 19, 28
Byrhtnoth 176

C

Ca 60 231
Caddis fly larva 10-11
Caesar, Julius 184
Cairbre, High King 187
Cairo 110
California 162
Californian condor 58
Camera 224
Camlann, Battle of 203
Camouflage 285
Campbell, Virginia 237
Canada 100-102
Canberra 119
Cane toad 171
Cannae, Battle of 184
Cape Town 110
Caracas 107
Carbon dioxide 172-173
Caribbean Sea 103
Carletonville 133
Carthage 144
Cartoon 271
Caspian Sea 115
Cassette tapes 221
Caterpillar 20-21
Catherine de Médici 288
Caucasus Mountains 92
Celts 184, 186
Central America 100, 104
Centre practice 299
Ceratium 72
Ceroc 310
CFCs 173
Champagne Castle Mountain 110
Chang River 116, 118
Channel Tunnel 132
Chaplin, Charlie 276
Cheyenne 196
Chile 104, 105

China 115, 116, 118, 155
China, Great Wall of 145
Chinese alligator 59
Cholera 169
Choreographers 306-307, 308
Choreology 307
Christian Church 249
Christians 192-193
Chrysler Building 127
Cinema 224
Citrus swallowtail butterfly 28
Classical tutu 305
Cleopatra, Queen 183
Click beetle 23
Clown anemone fish 64
CN Tower 127
Cobra 45
Cochineal bug 17
Cockroach 8
Cod 71
Coelacanth 87
Coherent light 274
Collingridge, Michael 238
Colombian horned toad 48
Colonel William Rankin 153
Colorado beetle 171
Colosseum 134
Colour blindness 269
Colour separation overlay 277
Colour television 225
Comet 174
Common house centipede 20
Common seal 70, 71
Compact disc 221
Complementary colours 269
Computer 226, 271, 274-275, 276-277,
    282-283, 286-286
Computer Aided Design 283
Concave mirror 281
Cones 268-269
Congo 109

Conquistadors 195
Contemporary dance 302-303
Converging light 281
Convex mirror 281
Cook, Mount 119
Copenhagen 97
Coppélia 291
Copperfield, David 278
Coral polyps 64, 65
Coral reefs 64, 65
Cordillera Mountains 100
Corps de ballet 300
Cotton stainer bug 31
Covens 248
Crab spider 27
Crabeater seal 76, 77
Crazy Horse 197
Crete 98
Cricket 22, 32
Croiset, Gerald 253
Crop circles 256
Crusaders 192-193
Crust 150
Cryptocleidus 88
Crystal Palace 122
Cuba 103
Cuchulainn 186
Cueva de Nerja 136
Cult dance 310
Cunningham, Merce 302
Custer, General 197
Cyclone 154-155

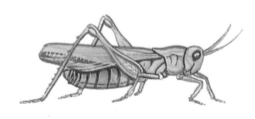

D

da Vinci, Leonardo 230, 280
Dab 67
Damselfly 9, 18
Dance classes 296
Dance companies 294-295, 301
Dance Theatre of Harlem, The 295
Darius, King 179
David, statue of 129
Dead Sea 114, 143
Death Valley 100, 143
Death's head hawkmoth 44
Death-watch beetle 33
Deep-sea angler fish 68
Deep-sea fish 39
Deep-sea shrimps 68
Demavend, Mount 115
Denmark 97, 234
Dermistid beetle 15
Desert 161
Desertification 161
Diadem butterfly 28-29
Diaghilev, Serge 289
Dinosaurs 173
Disco 311
Disease 168-169
Diverging light 281
Dixon, Jeane 253
Dodoma 111
Dogwhelk 67
Dolphins 78, 79
Dominoes 251
Dormant 150
Downing Street 241
Dowsing 254
Dr Charles Richter 148
Dragonfly 18
Drakensburg Mountains 110
Dropping Well 137
Drought 160-160, 162

Dugong 60
Duncan, Isadora 289, 293
Dung beetle 46
Dust Bowl 160
Dutch elm disease 171
Dyke 157

E

Earhart, Amelia 247
Earth 174
Earthquake 148-149, 158
Earthworm 9, 24
Earwig 34
East Germany 95
Easter Island 128
Eclipses 147
Ecuadorian erenus butterfly 28
Edison, Thomas 220, 224, 228
Edward I, King 201
Edward, Prince of Wales 252
Egypt 110
Eiffel Tower 126
Eiffel, Alexandre-Gustave 126
El Cid 193
Elasmosaurus 90
Elbe River 95
Elbrus, Mount 92, 99
Electric lift 238
Electric locomotive 207
Electric motor 229
Electron microscope 212
Electronic telephone exchanges 223
Elephant 36-37
Elephant seal 50-51, 76
Elm bark beetle 34
Emperor dragonfly 18
Emperor penguin 70
Empire State Building 127, 153
Enchaînement 300
Endoscope 213

English warriors 176, 187
Ephyra 71
Epidaurus theatre 135
Eruption 150
Escher, Maurits C 265
Estuary crocodile 84
Eternal peace 243
Etna, Mount 98
Etruscans 182
Euglandina rosea snail 13
Europe 92-7, 99, 108
European elm bark beetle 171
Everest, Mount 112, 116, 118
Ewing, Jock 239
Extinct 150

F

Facsimile machines 223
Fairy fly 19
Fairy penguin 70
False scorpion 58
Famine 160, 170
Fandango 313
Fashion designer 282
Fault 149
Fianna, The 187
Field of vision 260, 272
Fille Mal Gardée, La 289
Filter 268
Fionn mac Cumhaill 187
Firefly 33
Five basic positions 298-299
Fjord 165
Flamenco 313
Flea 16, 22
Flight simulator 282
Flood 156-157
Floor movements 302
Flower mantis 26-27
Flushing toilet 228

Fly 19, 47
Fly larva 25
Flying Dutchman, The 259
Flying fish 86
Flying fox 40
Flying saucer 244
Flying shuttle 215
Fokine, Mikhail 291, 307
Fonteyn, Margot 293
Forbidden City 123
Forkbeard, Sweyn 188
Forked lightning 153
Fossil fuels 173
Fossils 87, 88
Four-eyed fish 86
Frame 270-271
France 94, 114
French Guiana 105
Frilled lizard 44-45
Frogs 245
Fuji, Mount 118
Full rigging 208

G

Galileo 213
Ganges River 112, 115
Gannet 83
Garibaldi, Giuseppe 201
Gaudí, Antoni 139
Gaugamela, Battle of 178
Geller, Uri 255
George V, King 259
Germany 95
Geronimo 197
Ghostly animals 232
Ghostly bat 233
Giant anteater 53
Giant earwig 59
Giant ground sloth 62
Giant Irish deer 63
Giant spider crab 38
Giant squid 38, 68
Gila monster 55
Gilgamesh 202
Giraffe 37
Giza, pyramids of 120
Glacial 165
Glacier 164-165
Glama River 96
Glamis Castle 233
Gliders 210
Glittertind Mountain 96
Global warming 173
Glover, Savion 303
Glow-worm 33
Golden huntsman spider 21
Golden-silk spider 29
Goliath beetle 37
Gorilla 37
Graham, Martha 289, 302
Gramophone 221
Grand Canyon 102, 142
Grand Coulee Dam 144

Grasshopper 22-23
Great Barrier Reef 64, 119, 131
Great Lakes 102
Great Plains 100
Great Salt Lake Viaduct 145
Great skua 82
Great Wall of China 191, 198
Great white shark 80
Greece 98
Green flash 284
Green turtle 84
Greenhouse effect 172-173
Greenhouse gas 172-173
Greenland 100
Grey seal 71
Grey whale 75
Grizzly bear 37
Guardian spirit 243
Guden river 97
Gulf of Mexico 100
Gulper eel 69
Gutenburg, Johannes 219

H

Haddock 71
Hadrian's Wall 144, 182
Hailstones 147, 152, 153
Halicarnassus 121
Hall of Mirrors 281
Halley's Comet 146
Hammerhead shark 52, 81
Hannibal 184
Harp seal 76
Harvest spider 20-21
Haunted computers 233
Hawaii 151
Hawaiian Islands 100
Hawksbill turtle 85
Headset 286
Heath Robinson, William 231

Heathrow airport 234
Helicopter 211
Henry VIII, King 232
Herring gulls 82
Hillary, Edmund 125
Himalayas 112, 115, 116
Hippopotamus 50
Hokkaido 118
Hologram 274
Honeybee 33
Honshu 118
Hooded seal 77
Horatius 182
Hornet 56
Horoscope 251
Horus 202
Hospitallers 192
Hot-air balloon 210
Hover fly 19
Hover fly larva 25
Hovercraft 209
Howler monkey 45
Huang river 157
Huascarán, Mount 107
Humber Bridge 145
Humphrey, Doris 302
Huns 180-181
Huntsman spider 21
Hurricane 154-155
Hurricane Andrew 154
Hurricane Gilbert 155
Hyaena 49
Hyaenodon 63
Hydaspes, Battle of 177
Hydra 60-61
Hydrofoil 209

I

I Ching 250
Ice Age 164-165
Ice breaker 167
Ice cap 173
Ice sheet 164
Iceberg 166
Iceberg airstrip 231
Icebergs 143
Iceni 185
Ichthyosaurus 88
Igloo 242
Iguana 61
Imperial angelfish 65
Imperial Ballet, The 289
Incas 194-195
India 112, 113, 115, 169
Indian Ocean 77, 87, 111
Indo-Pacific crocodile 48
Indonesia 116
Influenza 169
Inoculation 168
Inquisition 249
Insect pests 170-171
Interactive Virtual Reality 286
Interglacial 165
Internal combustion engine 205
Iran 115
Irish dancing 313
Irrigation channels 161
Israel 114
Isthmus of Suez 108
Italy 92, 98

J

Jabal Katrinah (mountain) 110
Jackson's chameleon 52
Jacquard loom 215
Jaffa, Battle of 192
Jamaica 103
Japan 117, 118, 149, 235
Japanese Dictyoploca moth
    caterpillar 42
Jason 203
Javan rhinoceros 58-59
Jazz dance 303, 307
Jellyfish 71
Jerusalem 114, 192-193
Jesus, statue of 128
Jet airliner 153, 211
Jet engine 205
Jewel beetle 21
Jitterbug 311
Jive 311
Jordan 114
Joss sticks 242
Jumping plant louse 23
Jumping spider 23, 29
Jupiter 174

K

Kambula, Battle of 176
Kanchenjunga (mountain) 115
Kano 111
Katydid 32-33
Kebernerkaise, Mount 96
Kennedy, John F 253
Khan, Genghis 190
Kilimanjaro, Mount 108, 111
Kinetoscope 224
King Ludwig of Bavaria 122
King Mausolus 121
King Nebuchadnezzar 121
Kingsnake 52
Kingston 103
Kirghiz 190
Koala 163
Komodo dragon 36
Kosciusko, Mount 119
Krakatoa 125, 151, 167
Krásnohorská 136
Krill 72
Kronosaurus 88
Kyushu 118

L

Labanotation 307
Ladybird beetle 10
Lake Baykal 99
Lambert Glacier 142
Lamprey 46-47
Lancashire 237
Landowski, Paul 128
Landscape architect 283
Landslide 158
Lantern bug 31
Lasers 274
Lateen sail 208
Latin dance 311
Lava 151
Leatherback turtle 84
Leech 13, 20, 47
Leonardo da Vinci 141
Leopard seal 71
Leper 168
Leper colony 168
Leprosy 168
Leukerbad 158
Levitation 255
Light bulb 228
Lightning 152-153, 162
Lightning conductor 153
Lightwater Valley Theme Park 134

Lima 107
Lincoln, Abraham 234
Lion fish 54-55, 65
Little Big Horn, Battle of 197
Loch Ness Monster 60, 257
Locust 56, 170
Lodgepole pine 163
Logan, Mount 102
Loggerhead sponge 38
Loire River 94
London 94, 237
London subway system 133
Long Man 128
Long-jawed spider 12
Look-out tower 162
Loom 215
Los Angeles 149
Louis XIV, King 288
Lugworm 67

M

Macedonians 178
Mackay effect 262
Mackenzie River 102
MacMillan, Kenneth 293
Macmillan, Kirkpatrick 207
MacMurrogh, Dermot 187
Madrid 95
Maeve, Queen 187
Maillot 304
Maiman, Theodore 274
Malaria 168
Malaysia 116
Maldives 112
Maldon, Battle of 176
Mammoth 63
Mammoth Cave system 136
Manatee 51
Manning, Matthew 237
Manta ray 81

Maori 177
Maoris 313
Margaret, Princess 233
Marie Celeste, The 246
Marine chronometer 217
Marine iguana 85
Masada 185
Mashed Potato, The 311
Masked crab 66
Mauna Loa 124
May bug 19
Mazurka 312
McKinley, Mount 100, 102
Mecca 113, 114
Mecca, Great Mosque at 139
Mechanical clock 216
Medical scanner 213
Mediterranean Sea 92, 94, 98, 108,
   112, 114, 115
Megamouth shark 90
Meiron, Mount 114
Merce Cunningham Dance
   Company 295
Merkit 190
Mermaid 91
Merv, City of 190
Meteor 174-175
Meteorites 147, 174-175
Metriorhynchus 89
Mexico 100, 101, 103
Mexico City 101, 103
Michelangelo 129
Microprocessor 227

Microscope 212
Microwave oven 229
Middle East 112, 113
Midge 19
Miller, Glenn 246
Millipede 14-15, 21
Mime 304
Mirage 146, 284
Mirror writing 280
Mirrors 243, 281, 286
Mississippi river 156
Mississippi-Missouri River 100, 102
Missouri river 156
Mitchell, Arthur 295
Mite 14
Moa 63
Modern dance 289, 302-303, 306, 310
Mole cricket 14
Moloch 52-53
Mona Lisa 141
Mongols 190-191
Mongoose 238
Mont Blanc 94, 98
Montpelier Road 241
Monument Valley 124
Morphing 277
Morris dancing 312
Morse code 222, 223
Moscow 99
Mosquito 17, 57
Moth 10
Motor car 206
Motorcycle 207
Mount Etna 151
Mount Everest 125
Mount Huascaran 159
Mount Pinatubo 150
Mount Rushmore 129
Mount Vesuvius 125
Mudslide 159
Mulhacen, Mount 95

Murray River 116, 119
Musicals 303
Musk ox 43
Muslims 192-193
Mussels 67

N

Naiman 190
Nakwakto Rapids 131
Narwhal 61, 79
Necker cube 264
Nematode 25
Nepal 112, 118
Net-throwing spider 12
Netherlands 97
New Delhi 115
New Guinea 116
New York 101
New Zealand 116, 117, 119
Newspapers 219
Newton, Isaac 213
Niagara Falls 102
Nigeria 111
Nijinsky, Vaslav 292
Nile, River 108, 110
Noah 156
Nohoch Na Chich 137
Normans 187
North America 100-103
North Carolina, USA 235
North Pole 70, 71
Northern lights 147
Norway 96
Notation 307
Nothosaurus 89
Noverre, Jean Georges 289
Nureyev, Rudolf 293
Nutcracker, The 290, 307

O

Oak gall wasp 35
Oil slick 172
Okinawa 235
Old-time dance 310
Oleander hawkmoth 16-17
Olympus, Mount 98
Optic nerve 260-261
Optical fibres 222
Orang-utan 42
Orange River 110
Orchestra 309
Orinoco River 107
Orizaba, Mount 103
Oslo 96
Ottawa 102
Owl butterfly 31
Ozone layer 173

P

Pachacuti 194
Pacific Ocean 74, 85, 102, 118, 119
Pack ice 167
Pagoda 138
Painted lady butterfly 18-19
Pakistan 112
Palming 278
Palmistry 250
Papustyla snail 13
Parallel lines 263, 265
Paraná River 106
Paris 94
Pas de deux 301, 315
Pasha butterfly 10, 11
Pavlova, Anna 293
Peacock butterfly 30-31, 285
Pelican 41
Pemba 111
Pen 218

Pendulum clock 216
Penguins 70, 71
Pepper's Ghost 276
Peppered moth 26
Perpetual motion machine 230
Persian Gulf 113
Persians 176-177
Perspective 265
Peru 107
Petipa, Marius 289, 307
Petrushka 291
Phonograph 220
Phototypesetting 219
Phrenology 251
Phyto-plankton 72
Picasso, Pablo 141
Picture writing 218
Pirouette 301
Pisa, Leaning Tower of 126

Placodus 89
Plague 168-169
Plankton 71, 72, 73, 74, 75, 78, 80
Plate 148-149
Plié 298
Po River 98
Pocahontas 196
Pointe shoes 300
Poison dart frog 54
Poland 99
Polar bear 49
Pollution 172-173
Poltergeist 236-237
Pompeii 125
Pond skater 22
Pontefract 238
Porcupine 42
Porcupine fish 51, 86
Ports de bras 299
Portuguese Man O'War jellyfish 54
Porus, King 177
Posture 298
Powered aircraft 211
Powhatan 196
Praying mantis 12-13, 31, 49
Prehistoric creatures 88, 89, 90
Pretoria 110
Prince of the Pagodas, The 293
Printed book 218
Printing press 219
Privet hawkmoth caterpillar 20-21
Propeller 209
Pseudoscorpion 20, 35
Psychic photography 255
Psychokinesis 255
Puffin 83
Pupil 260
Puss moth caterpillar 30
Pyramids 257
Python 36

Q

Quartz watch 217
Quelea bird 170
Quetzalcoatlus 63

R

Rabbits 171
Radio 223
Radio telescopes 213
Radiolaria 72
Raft spider 22
Rainbows 268, 284
Rameses II 128
Rattlesnake 55
Raynham Hall 240
Rays 80, 81
Red Cloud 196
Red Sea 170-171
Red wolf 59
Redshank 67
Redshirts 201
Reflected light 280
Reflecting telescope 213
Refracted light 280, 284
Refrigerating machines 229
Reptiles 84, 85, 88
Réseau Jean Bernard 136
Retina 261, 269
Rhine River 95
Rhodes, Colossus of 121
Richard the Lionheart 192
Richter Scale 5
Ridley turtle 85
Rio Grande River 103
River Zambezi 130
Riyadh 114
Robber fly 17, 40
Robber fly 40
Roberts, Morgan 252

Rock 'n' Roll 311
Rock of Cashel 186
Rockpools 66, 67
Rocky Mountains 100, 102
Rods 268
Romans 182-186
Rome 98
Röntgen, Wilhelm 213
Rorke's Drift, Battle of 176
Royal Ballet School, The 315
Royal Ballet, The 295
Royal Danish Ballet Company, The 294
Royal ghosts 232
Rub Al-Khali (desert) 114
Rudder 209
Rufiji River 111
Runes stones 250
Russia 92, 99
Rysy Peak 99

S

Sabretooth cat 62-63
Sacasahuaman 194
Sagrada Familia 139
Sahara Desert 108, 143
Sahel, the 161
Sailfish 87
Sailing boats 208
Saladin 193
Salem 248
Samarkand, City of 199
Samurai 198
San Andreas fault 149
San Francisco 149
Sandwasp 35
Sarawak Chamber 137
Sardinia 98
Sarmatians 202
Satellite television 225

Saudi Arabia 112, 114
Sawfish 53
Scandinavia 93, 96, 97
Scarab beetle 14
Scorpion 8, 48
Scorpion fish 66
Scottish Reel 313
Scottish warriors 201
Sea anemone 43, 64, 65
Sea birds 82, 83
Sea dangers 166-167
Sea dragon 87
Sea horse 64
Sea reptiles 84
Sea serpent 91
Sea urchin 54
Seals 70, 71, 76, 77
Seashore 66, 67
Sei whale 74
Seikan Tunnel 133
Semaphore 222
Sennet, Max 276
Serengeti Plain 111
Serios, Ted 255

Seth 202
Severn, River 94
Seychelles 108
Shadow clocks 216
Shaka 176
Sharks 80, 81, 90
Sheet lightning 152
Shepherd's beaked whale 78
Shield bug 29
Shih Huang-ti, Emperor 198
Shikoku 118
Shinano-gawa (river) 118
Shoemaker-Levy 9 174
Shooting stars 174
Show dancing 303
Shrimps 72
Sicily 98
Sierra Nevada Mountains 95
Sigurd 203
Silicon chip 227
Silk moth 33
Sinclair C5 231
Sioux 196-197
Sitting Bull 196-197
Skunk 47
SkyDome 135
Sleeping Beauty, The 289, 307
Sleight of hand 278
Sloth 43
Slug 25
Smaller banded snail 8-9
Snail 8, 9, 13, 25
Soil centipede 25
Sole 69
South Africa 109, 110
South Africa 235
South African grasshopper 31
South America 103-107
South Pole 70, 71
Southend Pier 135
Soviet Union 92

Spacecraft 245
Spain 95, 103
Spartacus 184
Spatial awareness 272
Special effects 309
Spectrum 268
Sperm whale 68, 79
Spider 9, 18
Spinning jenny 214
Spinning machine 214
Spinning wheel 214
Spontaneous human combustion 257
Springtail 23
Square Dance 306, 313
Squid 71
Sri Lanka 112, 113
St Basil's Cathedral 139
St Elmo's Fire 147
St Gotthard Tunnel 133
St Lucia racer 58
Stag beetle 44
Stag beetle larva 15
Stage make-up 305
Stage manager 308
Stained glass windows 141
Stalactites 136-137
Stalagmites 136-137
Steam engine 205
Steam locomotive 206
Steam machine 204
Steam vehicle 207
Steam-powered boats 209
Steamboat Geyser 131
Steamer ducks 83
Stereogram 274-275
Stick insect 27, 285
Stingray 55, 81
Stockholm 96
Stonefish 65
Stonehenge 138
Strait of Gibraltar 108

Stravinsky, Igor 307
Striober, Whitley 244
Strongbow 187
Sudan 108
Superdome 135
Superimposition 277
Swallowtail butterfly 19
Swan Lake 306, 307
Swan, Joseph 228
Sweden 96
Swordfish 86
Sydney Harbor Bridge 145
Sydney Opera House 134
Sylphide, La 290, 292
Sylphides, Les 307
Syria 112

T

Table Mountain 110
Taglioni, Marie 292
Tagus, River 95
Tailor ant 35
Tales of Beatrix Potter, The 290
Talismans 243
Tamerlane 199
Tanystropheus 89
Tap dancing 302
Tape recorder 220
Tarantula spider 43
Tartar 190
Tchaikovsky, Pyotr Ilyich 307
Tedworth 236
Tehran 115
Telegraph 222
Telephone 223
Telephone exchange 223
Telescope 213, 225
Television 270-15
Television transmitter 225
Templars 192

Temujin 190
Tennessee, USA 247
Tenochtitlán 195
Tenzing, Sherpa 125
Termite 15, 34
Teutonic 192
Thames barrier 156
Tharp, Twyla 307
Theodora, Empress 141
Thermionic valve 226
Three dimensions 264-9, 273, 274-275, 283, 286
Thresher shark 81
Thrip 17
Thunder 152-153
Thunderstorm 152-153

Tick 16
Tide 66, 67
Tierra Del Fuego 106
Tiger 37
Tiger beetle 13
Tiger shark 38-39
Time-lapse photography 270
Timur the Lame 199
Titanic 166, 252
Tokyo 118
Toothed whales
Tornado 155
Tornado Alley 155
Tornadoes 146
Toussaint L'Ouverture, 200
Toxic waste 172
Transistor 227
Trap-door spider 12, 58
Tree cricket 32
Treehopper 22
Tribar 264
Trufac 192
Tsunamis 167
Turbine 205
Turkey 112
Turpin, Dick 234
Turtles 84, 85, 91
Tussock moth caterpillar 28-29
Tutus 305
Twist, The 311
Two dimensions 264-9
Typhoon 154

U

Ucayli River 107
Ultra-violet 173
Unidentified flying objects 244
United Kingdom 94
Ural Mountains 116
USA 100, 101, 102, 103, 108

V

Vacuum cleaner 229
Valencia 193
Valhalla 189
Vampire bat 46
Vatican City 92, 98
Velociraptor 62
Venezuela 107
Venice, City of 180
Vercingetorix 184
Versailles, Palace of 123
Vertical take off and landing aircraft 211
Vesuvius, Mount 98
Vicos Gorge 142
Victoria Falls 130
Video recorders 225
Videotape 225
Vietnamese pot-bellied pig 50
Vikings 176, 188-189
Viper fish 69
Vistula River 99
Vivar, Rodrigo di 193
Volcano 150-151
Volga River 92, 99
VR Glove 286
Vulture 46-47

W

Waikato River 119
Waimangu Geyser 131
Walpole, Dorothy 240
Walrus 39
Walt Disney World 134
Waltz, The 310
Wand 278
Wandering albatross 82, 83
Warsaw 99
Washington DC 102

Wasp 41
Wasp beetle 29
Water clock 216
Water vapour 154
Water wheels 204
Waterspout 146, 166-167
Wellington 119
West Germany 95
West Indies 100, 101
Whale shark 80
Wheels 206
Whirligig beetle 23
Wilhelm, Mount 116
Winchester, Sarah 123
Windmills 205
Winkle 67
Winter Solstice 249
Witch doctor 249
Witchcraft 248
Wolf 57
Wolf spider 18
Woodlouse-eating spider 21
World War I 158, 169
Wright, Florence 239

X

X-rays 213

Y

Yding Skovhoj Mountain 97
Yellow lines 283
Yellowstone Park 163
Yeti 256

Z

Zaïre 109
Zanzibar 111
Zebra 285
Zeus, statue of 120
Zhengzhou 157
Zoetrope 270
Zugspitze Mountain 95
Zulu 176

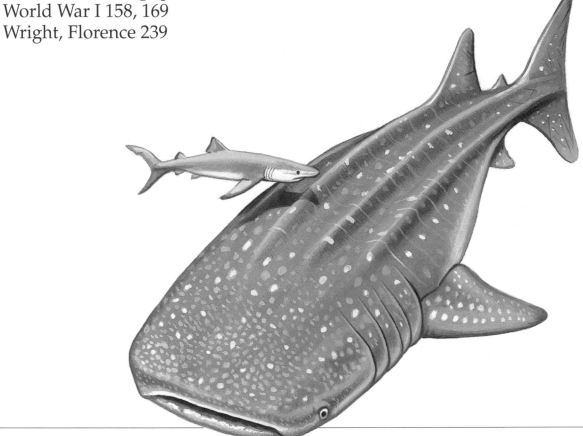

This book was created by Zigzag Publishing,
a division of Quadrillion Publishing Ltd., Godalming Business Centre,
Woolsack Way, Godalming, Surrey GU7 1XW England

Written by
Moira Butterfield, Fiona Corbridge, Jon Day, Gerald Legg, Rupert Matthews,
Duncan Muir, Maggie Tucker, Chris Oxlade and Carol Watson

Consultants:
Keith Lye, John Becklake, Richard Thames, Laura Wade

Editors:
Kay Barnham, Helen Burnford, Paul Harrison,
Fiona Mitchell, Philippa Moyle,
Hazel Songhurst and Nicola Wright

Originally published in eleven separate volumes from the Zigzag Factfinder series:
*Minibeasts, Monster Animals, Fantastic Sea Creatures, Countries, Wonders of the World,
Natural Disasters, Warriors, Inventions, Supernatural, Optical Illusions, Ballet and Dance.*
Copyright © 1997 Quadrillion Publishing Ltd

Colour separations: RCS Graphics Ltd, Leeds and
Sussex Repro, Portslade England and Proost, Belgium
Printed and bound in India

ISBN 1-85833-773-9
8503